Computer Basics

ABSOLUTE BEGINNER'S GUIDE

Michael Miller

800 East 96th Street,
Indianapolis, Indiana 46240

Computer Basics Absolute Beginner's Guide, Windows 8 Edition, Sixth Edition

ISBN-13: 978-0-7897-5001-3
ISBN-10: 0-7897-5001-5

First Printing September 2012

Trademarks

All terms mentioned in this book that are known to be trademarks or service marks have been appropriately capitalized. Que Publishing cannot attest to the accuracy of this information. Use of a term in this book should not be regarded as affecting the validity of any trademark or service mark.

Warning and Disclaimer

Every effort has been made to make this book as complete and as accurate as possible, but no warranty or fitness is implied. The information provided is on an "as is" basis. The author and the publisher shall have neither liability nor responsibility to any person or entity with respect to any loss or damages arising from the information contained in this book.

Bulk Sales

Que Publishing offers excellent discounts on this book when ordered in quantity for bulk purchases or special sales. For more information, please contact

U.S. Corporate and Government Sales
1-800-382-3419
corpsales@pearsontechgroup.com

For sales outside of the U.S., please contact

International Sales
international@pearsoned.com

Editor-in-Chief
Greg Wiegand

Acquisitions Editor
Michelle Newcomb

Development Editor
Charlotte Kughen

Managing Editor
Sandra Schroeder

Project Editor
Seth Kerney

Indexer
Lisa Stumpf

Proofreader
Debbie Williams

Technical Editor
Vince Averello

Publishing Coordinator
Cindy Teeters

Cover Designer
Anne Jones

Compositor
Bumpy Design

Contents at a Glance

Table of Contents

About the Author

Michael Miller is a successful and prolific author with a reputation for practical advice and technical accuracy and an unerring empathy for the needs of his readers.

Mr. Miller has written more than 100 best-selling books over the past two decades. His books for Que include *Facebook for Grown-Ups*, *My Pinterest*, *Easy Computer Basics*, *Windows 7 Your Way*, *How Windows Vista Works*, *Absolute Beginner's Guide to eBay*, and *The Ultimate Digital Music Guide*. He is known for his casual, easy-to-read writing style and his practical, real-world advice—as well as his ability to explain a wide variety of complex topics to an everyday audience.

You can email Mr. Miller directly at abg@molehillgroup.com. His website is located at www.molehillgroup.com.

Dedication

To Sherry—finally and forever.

Acknowledgments

Thanks to the usual suspects at Que Publishing, including but not limited to Greg Wiegand, Michelle Newcomb, Charlotte Kughen, Seth Kerney, and technical editor Vince Averello.

We Want to Hear from You!

As the reader of this book, *you* are our most important critic and commentator. We value your opinion and want to know what we're doing right, what we could do better, what areas you'd like to see us publish in, and any other words of wisdom you're willing to pass our way.

We welcome your comments. You can email or write to let us know what you did or didn't like about this book—as well as what we can do to make our books better.

Please note that we cannot help you with technical problems related to the topic of this book.

When you write, please be sure to include this book's title and author as well as your name, email address, and phone number. I will carefully review your comments and share them with the author and editors who worked on the book.

Email: feedback@quepublishing.com

Mail: Que Publishing
       ATTN: Reader Feedback
       Que Publishing
       800 East 96th Street
       Indianapolis, IN 46240 USA

Reader Services

Visit our website and register this book at quepublishing.com/register for convenient access to any updates, downloads, or errata that might be available for this book.

INTRODUCTION

Because this is the *Absolute Beginner's Guide to Computer Basics*, let's start at the absolute beginning, which is this: Computers aren't supposed to be scary. Intimidating? Sometimes. Difficult to use? Perhaps. Inherently unreliable? Most definitely. (Although they're much better than they used to be.)

But scary? Definitely not.

Computers aren't scary because there's nothing they can do to hurt you (unless you drop your notebook PC on your foot, that is). And there's not much you can do to hurt them, either. It's kind of a wary coexistence between man and machine, but the relationship has the potential to be beneficial—to you, anyway.

Many people think that they're scared of computers because they're unfamiliar with them. But that isn't really true.

You see, even if you've never actually used a computer before, you've been exposed to computers and all they can do for the past three decades or so. Whenever you make a deposit at your bank, you're working with computers. Whenever you make a purchase at a retail store, you're working with computers. Whenever you watch a television show or read a newspaper article or look at a picture in a magazine, you're working with computers.

That's because computers are used in all those applications. Somebody, somewhere, is working behind the scenes with a computer to manage your bank account and monitor your credit card purchases.

In fact, it's difficult to imagine, here in the twenty-first century, how we ever got by without all those keyboards, mice, and monitors. (Or, for that matter, the Internet.)

However, just because computers have been around for awhile doesn't mean that everyone knows how to use them. It's not unusual to feel a little trepidation the first time you sit down in front of that intimidating display and keyboard. Which keys should you press? What do people mean by double-clicking the mouse? And what are all those little pictures onscreen?

As foreign as all this might seem at first, computers really aren't that hard to understand—or use. You have to learn a few basic concepts, of course (all the pressing and clicking and whatnot), and it helps to understand exactly what part of the system does what. But once you get the hang of things, computers really are easy to use.

Which, of course, is where this book comes in.

Absolute Beginner's Guide to Computer Basics, Windows 8 Edition, will help you figure out how to use your new computer system. You'll learn how computers work, how to connect all the pieces and parts (if your computer has pieces and parts, that is; not all do), and how to start using them. You'll learn about computer hardware and software, about the Microsoft Windows 8 operating system, and about the Internet. And after you're comfortable with the basic concepts (which won't take too long, trust me), you'll learn how to actually do stuff.

You'll learn how to do useful stuff, such as writing letters, scheduling appointments, and managing your finances; fun stuff, such as listening to music, watching movies, and viewing digital photos; online stuff, such as searching for information, sending email, and keeping up with friends and family via Facebook and other social networks; and essential stuff, such as copying files, troubleshooting problems, and protecting against malware and computer attacks.

All you have to do is sit yourself down in front of your computer, try not to be scared (there's nothing to be scared of, really), and work your way through the chapters and activities in this book. And remember that computers aren't difficult to use, they don't break easily, and they let you do all sorts of fun and useful things once you get the hang of them. Really!

How This Book Is Organized

This book is organized into eight main parts, as follows:

- **Part I, "Getting Started,"** discusses all the different types of computers available today; describes all the pieces and parts of desktop, notebook, and tablet PCs; and how to connect everything to get your new system up and running.

- **Part II, "Using Windows,"** introduces the backbone of your entire system, the Microsoft Windows operating system—in particular, Windows 8. You'll learn how Windows 8 works, and how to find things on the new Start screen and beyond. You'll also learn how to use Windows to perform basic tasks, such as copying and deleting files and folders.

- **Part III, "Setting Up the Rest of Your Computer System,"** talks about all those things you connect to your computer—printers, scanners, external hard drives, USB thumb drives, and the like. You'll also learn how to connect your new PC to other computers and devices in a home network.

- **Part IV, "Using the Internet,"** is all about going online. You'll discover how to connect to the Internet and surf the Web with Internet Explorer. You'll also learn how to shop and sell online, search and do research, and even manage your finances over the Internet. This is the fun part of the book.

- **Part V, "Communicating Online,"** is all about keeping in touch. You'll find out how to send and receive email, of course, but also how to get started with social networking, on Facebook, Pinterest, Twitter, and other networks. It's how everyone's keeping in touch these days.

- **Part VI, "Working with Apps,"** tells you everything you need to know about using what we used to call software programs and now call "apps." You'll learn how apps work, which apps are included in Windows 8, and where to find more apps. (This last bit covers Microsoft's new Windows Store, which is where a lot of fun apps can be had.)

- **Part VII, "Doing Fun and Useful Things with Your PC,"** brings more fun—and a little work. You'll learn all about getting productive with Microsoft Office, as well as how to manage your schedule with the Windows Calendar app. You'll also discover how to use your PC to manage, edit, and view digital photos; listen to music, both on your PC and over the Internet; manage the music on your iPhone or iPod; watch downloaded videos; and view movies and TV shows online. Like I said, fun and useful stuff.

- **Part VIII, "Keeping Your System Up and Running,"** contains all the boring (but necessary) information you need to know to keep your new PC in tip-top shape. You'll learn how to protect against Internet threats (including viruses, spyware, and spam), as well as how to perform routine computer maintenance. You'll even learn how to troubleshoot problems and, if necessary, restore, refresh, or reset your entire system.

Taken together, the 32 chapters in this book will help you progress from absolute beginner to experienced computer user. Just read what you need, and before long you'll be using your computer like a pro!

Which Version of Windows?

This edition of the *Absolute Beginner's Guide to Computer Basics* is written for computers running the latest version of Microsoft's operating system, dubbed Windows 8. If you're running previous versions of Windows, you'll be better off with previous editions of this book. In particular, the book's Fifth Edition is written for Windows 7 users, the Fourth Edition is written for Windows Vista users, and the Third Edition is written for Windows XP users. Search them out if you're using one of these older versions of Windows.

By the way, you'll see in various places in this book references to Windows 8's new Metro interface. Well, I'm calling it Metro, because that's what Microsoft called it throughout the long, drawn out development process. For some reason, however, Microsoft quit calling it Metro right before they started shipping copies of Windows 8 to the market. Microsoft now just calls the new flat, tiled interface the "Windows 8 interface." Okay, but I'm still calling it Metro. So when you see references to the Metro interface or Metro-style apps, you know what I'm talking about.

Conventions Used in This Book

I hope that this book is easy enough to figure out on its own, without requiring its own instruction manual. As you read through the pages, however, it helps to know precisely how I've presented specific types of information.

Menu Commands

Most computer programs operate via a series of pull-down menus. You use your mouse to pull down a menu and then select an option from that menu. This sort of operation is indicated like this throughout the book:

> Select File, Save

or

> Right-click the button and select Properties from the pop-up menu.

All you have to do is follow the instructions in order, using your mouse to click each item in turn. When submenus are tacked onto the main menu, just keep clicking the selections until you come to the last one—which should open the program or activate the command you want!

By the way, since Windows 8 is optimized for touchscreen devices, I also include touchscreen instructions where practical. As you'll learn throughout the book, if you have a touchscreen PC, there's a whole lot of screen-based gestures and commands you can use to do what you need to do.

Shortcut Key Combinations

When you're using your computer keyboard, sometimes you have to press two keys at the same time. These two-key combinations are called *shortcut keys* and are shown as the key names joined with a plus sign (+).

For example, Ctrl+W indicates that you should press the W key while holding down the Ctrl key. It's no more complex than that.

Web Page Addresses

This book contains a lot of web page addresses. (That's because you'll probably be spending a lot of time on the Internet.)

Technically, a web page address is supposed to start with http:// (as in http://www.molehillgroup.com). Because Internet Explorer and other web browsers automatically insert this piece of the address, however, you don't have to type it—and I haven't included it in any of the addresses in this book.

Special Elements

This book also includes a few special elements that provide additional information not included in the basic text. These elements are designed to supplement the text to make your learning faster, easier, and more efficient.

TIP A *tip* is a piece of advice—a little trick, actually—that helps you use your computer more effectively or maneuver around problems or limitations.

 NOTE A *note* is designed to provide information that is generally useful but not specifically necessary for what you're doing at the moment. Some are like extended tips—interesting, but not essential.

 CAUTION A *caution* tells you to beware of a potentially dangerous act or situation. In some cases, ignoring a caution could cause you significant problems—so pay attention to them!

Let Me Know What You Think

I always love to hear from readers. If you want to contact me, feel free to email me at abg@molehillgroup.com. I can't promise that I'll *answer* every message, but I do promise that I'll *read* each one!

If you want to learn more about me and any new books I have cooking, check out my Molehill Group website at www.molehillgroup.com. Who knows, you might find some other books there that you would like to read.

HOW PERSONAL COMPUTERS WORK

Chances are you're reading this book because you just bought a new computer, are thinking about buying a new computer, or maybe even had someone give you his old computer. (Nothing wrong with high-tech hand-me-downs!) At this point you might not be totally sure what it is you've gotten yourself into. Just what is this mess of boxes and cables, and what can you—or should you—do with it?

This chapter serves as an introduction to the entire concept of personal computers in general—what they do, how they work, that sort of thing—and computer hardware in particular. It's a good place to start if you're not that familiar with computers or want a brief refresher course in what all those pieces and parts are and what they do.

Of course, if you want to skip the background and get right to using your computer, that's okay, too. For step-by-step instructions on how to connect and configure a new desktop PC, go directly to Chapter 2, "Setting Up and Using a Desktop Computer." Or, if you have a new notebook or tablet PC, go to Chapter 3, "Setting Up and Using a Notebook or Tablet Computer." Everything you need to know should be in one of those two chapters.

What Your Computer Can Do

What good is a personal computer, anyway?

Everybody has one, you know. (Including you, now!) In fact, it's possible you bought your new computer just so that you wouldn't feel left out. But now that you have your very own personal computer, what do you do with it?

Good for Getting Online

Most of what we do on our computers these days is accomplished via the Internet. We find our friends online; we find useful information online; we find movies and music online; we play games online; we even shop and do our banking online. Most of these activities are accomplished by browsing something called the World Wide Web (or just the "Web"), which you do from something called a web browser. Now that you have a new computer and (hopefully) an Internet connection at home, you won't feel left out when people start talking about "double-u double-u double-u" this and "dot-com" that—because you'll be online, too.

 NOTE Learn more about getting online in Chapter 11, "Connecting to the Internet—at Home and On the Road."

Good for Social Networking

One of the most popular online activities these days involves something called social networking. A *social network* is a website where you can keep informed as to what your friends and family are doing, and they can see what you're up to, too. There are several social networks you can use, but the most popular are Facebook, Pinterest, Twitter, and LinkedIn. You can join one or more of these and start sharing your life online.

 NOTE Learn more about Facebook in Chapter 17, "Social Networking with Facebook." Learn more about other social networks in Chapter 18, "More Social Networking with Google+, Pinterest, LinkedIn, and Twitter."

Good for Communicating

Your new computer is also great for one-to-one communication. Want to send a note to a friend? Or keep your family informed of what's new and exciting? It's easy enough to do, thanks to your new computer and the Internet. You can drop a note via email or keep 'em posted via Facebook or some similar social networking site.

 NOTE Learn more about communicating with email in Chapter 16, "Sending and Receiving Email."

Good for Sharing Photos and Home Movies

You can also use your computer to store and share your favorite photos and home movies. When you upload a picture, all your friends can view it online. You can even touch up the photo before you share it. Pretty nifty.

 NOTE Learn more about digital photos in Chapter 25, "Viewing and Sharing Digital Photos."

Good for Entertainment

For many people, a personal computer is a hub for all sorts of entertainment. You can use your computer to watch movies on DVDs, listen to music on CDs, or even go online to watch TV shows and movies. You can also go online to purchase and download new music, or listen to all your favorite tunes in real time via streaming music services.

 NOTE Learn more about listening to music with your PC in Chapter 26, "Playing Music in Windows." Learn more about watching TV and movies on your PC in Chapter 30, "Watching TV and Movies Online."

Good for Keeping Informed

Entertainment is fun, but it's also important to stay informed. Well, your computer is a great gateway to tons of information, both old and new. You can search for just about anything you want online, or use your computer to browse the latest news headlines, sports scores, and weather reports. All the information you can think of is online somewhere, and you use your computer to find and read it.

NOTE Learn more about staying informed online in Chapter 12, "Using Internet Explorer to Surf the Web."

Good for Work

A lot of people use their home PCs for work-related purposes. You can bring your work (reports, spreadsheets, you name it) home from the office and finish it on your home PC, at night or on weekends. Or, if you work at home, you can use your computer to pretty much run your small business—you can use it to do everything from typing memos and reports to generating invoices and setting budgets.

In short, anything you can do with a normal office PC, you can probably do on your home PC.

NOTE Learn more about using your computer for office work in Chapter 23, "Doing Office Work."

Good for Play

All work and no play make Jack a dull boy, so there's no reason not to have a little fun with your new PC. There are a lot of cool games (from Angry Birds to solitaire) online, plus you can purchase all manner of computer games to play, if that's what you're into. There's a lot of fun to be had with your new PC!

NOTE This book is written for users of relatively new personal computers—in particular, PCs running the Microsoft Windows 8 operating system. If you have an older PC running an older version of Windows, most of the advice here is still good, although not all the step-by-step instructions will apply.

Inside a Personal Computer

As we'll discuss momentarily, there are lots of different types of personal computers—desktops, notebooks, tablets, and the like. What they all have in common is a core set of components—the computer *hardware*. Unlike computer *software*, which describes the programs and applications you run on your computer, the hardware is comprised of those parts of your system you can actually see and touch.

Well, you could see the parts if you opened up the case, which you can't always do. Let's take a virtual tour inside a typical PC, so you can get a sense of how the darned thing works.

The Motherboard: Home to Almost Everything

Inside every PC are all manner of computer chips and circuit boards. Most of these parts are connected to a big board called a *motherboard*, because it's the "mother" for the computer's microprocessor and memory chips, as well as for all other internal components that enable your system to function. On a traditional desktop PC, the motherboard is located near the base of the computer, as shown in Figure 1.1; on an all-in-one desktop, it's built into the monitor unit; on a notebook PC, it's just under the keyboard; and on a tablet or hybrid model, it's built into the touchscreen display.

FIGURE 1.1

What a typical desktop PC looks like on the inside—a big motherboard with lots of add-on boards attached.

On a traditional desktop PC, the motherboard contains several slots, into which you can plug additional *boards* (also called *cards*) that perform specific functions. All-in-one and notebook PC motherboards can't accept additional boards, and thus aren't expandable like PCs that have separate system units.

Most desktop PC motherboards contain six or more slots for add-on cards. For example, a video card enables your motherboard to transmit video signals to your monitor. Other available cards enable you to add sound and modem/fax capabilities to your system. (On an all-in-one or notebook PC, these video and audio functions are built into the motherboard, rather than being on separate cards.)

Microprocessors: The Main Engine

We're not done looking at the motherboard just yet. That's because, buried somewhere on that big motherboard is a specific chip that controls your entire computer system. This chip is called a *microprocessor* or a *central processing unit (CPU)*.

The microprocessor is the brains inside your system. It processes all the instructions necessary for your computer to perform its duties. The more powerful the microprocessor chip, the faster and more efficiently your system runs.

Microprocessors carry out the various instructions that let your computer compute. Every input and output device connected to a computer—the keyboard, printer, monitor, and so on—either issues or receives instructions that the microprocessor then processes. Your software programs also issue instructions that must be implemented by the microprocessor. This chip truly is the workhorse of your system; it affects just about everything your computer does.

Different computers have different types of microprocessor chips. Many IBM-compatible computers use chips manufactured by Intel. Some use Intel-compatible chips manufactured by AMD and other firms. But all IBM-compatible computers that run the Windows operating system use Intel-compatible chips.

In addition to having different chip manufacturers (and different chip families from the same manufacturer), you'll run into microprocessor chips that run at different speeds. CPU speed today is measured in *gigahertz (GHz)*. A CPU with a speed of 1GHz can run at one *billion* clock ticks per second! The bigger the gigahertz number, the faster the chip runs.

It gets better. Many chips today incorporate so-called *dual-core* or *quad-core* chips. What this means is that a single chip includes the equivalent of two (dual-core) or four (quad-core) CPUs. That's like doubling or quadrupling your processing power! The more cores, the better—especially for processor-intensive tasks, such as editing digital video files.

If you're still shopping for a new PC, look for one with the combination of a powerful microprocessor and a high clock speed for best performance. And don't forget to count all the cores; a dual-core chip with two 1.8GHz CPUs is more powerful than a single-core chip with a 2.0GHz CPU.

Computer Memory: Temporary Storage

Before a CPU can process instructions you give it, your instructions must be stored somewhere, in preparation for access by the microprocessor. These instructions—along with other data processed by your system—are temporarily held in the computer's *random access memory (RAM)*. All computers have some amount of memory, which is created by a number of memory chips. The more memory that's available in a machine, the more instructions and data that can be stored at one time.

Memory is measured in terms of *bytes*. One byte is equal to approximately one character in a word processing document. A unit equaling approximately one thousand bytes (1,024, to be exact) is called a *kilobyte (KB)*, and a unit of approximately one thousand (1,024) kilobytes is called a *megabyte (MB)*. A thousand megabytes is a *gigabyte (GB)*.

Most computers today come with at least 4GB of memory, some with much more. To enable your computer to run as many programs as quickly as possible, you need as possess enough memory, its CPU must constantly retrieve data from permanent storage on its hard disk. This method of data retrieval is slower than retrieving instructions and data from electronic memory. In fact, if your machine doesn't have enough memory, some programs will run very slowly (or you might experience random system crashes), and other programs won't run at all!

Hard Disk Drives: Long-Term Storage

Another important physical component inside your system unit is the *hard disk drive*. The hard disk permanently stores all your important data. Some hard disks today can store up to 2 *terabytes* (TB) of data—that's 2,000GB—and even bigger hard disks are on the way. (Contrast this to your system's RAM, which temporarily stores only a few gigabytes of data.)

A hard disk consists of numerous metallic platters. These platters store data *magnetically*. Special read/write *heads* realign magnetic particles on the platters, much like a recording head records data onto magnetic recording tape.

However, before data can be stored on a disk, including your system's hard disk, that disk must be *formatted*. A disk that has not been formatted cannot accept data. When you format a hard disk, your computer prepares each track and sector of the disk to accept and store data magnetically. Fortunately, hard disks in new PCs are preformatted, so you don't have to worry about this. (And, in most cases, your operating system and key programs are preinstalled.)

CAUTION If you try to reformat your hard disk, you'll erase all the programs and data that have been installed—so don't do it!

One unique aspect of many netbooks and ultrabooks is that they don't have traditional hard disk storage. Instead, they use solid state flash memory for long-term storage. These types of PCs typically have much less onboard storage than you get with hard disk models, but that makes them a lot smaller and lighter.

CD/DVD Drives: Storage on a Disc

Not all the storage on your PC is inside the system unit. As you can see in Figure 1.2, most PCs feature a combination *CD/DVD drive* that lets you play audio CDs and movie DVDs, install CD- or DVD-based software programs, and burn music, movies, or data to blank CD or DVD discs.

FIGURE 1.2

Store tons of data on a shiny CD or DVD data disc.

Computer CD discs, called CD-ROM discs (the ROM stands for "read-only memory), look just like the compact discs you play on your audio system. They're also similar in the way they store data (audio data in the case of regular CDs; computer data in the case of CD-ROMs).

NOTE The *ROM* part of CD-ROM means that you can only read data from the disk; unlike normal hard disks and diskettes, you can't write new data to a standard CD-ROM. However, most PCs include recordable (CD-R) and rewritable (CD-RW) drives that *do* let you write data to CDs—so you can use your CD drive just like a regular disk drive.

If you need even more storage, consider writing to blank DVD discs. A DVD can contain up to 4.7GB of data (for a single-layer disc) or 8.5GB of data (for a double-layer disc). Compared to 700MB of storage for a typical CD-ROM, this makes DVDs ideally suited for large applications or games that otherwise would require multiple CDs. Similar to standard CD-ROMs, most DVDs are read-only—although all DVD drives can also read CD-ROMs.

Some high-end PCs do the standard DVD one step better and can read and write high-definition DVDs in the *Blu-ray* format, which lets you store 25GB or more of data on a single disc. Although that storage for PC data might be overkill, it might be nice to play high-definition Blu-ray movies on your PC.

By the way, those smaller and lighter netbooks, ultrabooks, and tablets get smaller and lighter by leaving out the CD/DVD drives. You can always add an external CD/DVD drive, but in most cases you can get by without the drive at all; just about anything you can find on CD or DVD is also available online for downloading.

Keyboards: Fingertip Input

Computers receive data by reading it from disk, accepting it electronically over a modem, or receiving input directly from you, the user. You provide your input by way of what's called, in general, an *input device*; the most common input device you use to talk to your computer is the keyboard.

A computer keyboard, similar to the one in Figure 1.3, looks and functions just like an old-fashioned typewriter keyboard, except that computer keyboards have a few more keys. Some of these keys (such as the arrow, PgUp, PgDn, Home, and End keys) enable you to move around within a program or file. Other keys provide access to special program features. When you press a key on your keyboard, it sends an electronic signal to your system unit that tells your machine what you want it to do.

FIGURE 1.3

A keyboard for a desktop PC.

Most keyboards that come with desktop PCs hook up via a cable to the back of your system unit, although some manufacturers make *wireless* keyboards that connect to your system unit via radio signals—thus eliminating one cable from the back of your system. Keyboards on notebook PCs are built into the main unit, of course, and are typically a little smaller than desktop PC keyboards; most notebook keyboards, for example, lack a separate numeric keypad for entering numbers.

On a Windows PC, there are a few extra keys in addition to the normal letters and numbers and symbols and such. Chief among these is the Windows key (sometimes called the *Winkey*), like the one shown in Figure 1.4, which has a little Windows logo on it. In Windows 8, many operating functions are initiated by pressing the Windows key either by itself or along with another key on the keyboard.

FIGURE 1.4

The Windows key on a computer keyboard.

 NOTE On some tablet and hybrid PCs, there's a Windows button instead of a Windows key.

Mice and Touchpads: Point-and-Click Input Devices

It's a funny name but a necessary device. A computer *mouse*, like the one shown in Figure 1.5, is a small handheld device. Most mice consist of an oblong case with a roller underneath and two or three buttons on top. When you move the mouse along a desktop, an onscreen pointer (called a *cursor*) moves in response. When you click (press and release) a mouse button, this motion initiates an action in your program.

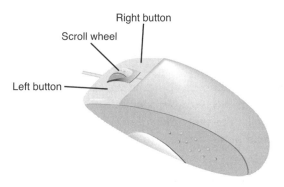

Right button

Scroll wheel

Left button

FIGURE 1.5

Roll the mouse back and forth to move the onscreen cursor.

Mice come in all shapes and sizes. Some have wires, and some are wireless. Some are relatively oval in shape, and others are all curvy to better fit in the palm of your hand. Some have the typical roller ball underneath, and others use an optical sensor to determine where and how much you're rolling. Some even have extra buttons that you can program for specific functions or a scroll wheel you can use to scroll through long documents or web pages.

Some newer mice also double as touch input devices. That is, you can tap and squeeze your fingers on a touch mouse much as you can on a touchscreen display. Obviously, you can also use a touch mouse like a traditional rolling and clicking mouse; the touch functionality is just a nice extra.

If you have a notebook PC, you don't have a separate mouse. Instead, most notebooks feature a *touchpad* pointing device that functions like a mouse. You move your fingers around the touchpad to move the onscreen cursor and then click one of the buttons underneath the touchpad the same way you'd click a mouse button.

 TIP If you have a portable PC, you don't have to use the built-in touchpad. Most portables let you attach an external mouse, which you can use in addition to the internal device.

If you're using a tablet or hybrid computer with a touchscreen display, you don't need a mouse at all. Instead, you control your computer by tapping and swiping the screen, using specific motions to perform specific operations. With a touchscreen computer, operation is fairly intuitive.

TIP How do you enter information if your tablet or touchscreen PC doesn't have a traditional keyboard? By using Windows 8's virtual onscreen keyboard, which pops up automatically when input is needed on a touchscreen device.

Network Connections: Getting Connected

If you have more than one computer in your home, you might want to connect them in a home network. A network enables you to share files between multiple computers, as well as connect multiple PCs to a single printer or scanner. In addition, you can use a home network to share a broadband Internet connection so that all your computers are connected to the Internet.

You can connect computers via either wired or wireless networks. Most home users prefer a wireless network, as there are no cables to run from one room of your house to another. Fortunately, connecting a wireless network is as easy as buying a wireless router, which functions as the hub of the network, and then connecting wireless adapters to each computer on the network. (And if you have a notebook PC, the wireless adapter is probably built-in.)

NOTE Learn more about wireless networks in Chapter 10, "Setting Up a Home Network."

Sound Cards and Speakers: Making Noise

Every PC comes with some sort of speaker system. Most desktop systems today let you set up separate right and left speakers, sometimes accompanied by a subwoofer for better bass. (Figure 1.6 shows a typical right-left-subwoofer speaker system.) Notebook PCs typically come with right and left speakers built in, but with the option of connecting external speakers if you want. You can even get so-called 5.1 surround sound speaker systems, with five satellite speakers (front and rear) and the ".1" subwoofer—great for listening to movie soundtracks or playing explosive-laden video games.

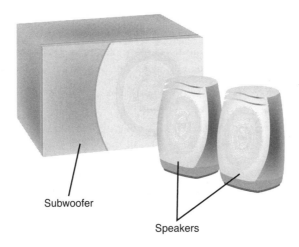

Subwoofer

Speakers

FIGURE 1.6

A typical set of right and left external speakers, complete with subwoofer.

All speaker systems are driven by a sound card or chip that is installed inside your system unit. If you upgrade your speaker system, you also might need to upgrade your sound card accordingly. (You can easily switch sound cards on a desktop PC, but it's really not an option on a notebook.)

Video Cards and Monitors: Getting the Picture

Operating a computer would be difficult if you didn't constantly receive visual feedback showing you what your machine is doing. This vital function is provided by your computer's monitor.

Most computer monitors today are built around an LCD display. On a notebook PC, this display is built into the unit; on a desktop PC, you connect a separate external monitor. You measure the size of a monitor from corner to corner, diagonally. Today's freestanding LCD monitors start at 15" or so and run up to 24" or larger.

A flat-screen LCD display doesn't take up a lot of desk space or use a lot of energy, both of which are good things. Many LCD monitors today come with a widescreen display that has the same 16:9 (or 16:10) aspect ratio used to display widescreen movies—which makes them ideal for viewing or editing movies on your PC.

NOTE Older computer monitors were built around a cathode ray tube, or CRT, similar to the picture tube found in normal television sets.

Know, however, that your computer monitor doesn't generate the images it displays. Instead, screen images are electronically crafted by a *video card* or chip installed inside your system unit. To work correctly, both the video card and monitor must be matched to display images of the same resolution.

Resolution refers to the size of the images that can be displayed onscreen and is measured in pixels. A *pixel* is a single dot on your screen; a full picture is composed of thousands of pixels. The higher the resolution, the sharper the resolution—which lets you display more (smaller) elements onscreen.

Resolution is expressed in numbers of pixels, in both the horizontal and vertical directions. Older video cards and monitors could display only 640×480 or 800×600 pixel resolution; you want a card/monitor combination that can display at least 1024×768 resolution—or, in the case of a widescreen monitor, 1280×800.

For most users, the video card or chip installed in their new PC works just fine. However, if you do a lot of heavy-duty gaming—especially with some of the newer graphics-intensive games—you might want to consider upgrading the video card in a desktop PC to one with more on-board memory, to better reproduce those cutting-edge graphics. And to display all of Windows 8's cutting-edge graphics, you need a card with a separate *graphics processing unit (GPU)*, which takes the graphics processing load off your PC's main CPU. The more graphics processing power, the better your system looks.

Other Parts of Your Computer System

The computer hardware itself is only part of your overall computer system. A typical PC has additional devices—such as printers—connected to it, and it runs various programs and applications to perform specific tasks.

Providing Additional Functionality with Peripherals

There are lots of other devices, called *peripherals*, you can connect to your computer. These items include

- **Printers**—A printer lets you make hardcopy printouts of documents and pictures.

 NOTE Learn more about printers and scanners in Chapter 8, "Working with Printers and Scanners."

- **Scanners**—These devices convert printed documents or pictures to electronic format.

- **Webcams**—These are small cameras (typically with built-in microphones) that let you send live video of yourself to friends and family.

- **Joysticks**—This is an alternative to a mouse that lets you play the most challenging computer games.

- **External hard drives**—These are just like the hard disks inside your computer, but they connect externally to help you back up your precious data.

 NOTE Learn more about using external hard disks in Chapter 9, "Adding Storage and Backup."

You can also hook up all manner of portable devices to your PC, including digital cameras, camcorders, and portable music players (such as the ubiquitous Apple iPod). You can even add the appropriate devices to connect multiple PCs in a network, which is useful if you have more than one computer in your house.

Fortunately, connecting a new device is as easy as plugging in a single cable. Whether you have a desktop or notebook PC, or even a tablet, most printers connect using a special type of cable called a USB cable. Almost all computers have multiple USB connections (sometimes called *ports*), so you can connect multiple peripherals via USB at the same time.

Doing What You Need to Do with Software and Apps

By themselves, the beige and black boxes that comprise a typical computer system aren't that useful. You can connect them and set them in place, but they won't do anything until you have some software to make things work.

As discussed earlier, computer hardware are those things you can touch—the keyboard, monitor, system unit, and the like. Computer *software*, on the other hand, is something you *can't* touch because it's nothing more than a bunch of electronic bits and bytes. These bits and bytes, however, combine into computer programs—sometimes called *applications* or just *apps*—that provide specific functionality to your system.

For example, if you want to crunch some numbers, you need a piece of software called a *spreadsheet* program. If you want to write a letter, you need a *word processing* program. If you want to make changes to some pictures you took with your digital camera, you need *graphics editing* software. And if you want to surf the Internet, you need a *web browser*.

In other words, you need separate software for each task you want to do with your computer. Fortunately, most new computer systems come with a lot of this software already installed. You might have to buy a few specific programs, but it shouldn't set you back a lot of money.

 NOTE Learn more about computer software and apps in Part VI of this book, "Working with Apps."

Making Everything Work—with Windows

Whatever program or app you're using at any given point in time, you interface with your computer via a special piece of software called an *operating system*. As the name implies, this program makes your system operate; it's your gateway to the hardware part of your system.

The operating system is also how your application software interfaces with your computer hardware. When you want to print a document from your word processor, that software works with the operating system to send the document to your printer.

Most computers today ship with an operating system called *Microsoft Windows*. This operating system has been around in one form or another for more than 25 years and is published by Microsoft Corporation.

Windows isn't the only operating system around, however. Computers manufactured by Apple Computing use a different operating system, called the *Mac OS*. Therefore, computers running Windows and computers by Apple aren't totally compatible with each other. Then there's *Linux*, which is compatible with most PCs sold today, but it's used primarily by über-techie types; it's not an operating system I would recommend for general users.

But let's get back to Windows, of which there have been several different versions over the years. The newest version is called *Microsoft Windows 8* because it's the eighth major version of the operating system, more or less. If you've just purchased a brand-new PC, this is probably the version you're using. If your PC is a little older, you might be running *Windows 7*, the immediate predecessor to Windows 8, or maybe even *Windows Vista* or *Windows XP*, both of which are much older.

To some degree, Windows is Windows is Windows; all the different versions do pretty much the same things. Windows 8, however, looks and functions much differently than previous versions; it's the first version designed for touchscreen operation, and it looks more like what you'd find on a smartphone than what you're used to on a computer desktop. In any case, you use Windows—whichever version you have installed—to launch specific programs and to perform various system maintenance functions, such as copying files and turning off your computer.

 NOTE You can learn more about Windows 8 in Chapter 4, "Getting to Know Windows 8."

Different Types of Computers

Although all computers consist of pretty much the same components and work in pretty much the same way, there are several different types to choose from. You can go with a traditional desktop computer, a smaller, more portable notebook model, a touchscreen tablet—or one that combines some or all of these features.

Let's look at the different types of computers you can choose from.

Desktop PCs

A *desktop PC* is one with a separate monitor that's designed to sit on your desktop, along with a separate keyboard and mouse. This type of PC is stationary; you can't take it with you. It sits on your desktop, perfect for doing the requisite office work.

Although all desktop PCs sit on your desktop, there are actually two different types of desktop units:

- **Traditional desktops**—A traditional desktop system, like the one shown in Figure 1.7, has a separate system unit that either sits on the floor or beside the monitor.

- **All-in-one desktops**—This newer type of desktop PC builds the system unit into the monitor for a more compact system, like the one shown in Figure 1.8. Some of these all-in-one PCs feature touchscreen monitors, so you can control them by tapping and swiping the monitor screen itself.

A lot of folks like the easier setup (no system unit to connect) and smaller space requirements of all-in-one systems. The only drawbacks I can see to these all-in-one desktops are the price (they're typically a bit more costly than traditional desktop PCs) and the fact that if one component goes bad, the whole system is out of commission. It's a lot easier to replace a single component than an entire system!

 NOTE Learn more about desktop PCs in Chapter 2.

FIGURE 1.7

A traditional desktop PC, complete with monitor, keyboard, mouse, and separate system unit. (Photo courtesy Acer.)

FIGURE 1.8

An all-in-one desktop system, with the system unit built into the monitor. (Photo courtesy HP.)

Notebook PCs

A *notebook PC*, sometimes called a *laptop*, combines a monitor, keyboard, and system unit in a single, compact case. This type of portable PC, like the one shown in Figure 1.9, can operate via normal electrical power or via a built-in battery; when using battery power, a notebook can be taken with you and used just about anywhere you choose to go.

FIGURE 1.9

A typical notebook PC. (Photo courtesy Sony.)

Just as there are several types of desktop PCs, there are also several types of notebooks, including the following:

- **Traditional notebooks**—These units have screens that run in the 14" to 16" range, and include decent-sized hard drives (200GB and up) and a combo CD/DVD drive. These are typically the least expensive notebooks because there's a lot of competition; this category is the most popular.

- **Desktop-replacement notebooks**—These are larger notebooks, with screens in the 17" range. They're not only bigger; they're also heavier, and the batteries don't last as long. As such, these notebooks really aren't designed for true portable use, but rather they replace traditional desktop PCs. Plus, these desktop-replacement models typically cost a bit more than traditional notebooks.

- **Ultrabooks**—An ultrabook is a smaller, thinner, and lighter notebook. Most ultrabooks have screens in the 12" to 14" range, don't have CD/DVD drives, and use solid state flash storage instead of hard disk storage. All this makes an ultrabook very fast and very easy to carry around without necessarily sacrificing computing power and functionality. However, all this new technology means ultrabooks cost a bit more than more traditional notebooks.

- **Netbooks**—This is the smallest type of notebook available, with screens in the 10" to 12" range. Netbooks, like ultrabooks, don't have CD/DVD drives or hard drives; they use solid state flash storage instead. However, netbooks typically use slower and less powerful microprocessors, which provide more battery life but less oomph to do more sophisticated operations. They also cost a lot less than other types of notebooks. Netbooks are great for checking email and doing small tasks on the go, but not for heavy duty office work.

 NOTE Learn more about notebook, tablet, and hybrid computers in Chapter 3.

With all these choices available, which type of notebook should you buy? It all depends.

Most users choose traditional notebooks, because they do everything you need them to do at a reasonable price. If you need more computing power but don't plan on taking your PC out of the house, then a desktop-replacement model might make sense. If you're a die-hard road warrior who likes to travel light, consider a more expensive but lighter weight ultrabook. And if all you need to do is check email and browse the Web while you're on the road, a netbook might be enough for you.

Tablet PCs

A tablet PC is a self-contained computer you can hold in one hand. Think of a tablet as the real-world equivalent of one of those communication pads you see on *Star Trek*; it doesn't have a separate keyboard, so you operate it by tapping and swiping the screen with your fingers.

No question about it, the most popular tablet today is the Apple iPad; no other model comes close in terms of number of users. The iPad, however, runs its own proprietary operating system (called iOS) and is thus incompatible with the hundreds of millions of Windows-based computers currently in use. That might not be important if all you do with your tablet is browse the Web, read books, and watch movies, but if you want to do more serious work—or read or work on documents created on a Windows computer—then using the iPad is somewhat problematic.

Sensing a need in the market (and wanting to grab some of that tablet revenue for itself), Microsoft designed the new Windows 8 operating system for touchscreen tablet use. A Windows 8 tablet, such as the one in Figure 1.10, looks and works just like a Windows 8 desktop or notebook PC; it's the same tiled interface, the same taps and swipes, the same everything.

FIGURE 1.10

A handheld tablet PC.

NOTE Most tablet PCs run a version of the operating system dubbed Windows RT. The only difference between Windows RT and desktop versions of Windows is that RT does not run traditional desktop software; it only runs newer Windows apps.

Tablets are great for consuming media and information, and they're pretty good for Web-based tasks, but they're not that great if you have to get serious work done; the lack of a true keyboard is a killer when you need to type long pieces of text and enter lots of numbers. Still, a Windows 8 tablet can easily supplement a more traditional PC for many types of tasks and is a strong competitor to Apple's iPad.

Hybrid PCs

A hybrid PC is the newest type of personal computer, a blend of the ultrabook and tablet form factors—literally. Think of a hybrid PC as an ultrabook with a touchscreen, or a tablet with a keyboard.

Most hybrid PCs, like the one in Figure 1.11, come with a swivel or fully removable keyboard, so you can type if you need to or get rid of the keyboard and use the touchscreen display as you would a tablet. The new Windows 8 operating system is optimized for this new type of PC, as many functions are touch enabled.

FIGURE 1.11

The Microsoft Surface hybrid tablet/ultrabook PC. (Photo courtesy Microsoft.)

With a hybrid PC, you use it like a touchscreen tablet when you're watching movies or browsing the Web, and like a notebook PC when you have office work to do. For many users, it's the best of both worlds.

 NOTE Microsoft's new Surface tablet is actually a kind of hybrid PC, especially when you consider the keyboard built into the tablet's case. Use the Surface without the keyboard and it's a tablet; open up the case and start typing on the keyboard, and it's kind of an ultrabook. Which, technically, makes it a hybrid—if old definitions are to be applied.

Which Type of PC Should You Choose?

Which type of PC is best for you? It really depends on how you think you'll use your new computer:

- If all you plan to do is check your Facebook feed, view some photos and movies, and maybe send the occasional email, then you don't really need a full keyboard and can make do with a tablet or hybrid PC.

- If you need to do more serious work, then a traditional desktop or notebook PC, complete with keyboard and mouse, is a must.

- If you plan to do all your computing in one spot, such as your home office, then a desktop PC can do the job.

- If you want more flexibility—and the ability to take your computer with you— then a notebook or hybrid model is a necessity.

As you can see, there are lots of choices, and even within these general types, more specific considerations to make. The price depends a lot on the amount of hard disk storage you get, the size of the display, the amount of internal memory, the speed of the microprocessor, and other technical details. And don't forget the design; make sure you choose a model you can personally live with, in terms of both style and functionality.

Don't Worry, You Can't Screw It Up—Much

I don't know why, but a lot of people are afraid of their computers. They think if they press the wrong key or click the wrong button they'll break something or will have to call an expensive repairperson to put things right.

This really isn't true.

The important thing to know is that it's really difficult to break your computer system. Yes, it's possible to break something if you drop it, but in terms of breaking your system through normal use, it just doesn't happen that often.

It *is* possible to make mistakes, of course. You can click the wrong button and accidentally delete a file you didn't want to delete or turn off your system and lose a document you forgot to save. You can even take inadequate security precautions and find your system infected by a computer virus. But in terms of doing serious harm just by clicking your mouse, it's unlikely.

So don't be afraid of the thing. Your computer is a tool, just like a hammer or a blender or a camera. After you learn how to use it, it can be a very useful tool. But it's *your* tool, which means you tell *it* what to do—not vice versa. Remember that you're in control and that you're not going to break anything, and you'll have a lot of fun—and maybe even get some real work done!

THE ABSOLUTE MINIMUM

Here are the key points to remember from this chapter:

- There are four main types of computer systems available today: desktops, notebooks, tablets, and hybrid models.

- Regardless of type, all personal computers are composed of various hardware components; in a desktop PC, they're separate devices, whereas notebook and tablet PCs combine them all into a single portable unit.

- You interface with your computer hardware via a piece of software called an operating system. The operating system on your new computer is probably some version of Microsoft Windows—Windows 8, Windows 7, Windows Vista, or Windows XP, depending on when you purchased the computer.

- You use specific software programs or apps to perform specific tasks, such as writing letters and editing digital photos.

- The brains and engine of your system is the system unit, which contains the microprocessor, memory, disk drives, and all the connections for your other system components.

- To make your system run faster, get a faster microprocessor or more memory.

- Data is temporarily stored in your system's memory; you store data permanently on some type of disk drive—typically a hard disk or CD/DVD drive.

2

SETTING UP AND USING A DESKTOP COMPUTER

Chapter 1, "How Personal Computers Work," gave you the essential background information you need to understand how your computer system works. With that information in hand, it's now time to connect all the various pieces and parts of your computer system—and get your PC up and running!

Of course, how you set up your computer depends on what type of computer you have. We examine notebook and tablet PCs in Chapter 3, "Setting Up and Using a Notebook or Tablet Computer;" in this chapter, we address the proper way to connect all the components of a traditional desktop PC.

Understanding the Components of a Desktop Computer System

A desktop PC is composed of several different pieces and parts. You have to properly connect all these components to make your computer system work.

On a traditional desktop PC, the most important piece of hardware is the *system unit*. This is the big, ugly box that houses your disk drives and many other components. Most system units, like the one in Figure 2.1, stand straight up like a kind of tower—and are, in fact, called either *tower* or *mini-tower* PCs, depending on the size.

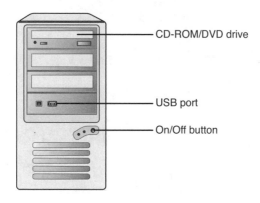

CD-ROM/DVD drive

USB port

On/Off button

FIGURE 2.1

A desktop PC system unit in a mini-tower configuration.

Know, however, that some desktop systems combine the system unit and the monitor into a single unit. These all-in-one desktops take up less space and, in some instances, provide touch-screen functionality that lets you use your fingers (instead of a mouse) to navigate the screen.

The system unit is where everything connects; it truly is the central hub for your entire system. For this reason, the back of the system unit typically is covered with all types of connectors. Because each component has its own unique type of connector, you end up with the assortment of jacks (called *ports* in the computer world) that you see in Figure 2.2.

As you've probably noticed, some PCs put some of these connectors on the front of the case, in addition to the back. This makes it easier to connect portable devices, such as an iPod music player or a digital video camcorder, without having to muck about behind your PC.

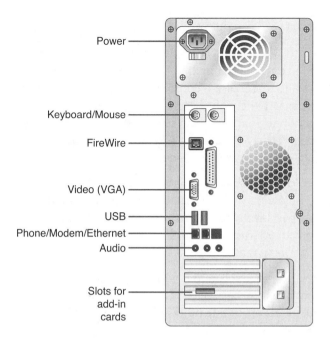

FIGURE 2.2

The back of a typical desktop PC system unit—just look at all those different connectors!

The connections are on the outside, but all the good stuff in your system unit is inside the case. With most system units, you can remove the case to peek and poke around inside.

To remove your system unit's case, make sure the unit is unplugged, and then look for some big screws or thumbscrews on either the side or back of the case. (Even better—read your PC's instruction manual for instructions specific to your unit.) With the screws loosened or removed, you should then be able to either slide off the entire case or pop open the top or back.

 CAUTION Always turn off and unplug your computer before attempting to remove the system unit's case—and be careful about touching anything inside. If you have any built-up static electricity, you can seriously damage the sensitive chips and electronic components with an innocent touch.

Before You Get Started

It's important to prepare the space where you'll be putting your new PC. Obviously, the space has to be big enough to hold all the components—though you don't have to keep all the components together. You can, for example, spread out your left and right speakers, place your subwoofer on the floor, and separate the printer from the main unit. Just don't put anything so far away that the cables don't reach. (And make sure you have a spare power outlet—or even better, a multi-outlet power strip—nearby.)

You also should consider the ergonomics of your setup. You want your keyboard at or slightly below normal desktop height, and you want your monitor at or slightly below eye level. Make sure your chair is adjusted for a straight and firm sitting position with your feet flat on the floor, and then place all the pieces of your system in relation to that.

Wherever you put your computer, you should make sure that it's in a well-ventilated location free of excess dust and smoke. (The moving parts in your computer don't like dust and dirt or any other such contaminants that can muck up the way they work.) Because your computer generates heat when it operates, you must leave enough room around the system unit for the heat to dissipate. *Never* place your computer (especially a desktop PC's system unit) in a confined, poorly ventilated space; your PC can overheat and shut down if it isn't sufficiently ventilated.

For extra protection to your computer, connect the PC's power cable to a surge suppressor rather than directly into an electrical outlet. A *surge suppressor*—which looks like a power strip but has an On/Off switch and a circuit breaker button— protects your PC from power-line surges that could damage its delicate internal parts. When a power surge temporarily spikes your line voltage (causing the voltage to momentarily increase above normal levels), a surge suppressor helps to keep the level of the electric current as steady as possible. Most surge suppressors also include circuit breakers to shut down power to your system in the event of a severe power spike.

TIP When you unpack your PC, be sure you keep all the manuals, discs, cables, and so forth. Put the ones you don't use in a safe place in case you need to reinstall any software or equipment at a later date.

CAUTION Before you connect *anything* to your computer, make sure that the peripheral is turned off.

Connecting a Traditional Desktop PC

Now it's time to get connected—which can be a bit of a chore for a traditional desktop computer system. (It's a lot easier for an all-in-one model, as you'll see in a moment.)

Connect in Order

Start by positioning your system unit so that you easily can access all the connections on the back. Then you need to carefully run the cables from each of the other components so that they're hanging loose at the rear of the system unit. Now you're ready to get connected.

It's important that you connect the cables in a particular order. To make sure that the most critical devices are connected first, follow these steps:

1. Connect your mouse to an open USB port on your computer.

2. Connect your keyboard to an open USB port on your computer.

 NOTE Some older mice and keyboards connect to separate mouse and keyboard connections on the back of your PC. Most newer mice and keyboards, however, connect via USB.

3. Connect your video monitor to the video connector on the back of your PC. Most monitors connect via a standard VGA connector, although some LCD monitors can connect via a digital DVI or HDMI connector, if one of those is present.

4. Connect the phono jack from your speaker system to the "audio out" or "sound out" connector on the back of your PC. Run the necessary cables between your right and left speakers and your subwoofer, as directed by the manufacturer. (If your speaker system connects via USB, which many newer ones do, just connect the USB cable from the main speaker to an open USB port on your computer.)

5. If you're connecting your computer to a wired router for network and Internet access, connect an Ethernet cable between the router and the Ethernet connector on the back of your computer. (If you're connecting to a wireless router and network, you can skip this step.)

6. If you have a printer, connect it to an open USB port on your computer.

NOTE Some older printers connect to a parallel port connector, sometimes labeled "printer" or "LPT1." Most newer printers, however, connect via USB.

7. Connect any other external devices to open USB ports on your PC.

8. Plug the power cable of your video monitor into a power outlet.

9. If your system includes powered speakers, plug them into a power outlet.

10. Plug any other powered external components, such as your printer, into a power outlet.

11. Connect the main power cable to the power connector on the back of your PC.

12. Plug your PC's power cable into a power outlet.

CAUTION Make sure that every cable is *firmly* connected—both to the system unit and the specific piece of hardware. Loose cables can cause all sorts of weird problems, so be sure they're plugged in really well.

Connect by Color

Most PC manufacturers color-code the cables and connectors to make the connection even easier—just plug the blue cable into the blue connector, and so on. If you're not sure what color cable goes to what device, take a look at the standard cable color coding in Table 2.1.

TABLE 2.1 Connector Color Codes

Connector	Color
VGA (analog) monitor	Blue
Digital monitor (DVI)	White
Video out	Yellow
Mouse	Green
Keyboard	Purple
Serial	Teal or turquoise
Parallel (printer)	Burgundy
USB	Black
FireWire (IEEE 1394)	Gray
Audio line out (right)	Red

TABLE 2.1   (continued)

Connector	Color
Audio line out (left)	White
Audio line out (headphones)	Lime
Speaker out/subwoofer	Orange
Right-to-left speaker	Brown
Audio line in	Light blue
Microphone	Pink
Gameport/MIDI	Gold
HDMI	Black

Connecting an All-in-One Desktop

Connecting an all-in-one desktop is somewhat easier than connecting one with a separate system unit simply because you have fewer components to deal with. You don't have to worry about connecting the monitor to the system unit because they're all one unit. Same thing typically with speakers, which are typically built into the monitor/system unit.

All you need to worry about connecting, then, are the keyboard and mouse, as well as any peripherals you might have. Follow these steps:

1. Connect your mouse to an open USB port on your computer.

2. Connect your keyboard to an open USB port on your computer.

3. If you're connecting your computer to a wired router for network and Internet access, connect an Ethernet cable between the router and the Ethernet connector on the back of your computer. (If you're connecting to a wireless router and network, you can skip this step.)

4. If you have a printer, connect it to an open USB port on your computer.

5. Connect any other external devices to open USB ports on your PC.

6. Plug any powered external components, such as your printer, into a power outlet.

7. Connect the main power cable to the power connector on the back of your PC.

8. Plug your PC's power cable into a power outlet.

Pretty simple—which is one of the advantages of all-in-one units.

Turning It On and Setting It Up

Now that you have everything connected, sit back and rest for a minute. Next up is the big step—turning it all on.

Getting the Right Order

It's important that you turn on things in the proper order. For a traditional desktop PC, follow these steps:

1. Turn on your video monitor.

2. Turn on your speaker system—but make sure the speaker volume knob is turned down (toward the left).

3. Turn on any other system components that are connected to your system unit—such as your printer, scanner, and so on. (If your PC is connected to an Ethernet network, make sure that the network router is turned on.)

4. Turn on your system unit.

Note that your system unit is the *last* thing you turn on. That's because when it powers on, it has to sense the other components of your system—which it can do only if the other components are plugged in and turned on.

For an all-in-one desktop, there's less to worry about. Just turn on any peripherals connected to the PC, such as your printer, and then press your PC's power button. It's a snap.

Powering On for the First Time

The first time you turn on your PC is a unique experience. A brand-new, out-of-the-box system has to perform some basic configuration operations, which include asking you to input some key information.

 NOTE For full installation, activation, and registration, your PC needs to be connected to the Internet—typically via a cable or DSL modem connected either to your PC or to a network hub or router.

This first-time startup operation differs from manufacturer to manufacturer, but it typically includes one or both of the following steps:

- **Windows Product Activation**—You might be asked to enter the long and nonsensical product code found on the label attached to the rear of a desktop PC system unit. Your system then connects to the Microsoft mother ship (via the Internet), registers your system information, and unlocks Windows for you to use. (Note that some manufacturers "pre-activate" Windows at the factory, so you might not have to go through this process.)

- **Windows Configuration**—During this process Windows asks a series of questions about your location, the current time and date, and other essential information. You also might be asked to create a username and password.

Many computer manufacturers supplement these configuration operations with setup procedures of their own. It's impossible to describe all the different options that might be presented by all the different manufacturers, so watch the screen carefully and follow all the onscreen instructions.

After you have everything configured, Windows finally starts, and then *you* can start using your system.

 NOTE Some installation procedures require your computer to be restarted. In most cases, this happens automatically; then the installation process resumes where it left off.

THE ABSOLUTE MINIMUM

Here are the key points to remember when connecting and configuring your new computer:

- Most peripherals connect to any USB port on your computer.

- Connecting an all-in-one unit is easier than connecting one with a separate system unit.

- Make sure your cables are firmly connected; loose cables are the cause of many computer problems.

- Connect all the cables to your system unit before you turn on the power.

- Remember to turn on your printer and monitor before you turn on the system unit.

- For full registration and activation, your computer needs to be connected to the Internet.

3

SETTING UP AND USING A NOTEBOOK OR TABLET COMPUTER

Setting up a notebook or tablet PC is considerably easier than setting up a traditional desktop system. Because everything is built into the unit's case, there's much, much less to connect!

Understanding Notebook and Hybrid PCs

Although desktop systems used to dominate the market, the most popular type of computer today is the notebook PC. A notebook PC does everything a larger desktop PC does, but in a more compact package.

A typical notebook PC combines all the various elements found in a desktop PC system into a single case and then adds a battery so that you can use it on the go. Many users find that portability convenient, even if it's just for using the computer in different rooms of the house.

As you can see in Figure 3.1, a notebook PC looks like a smallish keyboard with a flip-up LCD screen attached. That's what you see, anyway; beneath the keyboard is a full-featured computer, complete with motherboard, CPU, memory chips, video and audio processing circuits, hard drive, and battery.

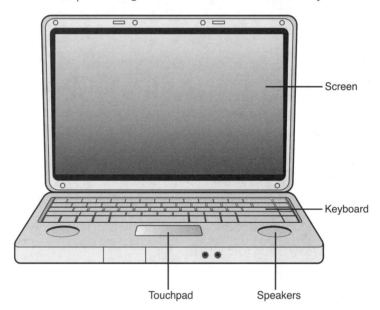

FIGURE 3.1

The important parts of a notebook PC.

When the screen is folded down, the keyboard is hidden and the PC is easy to carry from place to place; when the screen is flipped up, the keyboard is exposed. On the keyboard is some sort of built-in pointing device, like a touchpad, which is used in place of a standalone mouse.

On hybrid PCs, the screen may flip or fold in a way to hide the keyboard and make the unit look like and function as a tablet. (It may be the keyboard doing the flipping, on some models.) Hybrid PCs have touchscreen displays, which you can operate with your fingers in either notebook or tablet mode.

If you look closely at a notebook or hybrid PC, you also see two built-in speakers, typically just above the top edge of the keyboard. Most notebooks also have an earphone jack, which you can use to connect a set of headphones or earbuds, the better to listen to music in a public place. (When you connect a set of headphones or earbuds, the built-in speakers are automatically muted.)

Somewhere on the notebook—either on the side or along the back edge—should be a row of connecting ports, like what's shown in Figure 3.2. Most notebooks have two or more USB connectors, an Ethernet connector (for connecting to a wired network), a VGA video connector (for connecting to an external display monitor), and perhaps an HDMI connector (for connecting to a living room TV).

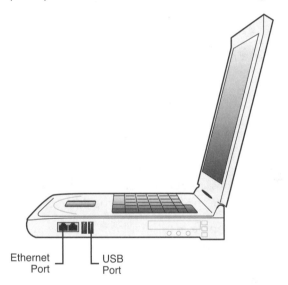

Ethernet Port   USB Port

FIGURE 3.2

Connecting ports on a notebook PC.

 NOTE Some notebooks include a DisplayPort port, which can be used to connect the PC to an external monitor. To do so, you use a special adapter that connects to the DisplayPort connector on one end and to a VGA, DVI, or HDMI connector on the other.

In addition, most traditional notebooks (but not ultrabooks or netbooks) have a built-in CD/DVD drive, typically on the side of the case. Some notebooks up the ante and include Blu-ray capability, as well. Press the little button to open the drive and insert a disc; push the drive back in to begin playing the CD or DVD.

Inside the notebook case are the guts of the computer—everything you have in a desktop PC's system unit but more compact. In fact, most notebooks have *more* inside than does a typical desktop; in particular, most notebook PCs have a built-in Wi-Fi adapter so that the notebook can connect to a wireless home network or public Wi-Fi hotspot.

In addition, virtually all notebook PCs come with some sort of built-in battery. That's because a portable PC is truly portable; in addition to running on normal AC power, a notebook PC can operate unplugged, using battery power. Depending on the PC (and the battery), you might be able to operate a laptop for three or four hours or more before switching batteries or plugging the unit into a wall outlet. That makes a notebook PC great for use on airplanes, in coffee shops, or anywhere plugging in a power cord is inconvenient.

Understanding Tablet PCs

A tablet PC is like a notebook without the keyboard. That is, you have a single, nonhinged unit with a display in the 7" to 10" range. The display is a touchscreen, which is how you operate the thing, by tapping and swiping your fingers across the screen.

Most Windows 8 tablets run a slimmed down version of the same operating system found on notebook and desktop PCs, dubbed Windows RT. (Other tablets run the full desktop version of Windows.) Window RT looks just like the notebook/desktop version, but doesn't run traditional desktop software programs, only newer purpose-specific apps found in Microsoft's online Windows Store.

Unlike the competing Apple iPad, Windows tablets feature a small selection of ports along the side of the unit. Depending on the model, you're likely to find one or more USB ports, as well as a headphone connector and full-size or mini HDMI connector. You can use the USB ports to connect all manner of peripherals, from printers to external hard drives. You use the headphone connector to connect a set of headphones or earbuds, of course. And you use the HDMI port to connect your tablet to an external monitor or living room TV.

Connecting Peripherals and Powering On

One nice thing about notebook PCs is that you don't have nearly as many pieces to connect to get your system up and running. Because the monitor, speakers, keyboard, mouse, and Wi-Fi adapter are all built into the notebook unit, the only things you really have to connect are a printer and a power cable. (And not even a printer, if you already have one connected elsewhere on your home network.)

Getting Connected

To get your notebook PC up and running, all you have to do is connect your printer or any other desired peripherals to a USB port on your computer. Then connect your notebook's power cable to a power strip or surge suppressor and press the power button. (You can even skip connecting to a power strip if you're running on internal batteries.)

Getting a tablet up and running is even simpler, as you probably won't have any peripherals to connect. Because the tablet runs on battery power, all you have to do is turn it on—after you've charged it up, of course.

Powering On for the First Time

As with a desktop PC, the first time you turn on a notebook or tablet computer is different from what you'll experience in later use. There are some basic configuration operations you need to perform.

 NOTE For full installation, activation, and registration, your PC needs to be connected to the Internet—typically via the unit's built-in Wi-Fi connection.

This first-time startup operation differs from manufacturer to manufacturer, but it typically includes one or both of the following steps:

- **Windows Product Activation**—You might be asked to input the long and nonsensical product code found on the label attached to the bottom of a notebook PC or back of a tablet. Your system then connects to Microsoft (via the Internet), registers your system information, and unlocks Windows for you to use. (Note that some manufacturers "pre-activate" Windows at the factory, so you might not have to go through this process.)

- **Windows Configuration**—During this process Windows asks a series of questions about your location, the current time and date, and other essential information. You also might be asked to create a username and password.

It's also possible that the computer manufacturer might supplement these configuration operations with setup procedures of its own. Just make sure you follow the onscreen instructions as best you can. After you have everything configured, Windows finally starts, and then you can start using your system.

THE ABSOLUTE MINIMUM

Here are the key points to remember when connecting and configuring your new computer:

- Notebook PCs contain all the components of a desktop PC, but in a smaller, more portable case—complete with battery.

- A tablet PC is just like a notebook, but without the keyboard.

- You don't have to connect anything to your notebook or tablet to get it up and running—save for the power cord, at least until the internal battery is charged up.

- Turning on a notebook or tablet is as simple as pressing the power button.

- For full registration and activation, your notebook or tablet needs to be connected to the Internet.

4

GETTING TO KNOW WINDOWS 8

As you learned in Chapter 1, "How Personal Computers Work," the software and operating system make your hardware work. The operating system for most personal computers is Microsoft Windows, and you need to know how to use Windows to use your PC. Windows pretty much runs your computer for you; if you don't know your way around Windows, you won't be able to do much of anything on your new PC.

Introducing Microsoft Windows

Microsoft Windows is a type of software called an *operating system*. An operating system does what its name implies—*operates* your computer *system*, working in the background every time you turn on your PC.

Equally important, Windows is what you see when you first turn on your computer, after everything turns on and boots up. Windows is your gateway to every program and app you run on your computer, and to all the documents and files you view and edit.

Welcome to Windows 8

If you've recently purchased a new PC, the version of Windows on your PC is probably Windows 8. Microsoft has released different versions of Windows over the years, and Windows 8 is the latest—which is why it comes preinstalled on most new PCs.

 NOTE If your computer is running an older version of Windows, you should pick up a previous edition of this book covering that operating system. The Fifth Edition of the book covers Windows 7; the Fourth Edition covers Windows Vista. You should be able to find these editions at Amazon.com and other online booksellers.

If you've used a previous version of Windows—such as Windows 7, Windows Vista, or Windows XP—on another PC, you'll immediately notice that Windows 8 looks and acts completely different from what you're used to. Don't worry, though; everything that was in the old Windows is still in the new Windows—it's just in a slightly different place, and you have to do something different to get to it.

 NOTE You can upgrade a computer running an older version of Windows to Windows 8—but you probably don't want to. Basic operation is so different in Windows 8 you'll face significant retraining time if you move to the new version.

The most different part of Windows 8 is the graphical user interface, or GUI. Where previous versions of Windows operated from something called the Windows desktop, Windows 8 hides the desktop (it's still there, just buried) and the old Start menu, and instead relies on a tile-based Start screen. The new Windows puts everything front and center; launching an app or opening a file is as easy as scrolling to the right tile and then clicking or tapping it.

The new Windows 8 interface isn't just for computers; it looks right at home on a touchscreen device, such as a tablet PC or smartphone—in fact, it's touch enabled. That means you can just as easily operate Windows 8 with a tap and a swipe of your finger (on a touchscreen device, that is) as you can with a mouse or keyboard.

 NOTE   Microsoft called the new Windows 8 interface the "Metro interface" during development.

The reason for Windows 8's new interface has to do with the overall industry movement toward touchscreen computing. Microsoft designed an interface (actually taken from its Windows Phone 7 operating system for smartphones) that works equally well on all types of computers and mobile devices. This makes it easier for you to switch from using a computer to a tablet to a smartphone; the Windows interface stays pretty much the same no matter what device you're using.

If you're a brand-new computer user, you'll find the Windows 8 interface easy to understand and even easier to use. If you've used other versions of Windows in the past, however, you might find the Windows 8 interface to be a little confusing; nothing looks the same and nothing is where you expect it to be. It requires a bit of relearning, but after you get past that, Windows 8 is actually quite easy to use.

Different Versions of Windows 8

Not to confuse you, but there are three different versions of Windows 8, each with a slightly different feature set. Which version you have depends on which was installed by your PC's manufacturer.

Most consumer-oriented PCs should be running the basic version, called simply Windows 8. This version is designed for home use and comes with all the functionality the average user needs.

Windows 8 Pro is designed for professional and business users. The primary additions to this version are features for large businesses and professional IT folks, such as BitLocker drive encryption and an encrypting file system (for greater security), as well as a group policy editor (for managing multiple PCs from a single location).

If you're running Windows on a tablet PC, chances are you're running Windows RT. This version of Windows is designed for this type of limited-functionality device, not for full-featured notebook and desktop computers. It's a lot like the basic Windows 8 version, but lacks the ability to run traditional desktop computer software.

It's likely, then, that your personal computer is running the basic Windows 8 version. That's also the version we focus on throughout this book.

TIP You can upgrade the basic version of Windows 8 to the Pro version within Windows itself. Open the Control Panel, click System and Security, then System, then Get More Features with a New Edition of Windows. Select the version you want, enter your payment information (the upgrade isn't free, sorry), then prepare to download and install the new version.

Starting and Logging into Windows 8

Starting your computer and logging into Windows 8 is a simple affair, albeit a bit different than in previous versions of Windows. It all starts when you push the power button on your PC.

Each time you turn on your computer, you should see a series of text messages flash across your screen. These messages are there to let you know what's going on as your computer *boots up.*

NOTE Technical types call the procedure of starting up a computer *booting* or *booting up* the system. Restarting a system (turning it off and then back on) is called *rebooting.*

After a few seconds (during which your system unit beeps and whirrs a little bit), the Windows Lock screen appears. As you can see in Figure 4.1, the Lock screen provides some basic information—today's date and the current time, Internet connection status, and power status—against a pretty photographic background while Windows waits for you to log on.

To log onto your Windows account, all you have to do is press any key on your keyboard or tap the screen. This displays your username, as shown in Figure 4.2.

Enter your password and then press the Enter key or click/tap the right-arrow button. After you're past this Lock screen, you're taken directly to the Windows Start screen, and your system is ready to use.

NOTE It's easy to configure Windows 8 for multiple users, each with their own account and settings; we'll discuss that in Chapter 5, "Personalizing Windows 8." If you only have a single user on the machine, only one name appears from the Lock screen.

FIGURE 4.1

The first thing you see in Windows 8—the Lock screen.

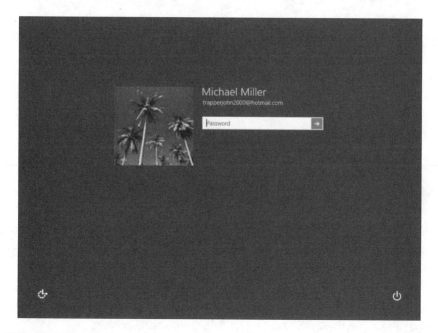

FIGURE 4.2

Select your username and enter your password to proceed.

Working Your Way Around the Start Screen

Everything in Windows 8 revolves around the Start screen. That's where you start out and where you launch new apps and software programs.

Examining the Parts of the Start Screen

As you can see in Figure 4.3, the main area of the Start screen consists of a series of *tiles*. Each tile represents a particular app, program, document, or function.

Tiles   Username and profile picture

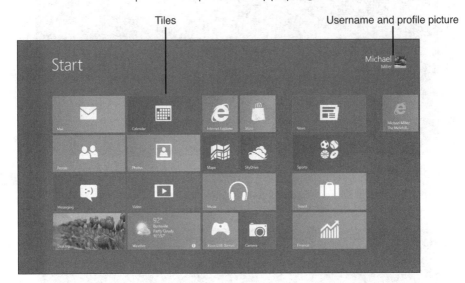

FIGURE 4.3

The Windows 8 Start screen.

NOTE Your Start screen probably looks a little different from the one in Figure 4.3, in particular the tiles you see. That's because every person's system is different, depending on the particular programs and apps you have installed on your PC.

Windows 8 tiles are big and colorful, ideal for viewing on a portable or touch-screen device. Tiles vary in size, with some spanning a single column and some spanning two columns; there's no real difference between a large and a small tile, other than the size.

At the top-left corner of the screen is the screen name—Start. Clicking this name doesn't do anything; the name just tells you where you are.

At the top-right corner of the screen is your name and profile picture. Click or tap your name to sign out of Windows, lock the screen, or change your account picture.

The bottom of the Start screen is empty until you move your mouse to this area or tap your finger here (if you have a touchscreen display). Then you see the horizontal scrollbar, shown in Figure 4.4, along with the Zoom button. Use the scrollbar to scroll left and right through additional tiles; click the Zoom button to see all the screens of tiles on your Start screen, in a minimized mode, as shown in Figure 4.5.

Left scroll button   Scrollbar   Right scroll button

FIGURE 4.4

The navigation elements at the bottom of the Start screen.

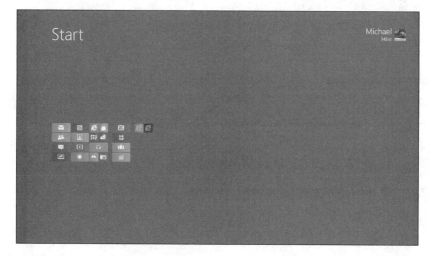

FIGURE 4.5

Zooming out to see all your Start screens.

NOTE Microsoft calls this ability to view all the Start screens in minimized mode *semantic zoom*. If you have a touchscreen display, you can perform this semantic zoom by "pinching" your thumb and first finger together to zoom out, or by "spreading" your thumb and finger to return to normal view. When you're zoomed out on the Start screen, you can then click or tap any individual screen of tiles to go to that screen.

Scrolling Through the Tiles

There are probably more tiles on your Start screen than will fit on a single screen of your computer display. To view all your Start tiles, you need to scroll the screen left or right. There are several ways to do this:

- **With your mouse**—Click and drag the horizontal scrollbar at the bottom of the screen, or click the right and left scroll arrows on either side of the scrollbar. If your mouse has a scroll wheel, you can use the scroll wheel to scroll right (down) or left (up) through the tiles.

- **With your keyboard**—To scroll one screen at a time, press the PageDown button (scroll right) or the PageUp button (scroll left). To scroll one tile at a time, press the left arrow or right arrow buttons.

- **With a touchscreen display**—Swipe the screen with your finger right to left to scroll right, or left to right to scroll left.

Opening a Tile

Remember that each tile on the Start screen represents a specific app or document. There are three ways to launch an app or open a document from these tiles:

- **With your mouse**—Click the tile, using the left mouse button.

- **With your keyboard**—Use your keyboard's arrow keys to highlight that tile and then press the Enter key.

- **With a touchscreen display**—Tap the tile with your finger.

Displaying the Charms Bar

Windows 8 has more functions up its sleeve, although they're not obvious during normal use. These are a series of system functions, called *Charms*, which are accessed from a Charms Bar that appears on the right side of the screen.

There are three ways to display the Charms Bar:

- **With your mouse**—Move your mouse to either the top-right or bottom-right corner of the screen.

- **With your keyboard**—Press Windows+C.

- **On a touchscreen display**—Swipe your finger from the right edge of the screen (to the left).

As you can see in Figure 4.6, the Charms Bar consists of the following icons:

- **Search**—Click this icon to search your computer for apps and documents. (We discuss the search function later in this chapter.)

- **Share**—If you're using a specific application, click this icon to share the content of the app with other users via email and other services.

- **Start**—Click this icon to return to the Start screen from any other location in Windows.

- **Devices**—Click this icon to configure the settings of any external devices connected to your computer.

- **Settings**—Click this icon to access and configure various Windows settings.

FIGURE 4.6

The Windows 8 Charms Bar.

 NOTE Whenever the Charms Bar is displayed, Windows also displays a notification panel (at the bottom left of the screen) with the current date and time, Internet connection status, and power status. This panel pretty much duplicates the information shown on the Windows 8 Lock screen.

Note that you can access the Charms Bar from *any* screen in Windows 8, even if you have an app displayed full screen. All you have to do is click or tap appropriately and the Charms Bar appears.

 TIP You can access more advanced system options, such as Network Connections, Power Options, and Device Manager, by moving your mouse to the lower-left corner of the screen and then right-clicking. A menu of advanced options displays; click an item to open it.

Returning to the Start Screen

Obviously, the Start screen is important; it's where you launch everything you want to do in Windows. Fortunately, it's easy to return to the Start screen at any time.

Actually, there are several different ways to return to the Start screen from any running app. You can

- Display the Charms Bar and click Start.

- Press the Windows key on your keyboard.

- Move your mouse to the lower-left corner of the app screen to display a thumbnail of the Start screen; click this thumbnail to return to the Start screen.

Displaying the Traditional Desktop

If you've used a previous version of Windows (or use a different Windows at work), you might wonder what happened to the Windows desktop. Well, it's still there in Windows 8; you just have to know where to look.

The desktop used to be the control center of Windows; it was where you launched all your programs and managed all your documents and files. That's changed in Windows 8, of course; everything now is done from the new tile-based Start screen. But if you're a more-experienced user you might be more comfortable using the old-style desktop, which is why it's still there in Windows 8—just not displayed as prominently as it used to be.

To display the traditional Windows desktop, all you have to do is click or tap the Desktop tile on the Start screen. This displays the Windows 8 version of the traditional desktop.

As you can see in Figure 4.7, the Windows 8 desktop doesn't contain as many elements as older desktops, and that's for a reason. You really don't use the desktop to open programs and documents; that's done with the new Start screen. So you don't need a Start menu or anything similar on the desktop. In fact, you only need the desktop to host traditional desktop programs.

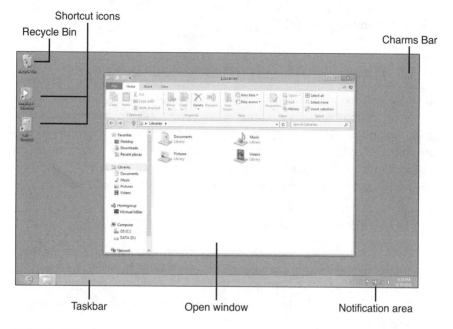

FIGURE 4.7

The Windows 8 desktop.

What's on the Windows 8 desktop? You'll see the following elements:

- **Taskbar**—Displays icons for your favorite applications and documents, as well as for any open window. By default, you'll see icons for Internet Explorer (the web browser for Windows) and File Explorer (the file management tool for Windows). Right-click an icon to see a Jump List of recent open documents and other operations for that application.

- **Notification area**—Previously known as the system tray, this part of the taskbar displays icons for a handful of key system functions, including the Action Center, power (on notebook PCs), networking/Internet, and audio (volume).

- **Shortcut icons**—These are links to software programs you can place on your desktop; a "clean" desktop includes just one icon—the one for the Windows Recycle Bin.

- **Recycle Bin**—This is where you dump any files you want to delete.

Again, if you're an experienced Windows user, you'll notice several items missing from this new desktop—including and especially the Start menu. If you want to open a program, you need to return to the Windows 8 Start screen and launch it from there. (Unless, that is, you've created a desktop shortcut for that item or "pinned" it to the taskbar.)

Learning Important Mouse Operations

To use Windows efficiently on a desktop or notebook PC, you must master a few simple operations with your mouse or touchpad, such as pointing and clicking, dragging and dropping, and right-clicking. (If you have a touchscreen PC, you can perform many of these same operations with your finger—which we discuss later in this chapter.) When you're using your mouse or touchpad in this fashion, you're moving the onscreen *cursor*—that pointer thing that looks like a little arrow.

Pointing and Clicking

The most common mouse operation is *pointing and clicking.* Simply move your computer's mouse or, on a notebook PC, drag your finger across the touchpad or other pointing device so that the cursor is pointing to the object you want to select, and then click the left mouse button once. Pointing and clicking is an effective way to select tiles, menu items, and the like.

Double-Clicking

In some instances, single-clicking doesn't launch or open an item, it merely selects it. In these instances, you need to *double-click* an item to activate an operation. This involves pointing at something onscreen with the cursor and then clicking the left mouse button twice in rapid succession.

Right-Clicking

Here's one of the secret keys to efficient Windows operation. When you select an item and then click the *right* mouse button, you often see a pop-up menu. This menu, when available, contains commands that directly relate to the selected object. So, for example, if you right-click a file icon, you see commands related to that file—copy, move, delete, and so forth.

Refer to your individual programs to see whether and how they use the right mouse button.

Dragging and Dropping

Dragging is a variation of clicking. To drag an object, point at it with the cursor and then press and hold down the left mouse button. Move the mouse without releasing the mouse button and drag the object to a new location. When you're finished moving the object, release the mouse button to drop it onto the new location.

You can use dragging and dropping to move files from one location to another.

Mouse Over

When you position the cursor over an item without clicking your mouse, you're *mousing over* that item. (This is sometimes called *hovering*.) Many operations require you to mouse over an item to display additional options or information.

Moving and Resizing Windows

In Windows 8, most newer apps launch full screen. However, traditional software programs operate within the traditional Windows desktop and display in individual onscreen windows. When you open more than one program in this fashion, you get more than one window—and your desktop can quickly become cluttered.

 TIP   The cursor changes shape—to a double-ended arrow—when it's positioned over the edge of a window.

There are many ways to deal with this sort of multiple-window desktop clutter. One way is to move a window to a new position. You do this by positioning your cursor over a blank area at the top of the window frame and then clicking and holding down the left button on your mouse. As long as this button is depressed, you can use your mouse to drag the window around the screen. When you release the mouse button, the window stays where you put it.

With Windows 8, you can quickly "snap" a window to the left or right side of the desktop. Just drag the window to the left side of the screen to dock it there and resize it to the left half of the desktop; drag the window to the right side of the screen to dock it on that side.

You also can change the size of most windows. You do this by positioning the cursor over the edge of the window—any edge. If you position the cursor on either side of the window, you can resize the width. If you position the cursor on the top or bottom edge, you can resize the height. Finally, if you position the cursor on a corner, you can resize the width and height at the same time.

After the cursor is positioned over the window's edge, press and hold down the left mouse button; then drag the window border to its new size. Release the mouse button to lock in the newly sized window.

Maximizing, Minimizing, and Closing Windows

Another way to manage a window on the Windows desktop is to make it display full screen. You do this by maximizing the window. All you have to do is click the Maximize button at the upper-right corner of the window, as shown in Figure 4.8.

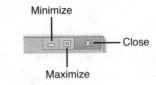

FIGURE 4.8

Use the Minimize, Maximize, and Close buttons to manage your desktop windows.

 TIP You can also "snap" a window full screen by using your mouse to drag the window to the top of the desktop. This automatically maximizes the window.

If the window is already maximized, the Maximize button changes to a Restore Down button. When you click the Restore Down button, the window resumes its previous (premaximized) dimensions.

If you would rather hide the window so that it doesn't clutter your desktop, click the Minimize button. This shoves the window off the desktop, onto the taskbar. The program in the window is still running, however—it's just not on the desktop. To restore a minimized window, all you have to do is click the window's icon on the Windows taskbar (at the bottom of the screen).

If what you really want to do is close the window (and close any program running within the window), just click the window's Close button.

 CAUTION If you try to close a window that contains a document you haven't saved, you're prompted to save the changes to the document. Because you probably don't want to lose any of your work, click Yes to save the document and then close the program.

Scrolling Through a Window

Many windows, whether full screen or otherwise, contain more information than can be displayed at once. When you have a long document or web page, only the first part of the document or page is displayed in the window. To view the rest of the document or page, you have to scroll down through the window using the various parts of the scrollbar (shown in Figure 4.9).

There are several ways to scroll through a window. To scroll up or down a line at a time, click the up or down arrow on the window's scrollbar. To move to a specific place in a long document, use your mouse to grab the scroll box (between the up and down arrows) and drag it to a new position. You can also click on the scrollbar between the scroll box and the end arrow, so that you scroll one screen at a time.

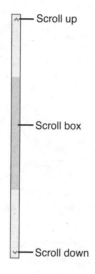

Scroll up

Scroll box

Scroll down

FIGURE 4.9

Use the scrollbar to scroll through long pages.

If your mouse has a scroll wheel, you can use it to scroll through a long document. Just roll the wheel back or forward to scroll down or up through a window. Likewise, some notebook touchpads let you drag your finger up or down to scroll through a window. And, of course, if you're using a touchscreen display, you can simply swipe your finger downward in the document to scroll down, or swipe upward to scroll up.

Using Dialog Boxes, Tabs, and Buttons

When Windows or a specific app requires a complex set of inputs, you are often presented with a *dialog box*. A dialog box is similar to a form in which you can input various parameters and make various choices—and then register those inputs and choices when you click OK. (Figure 4.10 shows the Save As dialog box, found in many Windows apps.)

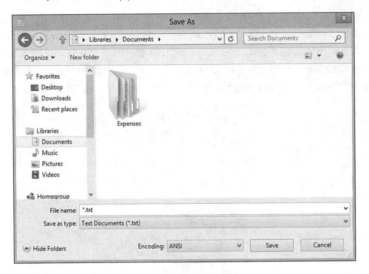

FIGURE 4.10

Use dialog boxes to control various aspects of your Windows applications.

Windows has several types of dialog boxes, each one customized to the task at hand. However, most dialog boxes share a set of common features, which include the following:

- **Buttons**—Most buttons either register your inputs or open an auxiliary dialog box. The most common buttons are OK (to register your inputs and close the dialog box), Cancel (to close the dialog box without registering your inputs), and Apply (to register your inputs without closing the dialog box). Click a button once to activate it.

- **Tabs**—These allow a single dialog box to display multiple "pages" of information. Think of each tab, arranged across the top of the dialog box, as a "thumbtab" to the individual page in the dialog box below it. Click the top of a tab to change to that particular page of information.

- **Text boxes**—These are empty boxes where you type a response. Position your cursor over the empty input box, click your left mouse button, and begin typing.

- **Lists**—These are lists of available choices; lists can either scroll or drop down from what looks like an input box. Select an item from the list with your mouse; you can select multiple items in some lists by holding down the Ctrl key while clicking with your mouse.

- **Check boxes**—These are boxes that let you select (or deselect) various stand-alone options.

- **Sliders**—These are sliding bars that let you select increments between two extremes, similar to a sliding volume control on an audio system.

 NOTE The operations presented in this chapter are described as they look and act by default in a typical Windows 8 installation. If you're using someone else's PC, things might not look or act exactly like this. It's normal for two different PCs to look and act a little differently because you can customize so many options for your own personal tastes—as you learn in Chapter 5.

Learning Important Touchscreen Operations

If you're using Windows on a computer or tablet with a touchscreen display, you use your fingers instead of a mouse to do what you need to do. To that end, it's important to learn some essential touchscreen operations.

Tapping

The touchscreen equivalent of clicking an item is tapping that item. That is, you tap a tile or button or menu item with the tip of your finger. Just tap and release, that's it to open an app or select an option.

Pressing and Holding

As you've learned, right-clicking an item with your mouse often displays additional information or options. The touchscreen equivalent of the right-click is to press and hold an item. Simply touch an item onscreen with your finger and hold it there until a complete circle appears on the display. You can then lift your finger, and a shortcut menu appears.

Flicking

With a touchscreen display, you can perform many common tasks with a simple flick of your finger across the screen. A flick is essentially a rapid swipe from one point to another. For example, an upward flick scrolls a page downward, and a downward flick scrolls a page upward.

Panning

You use panning to scroll down or through a long page or series of screens. Simply touch and drag the page with one or more fingers in the direction you want to pan.

Zooming

You use two fingers to zoom into or out of a given screen—that is, to make a selection larger (zooming in) or smaller (zooming out) onscreen.

To zoom out, use two fingers (or your thumb and first finger) to touch two points on the item, and then move your fingers in toward each other, as if you're pinching the screen. To zoom in, use your fingers to touch two points on the item, and then move your fingers apart from each other, as if you're stretching the screen.

Rotating

You can use your fingers to rotate a picture or other item on the screen in a circular motion, either clockwise or counter-clockwise. Simply use two fingers to touch two points on the item, then turn your fingers in the direction you want to rotate it.

Getting Help in Windows

When you can't figure out how to perform a particular task, it's time to ask for help. In Windows 8, you get help through the Help and Support Center.

To launch the Help and Support Center, follow these steps:

1. Press the Windows key to display the Start screen.

2. Right-click anywhere on the Start screen to display the App Bar at the bottom of the screen.

3. Click or tap All Apps.

4. When the Apps screen appears, scroll to the Windows System section and tap or click Help and Support.

A Help and Support window opens on the Windows desktop, as shown in Figure 4.11. From here you can search for specific answers to your problems, browse the table of contents, connect to another computer for remote assistance, go online for additional help, and troubleshoot any problems you might be having. Click the type of help you want, and follow the onscreen instructions from there.

FIGURE 4.11

Windows 8's Help and Support Center.

Shutting Down Windows—And Your Computer

You've probably already noticed that Windows starts automatically every time you turn on your computer. Although you see lines of text flashing onscreen during the initial startup, Windows loads automatically and goes on to display the Windows desktop.

 CAUTION Do *not* turn off your computer from your computer's main power button without first shutting down Windows. You could lose data and settings that are temporarily stored in your system's memory.

When you want to turn off your computer, you do it through Windows. In fact, you don't want to turn off your computer any other way—you *always* want to turn off things through the official Windows procedure.

To shut down Windows and turn off your PC, follow these steps:

1. Display the Charms Bar and click or tap Settings.

2. When the Settings panel appears, as shown in Figure 4.12, click or tap Power to display the pop-up menu.

3. Click or tap Shut Down.

FIGURE 4.12

Powering off Windows 8.

That's it. If you have a desktop PC, you then need to manually turn off your monitor, printer, and other peripherals.

THE ABSOLUTE MINIMUM

This chapter gave you a lot of background about Windows 8—your new PC's operating system. Here are the key points to remember:

- You use Windows to manage your computer system and run apps and programs.

- Most functions in Windows are activated by clicking or tapping a tile, icon, or button.

- The most popular apps and accessories on your system are displayed as clickable tiles on the Start screen. You can display the Start screen at any time by pressing the Windows button on your computer keyboard.

- You access key system functions via the Charms Bar, which you display by pressing Windows+C on your keyboard.

- You can complete most operations in Windows 8 using your computer keyboard, mouse, or—on touchscreen displays—a tap or swipe of your finger on the touchscreen.

- Desktop software programs are typically run on the traditional Windows desktop, which you open from the Start screen.

PERSONALIZING WINDOWS 8

When you first turn on your new computer system, you see the Windows Start screen as Microsoft (or your computer manufacturer) set it up for you. If you like the way it looks, great. If not, you can change it.

Windows presents a lot of different ways to personalize the look and feel of your system. In fact, one of the great things about Windows is how quickly you can make Windows look like *your* version of Windows, different from anybody else's.

Personalizing the Start Screen

Let's start by learning how to configure your own personal Start screen. As you know, the Start screen, shown in Figure 5.1, is your own personal home base in Windows 8; it consists of a number of tiles that you use to open apps and files. You can change the background color of the start screen, as well as determine which tiles are displayed—and how.

FIGURE 5.1

The Windows 8 Start screen.

Changing the Background Color

When you configured Windows when you first turned on your new computer, you were asked to choose a color scheme. This color scheme is what you see when you display the Windows Start screen.

Fortunately, you're not locked into your initial choice. You can change the color scheme for your Start screen (and various subsidiary screens) at any time. Just follow these steps:

1. Display the Charms Bar and click or tap Settings to display the Settings panel.

2. Click or tap Change PC Settings to display the PC Settings page, shown in Figure 5.2.

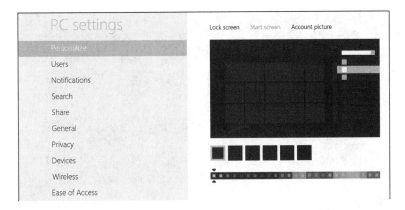

FIGURE 5.2

Personalizing the Start screen color scheme.

3. Click or tap Personalize in the left column.

4. Click or tap Start Screen in the right panel.

5. Drag the background color slider to the color you want.

6. Click or tap the desired background pattern.

That's it. The changes you make are immediate and interactive. You don't have to "save" them; they're applied automatically.

Making a Tile Larger or Smaller

The Start screen is composed of dozens of individual tiles, each representing an app, program, operation, or file. There are several ways to personalize the Start screen by changing how these tiles are displayed.

For instance, tiles can be either one- or two-column width. To change the width of a given tile, follow these steps:

1. Right-click the tile (or press and hold it on a touchscreen) you want to change. This adds a check mark to the tile and displays the pop-up bar at the bottom of the screen, as shown in Figure 5.3.

2. Click or tap Smaller to make a large tile smaller; click or tap Larger to make a small tile larger.

FIGURE 5.3

Changing the size of the Video tile.

Rearranging Tiles

If you don't like where a given tile appears on the Start screen, you can rearrange the order of your tiles. To move a tile, use your mouse (or, on a touchscreen display, your finger) to click and drag a given tile to a new position.

Removing a Tile

You might find that there are one or more tiles on your Start screen that you never use. You can remove unused tiles to get them out of your way and make room for additional tiles. Follow these steps:

1. Right-click the tile (or press and hold it on a touchscreen) you want to delete. This adds a check mark to the tile and displays the pop-up bar at the bottom of the screen.

2. Click or tap Unpin from Start.

Adding a New Tile

If you accidently remove a tile from the Start screen, or you want to add a tile for an app that isn't already there, you can do so. To add a new tile, follow these steps:

1. Press the Windows key to display the Start screen.

2. Right-click anywhere on the Start screen (or press Windows+Z) to display the Options Bar at the bottom of the screen.

3. Click or tap All Apps.

4. When the Apps screen appears, right-click the item you want to add (or press and hold it on a touchscreen); this displays the Options Bar at the bottom of the screen, as shown in Figure 5.4.

5. Click or tap Pin to Start.

The new tile appears at the end of your existing tiles on the Start screen. You can move it to a new position by clicking and dragging it with your mouse or finger.

FIGURE 5.4

Adding a new tile to the Start screen.

Turning On or Off a Live Tile

Many tiles are "live," meaning that they display the current information or a selected document for that app. For example, the Weather tile displays the current weather conditions; the Photos tile displays a slideshow of photographs stored on your computer.

To turn off a live tile—that is, to display the default tile icon—follow these steps:

1. Right-click the tile (or press and hold it on a touchscreen) you want to change; this adds a check mark to the tile and displays the pop-up bar at the bottom of the screen, shown in Figure 5.5.

2. Click or tap Turn Live Tile Off.

To turn on a live tile, repeat these steps but select Turn Live Tile On.

FIGURE 5.5

Turning "off" the live Weather tile.

Personalizing the Lock Screen

You can also personalize the Lock screen, shown in Figure 5.6, which you see when you first start or begin to log into Windows. You can change the background picture, as well as add informational apps to the screen.

FIGURE 5.6

The Windows 8 Lock screen.

Changing the Lock Screen Background

To change the background picture you see on the Lock screen, follow these steps:

1. Display the Charms Bar and click or tap Settings to display the Settings panel.

2. Click or tap Change PC Settings to display the PC Settings page, shown in Figure 5.7.

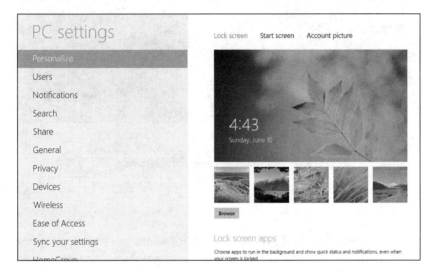

FIGURE 5.7

Personalizing the background image on the Lock screen.

3. Click or tap Personalize in the left column.

4. Click or tap Lock Screen in the right panel.

5. Click or tap the thumbnail for the picture you'd like to use.

   OR

6. To use your own picture as the background, click or tap the Browse button.

7. When the Files screen appears, as shown in Figure 5.8, navigate to and click or tap the picture you want to use, then click or tap the Choose Picture button.

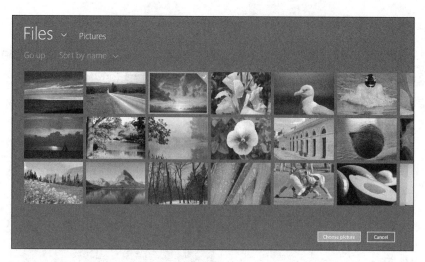

FIGURE 5.8

Selecting your own picture for the Lock screen background.

Adding Apps to the Lock Screen

The Lock screen can display a number of apps that run in the background and display useful or interesting information, even while your computer is locked. By default you see the date/time, power status, and connection status, but it's easy to add the following apps to the Lock screen:

- Calendar
- Mail
- Messaging
- Weather

To add one or more of these apps to your Lock screen, follow these steps:

1. Display the Charms Bar and click or tap Settings to display the Settings panel.
2. Click or tap Change PC Settings to display the PC Settings page.
3. Click or tap Personalize in the left column.
4. Click or tap Lock Screen in the right panel.
5. Scroll down the Lock Screen panel to the Lock Screen Apps section, shown in Figure 5.9.

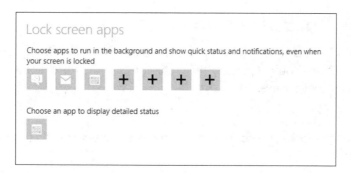

FIGURE 5.9

Selecting apps for the Lock screen.

6. Click or tap a + button to display the Choose an App panel, shown in Figure 5.10.

7. Click or tap the app you want to add.

FIGURE 5.10

Choosing a Lock screen app.

 TIP You can also opt for one of the apps to display detailed live information. For example, you might want the Lock screen to display current weather conditions from the Weather app, or upcoming appointments from the Calendar app. To select which app displays detailed information, click or tap the app button in the Choose an App to Display Detailed Status section. When the Choose an App panel appears, click or tap the app you want.

Changing Your Account Picture

When you first configured Windows, you picked a default image to use as your profile picture. You can, at any time, change this picture to something more to your liking. Follow these steps:

1. Press the Windows key or button to return to the Start screen.

2. Click or tap your account name in the top-right corner to display the pop-up menu.

3. Click or tap Change Account Picture.

4. When the PC Settings page appears, make sure that Personalize is selected in the left column and Account Picture is selected in the right panel, as shown in Figure 5.11.

FIGURE 5.11

Changing your account picture.

5. Click or tap the Browse button.

6. When the Files screen appears, navigate to and click or tap the picture you want, then click or tap the Choose Image button.

 TIP If your computer has a webcam, you can take a picture with your webcam to use for your account picture. From the Account Picture page, click or tap the Camera button and follow the onscreen directions from there.

Configuring Other Windows Settings

There are many other Windows system settings that you can configure. In most cases, the default settings work just fine and you don't need to change a thing. However, you *can* change these settings, if you so desire.

You configure most of these settings from the PC Settings screen, which you get to by following these steps:

1. Display the Charms Bar and click or tap Settings to display the Settings panel.

2. Click or tap Change PC Settings.

The PC Settings screen offers a number of different tabs or panels. You display a given panel by selecting that tab in the left side of the screen, as shown in Figure 5.12.

Table 5.1 details the settings available on each tab.

PC settings

Personalize

Users

Notifications

Search

Share

General

Privacy

Devices

Wireless

Ease of Access

Sync your settings

FIGURE 5.12

The various tabs of the PC Settings screen.

TABLE 5.1 PC Settings Tabs

Tab	Settings
Personalize	Configure the Windows Lock screen, Start screen, and account picture.
Users	Change your account sign-in options and add new users to this computer.
Notifications	Determine which apps can display notifications in Windows.
Search	Determine which apps can be searched from within Windows, as well as delete your search history.
Share	Choose apps to share and configure sharing display options.
General	Change system time, enable/disable app switching, configure spell check, change system language, refresh or reset your entire system, and configure advanced startup options.
Privacy	Let apps use your current location, name, and account picture.
Devices	Configure system devices and add new devices to your system.
Wireless	Configure your system's Wi-Fi connection.
Ease of Access	Configure accessibility options.
Sync Your Settings	Synchronize your system settings with other computers you might be using; also determines which settings to sync.
HomeGroup	Configure sharing options for your home network.
Windows Update	Configure automatic downloading of system updates.

We discuss these settings as relevant throughout this book. Note, however, that you don't need to bother with most of these settings—even though it's good to know where they are, just in case!

Using the Traditional Control Panel

Even more configuration settings are found in the Windows Control Panel. The Control Panel is a holdover from older versions of Windows, but it's still a good way to access various system settings—even if most of those settings duplicate those found on Windows 8's PC Settings page.

To open the Control Panel, follow these steps:

1. From the Start screen, click or tap the Desktop tile to open the traditional Windows desktop.

2. Display the Charms Bar and click or tap Settings to display the Settings panel.

3. Click or tap Control Panel.

 NOTE The Settings panel you display from the Charms Bar differs from app to app and within different parts of Windows. For example, the Settings panel displayed from the Windows desktop lists options specific to the desktop; the Settings panel displayed from the Start screen lists options for Windows in general.

Figure 5.13 shows the Windows 8 Control Panel, which runs on the traditional Windows desktop. You can click a major category, such as System and Security or Network and Internet, to access related configuration settings. Or you can click or tap one of the key settings under a major heading to go directly to that setting.

FIGURE 5.13

The Windows 8 Control Panel.

After you click or tap through the various links, you eventually end up with a specific configuration utility displayed onscreen. Each type of configuration setting uses a different utility; you might see a full-fledged window full of controls, or a smaller dialog box with a few options to check. Whatever you see onscreen, select the options you want and then click OK to apply the settings you've selected.

Setting Up Additional Accounts

Chances are you're not the only person using your computer; it's likely that you'll be sharing your PC with your spouse and kids, at least to some degree. Fortunately, you can configure Windows so that different people using your computer sign on with their own custom settings—and access to their own personal files.

The way to do this is to assign each user in your household his own password-protected *user account*. Anyone trying to access another user's account and files without the password is denied access.

Windows 8 lets you create two different types of user accounts—online and local.

An online account is linked to a new or existing Microsoft Account (previously known as a Windows Live account), and it lets you synchronize your account settings between multiple computers. (That is, you can log into another Windows 8 computer with your Microsoft Account and see the same Start screen and apps you have on your home computer.) The only downside to this type of account is that your computer has to be connected to the Internet for you to log on.

The second type of account is a local account exclusive to your current computer. With a local account, you don't have to be connected to the Internet to log into your computer.

 TIP If your main account on your computer is linked to your Microsoft Account, you might want to create a second, local account for yourself for more private operation.

When you set up an account, you can choose from three different ways to log in. You can log into an account with a traditional password, with a PIN code, or with something new, called a picture password. The following sections look at all these options.

Setting Up a New Account with a Microsoft Account

By default, Windows likes to create new accounts linked to a Microsoft Account. So if you have a Hotmail, Xbox Live, Windows Phone, or other Microsoft account, you can use that account to log into your Windows 8 computer.

The advantage of setting up a Microsoft Account is that you can use the same username and password for multiple devices and services. Your Windows settings also follow you from device to device; it's a little like taking the same computer with you wherever you go, even if you're using a different computer.

For that reason, creating a Windows user account linked to your Microsoft Account is the way to go. Here's how to do it:

1. Display the Charms Bar and click or tap Settings to display the Settings panel.

2. Click or tap Change PC Settings to display the PC Settings page, shown in Figure 5.14.

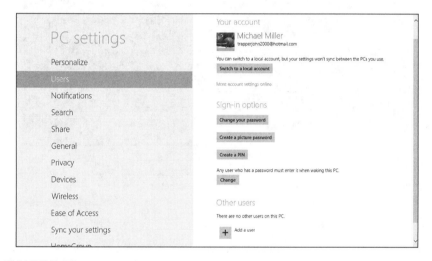

FIGURE 5.14

Creating a new user account.

3. Click or tap Users in the left column.

4. Scroll to the Other Users section and click or tap the Add a User button.

5. When the Add a User screen appears, as shown in Figure 5.15, enter the person's email address into the Email Address box. If this person currently has a Microsoft Account, such as a Hotmail account, use the email address for that account.

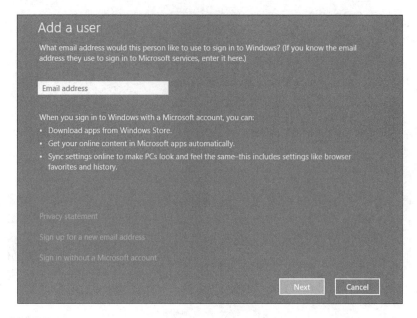

FIGURE 5.15

Entering the email address for your new user account.

6. Click or tap the Next button.

7. If you entered an email address that was not associated with an existing Microsoft Account, you're prompted to enter additional information (first name, last name, ZIP Code, and so forth) to create a new account. Do so and then click the Next button.

8. When the final screen appears, as shown in Figure 5.16, click the Finish button.

 TIP If you're adding an account for a child, check the Is This a Child's Account option to turn on Windows' Family Safety features.

This new user is now able to sign in to Windows from the Lock screen.

FIGURE 5.16

A new user account has been created.

Setting Up a New Local Account

If a new user does not have an existing Microsoft Account of any kind and does not want one, or if the user only needs access to this particular PC, you can create a local account for this person. The nice thing about a local account is that the computer does not have to be online for the user to log in and use the PC.

Follow these steps to create a new local account:

1. Display the Charms Bar and click or tap Settings to display the Settings panel.

2. Click or tap Change PC Settings to display the PC Settings page.

3. Click or tap Users in the left column.

4. Scroll to the Other Users section and click or tap the Add a User button.

5. When the Add a User screen appears, go to the bottom of the screen and click or tap Sign In Without a Microsoft Account.

6. Click or tap the Local Account button.

7. Enter the desired username into the User Name box, as shown in Figure 5.17.

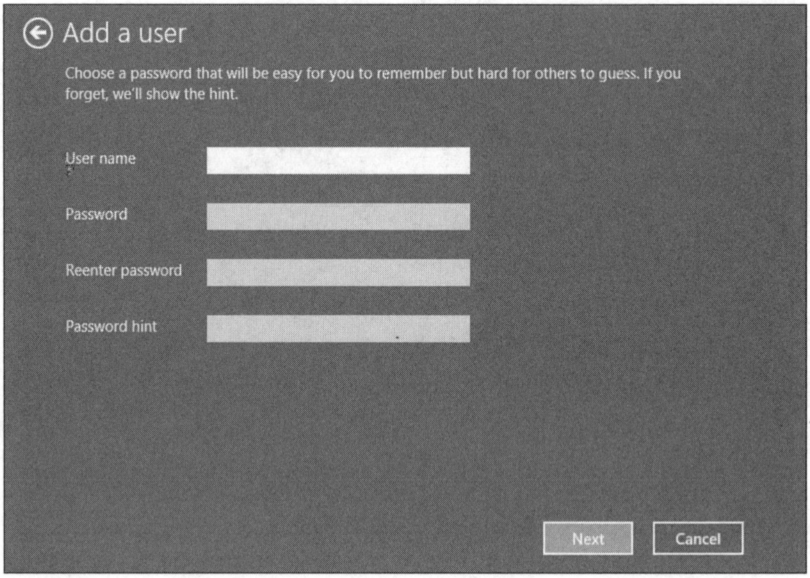

FIGURE 5.17

Creating a new local account.

8. Enter the desired password into the Password box and then re-enter it into the Retype Password box.

9. Enter some sort of hint about the password into the Password Hint box.

10. Click or tap the Next button.

11. When the final screen appears, click or tap the Finish button.

Switching a Microsoft Account to a Local Account

If you created your initial Windows user account as one linked to a Microsoft Account, you might later decide that you'd rather have a local account instead. Although you can certainly create two different accounts (Microsoft Account and local) on the same PC, you can also switch an existing Microsoft Account to a local account.

Here's how you do it:

1. Display the Charms Bar and click or tap Settings to display the Settings panel.

2. Click or tap Change PC Settings to display the PC Settings page.

3. Click or tap Users in the left column.

4. Click or tap the Switch to a Local Account button.

5. Enter your current password and click or tap the Next button.

6. Accept the current username or enter a new one on the Change to a Local Account screen that appears, as shown in Figure 5.18.

FIGURE 5.18

Changing an online account to a local account.

7. Enter your current password into the Password box and then re-enter it into the Retype Password box.

8. Enter some sort of hint about the password into the Password Hint box.

9. Click or tap the Next button.

10. When the final screen appears, as shown in Figure 5.19, click or tap the Sign Out and Finish button.

Windows signs you out of your current account and displays the Lock screen. Click or tap the Lock screen and sign in as normal.

FIGURE 5.19

Finishing the switch to a local account.

Logging in with a Traditional Password

By default, you log into Windows 8 using a traditional password consisting of some combination of letters and numbers. Use your keyboard to enter the password when prompted.

Logging in with a PIN Code

Windows 8 also lets you log into your computer using a shorter numeric PIN, in much the same way you log into your smartphone. (In fact, this feature was added for those smartphones and tablets running the Windows operating system.)

To create a PIN for your Windows account, follow these steps:

1. Display the Charms Bar and click or tap Settings to display the Settings panel.

2. Click or tap Change PC Settings to display the PC Settings page.

3. Click or tap Users in the left column.

4. Click or tap the Create a PIN button.

5. Enter your current password and click or tap the OK button.

6. Enter the desired four-number PIN and then click or tap the Finish button on the Create a PIN panel, as shown in Figure 5.20.

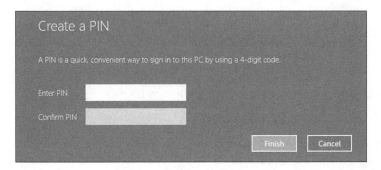

FIGURE 5.20

Creating a PIN for your Windows account.

When you next log into your computer, you're prompted to enter your PIN instead of your password, as shown in Figure 5.21. Enter the four-number PIN (you don't have to press Enter when done) to log in.

FIGURE 5.21

Signing in with a PIN.

TIP If you'd prefer to sign in with your password, click or tap Sign-In Options and proceed from there.

Logging in with a Picture Password

Windows 8 also lets you log in with something called a *picture password*. This is a picture that you select, and you trace over the picture with your finger to sign in. This type of log in is specifically designed for touchscreen use; it is not suited for mouse or keyboard use.

To create a picture password, follow these steps:

1. Display the Charms Bar and tap Settings to display the Settings panel.

2. Tap Change PC Settings to display the PC Settings page.

3. Tap Users in the left column.

4. Tap the Create a Picture Password button.

5. Enter your current password and tap the OK button.

6. Tap the Choose Picture button.

7. from the Files screen, navigate to and select the picture you want to use and then tap the Open button.

8. When the How's This Look? screen appears, tap the Use This Picture button.

9. Draw three gestures on the picture on the Set Up Your Gestures screen, as shown in Figure 5.22. Ideally, your gestures trace all or part of the image. Remember, you need to be able to repeat these gestures each time you log into Windows.

FIGURE 5.22

Setting up your gestures for your picture password.

10. When prompted, confirm (repeat) the gestures.

11. When the final screen appears, tap the Finish button.

When you log into Windows with a picture password, you see the image you selected. To log in, you have to retrace your original gestures across the picture. After you do so, you're logged in.

FIGURE 5.23

Logging into Windows with a picture password.

Switching Users

If other people are using your computer, they might want to log in with their own accounts. To switch users on a Windows 8 computer, follow these steps:

1. Press the Windows key to return to the Start screen.

2. Click or tap your username and picture in the top-right corner to display the pop-up menu.

3. Click or tap the desired user's name.

4. Enter the new user's password and then press Enter or click or tap the next arrow.

Logging Out

When you switch users, both accounts remain active; the original user account is just suspended in the background. If you'd rather log out completely from a given account and return to the Windows Lock screen, follow these steps:

1. Press the Windows key to return to the Start screen.

2. Click or tap your username and picture in the top-right corner to display the pop-up menu.

3. Click or tap Sign Out.

Logging In with Multiple Users

In Chapter 4, "Getting to Know Windows 8," you learn how to log into Windows when your computer first starts up. If you have more than one user assigned to Windows, however, the log in process is slightly different. Follow these steps:

1. From the Windows Lock screen, press any key on your keyboard or gently tap the screen.

2. By default, the logon screen lists the main user of this computer; click or tap the left arrow to display a list of all the users registered for this computer, as shown in Figure 5.24.

3. Click or tap your username.

Lew Archer   Michael Miller   Spenser

FIGURE 5.24

Logging into Windows with multiple users.

4. Your personal log in screen displays. Enter your password and then press the Enter key or click or tap the right arrow button.

Windows now displays your personal Start screen.

THE ABSOLUTE MINIMUM

Here are the key points to remember from this chapter:

- In Windows 8 you can personalize the tiles and colors of the Start screen, the background picture and apps on the Lock screen, and your profile picture.

- Most Windows settings are configured from the PC Settings screen—although you can also use the traditional Control Panel for this purpose.

- If you have multiple users in your household, you can create a user account for each person and assign each user his own password. A user account can be based on an existing Microsoft Account or be local to this computer.

- You can choose to log in with a traditional alphanumeric password, a four-number PIN, or a touch-enabled picture password.

6

WORKING WITH FILES, FOLDERS, AND DISKS

Managing the data stored on your computer is vitally important. After you've saved a file, you might need to copy it to another computer, move it to a new location on your hard drive, rename it, or even delete it. You have to know how to perform all these operations—which means learning how to work with files, folders, and disks in Windows.

Understanding Files and Folders

All the information on your computer is stored in *files*. A file is nothing more than a collection of digital data. The contents of a file can be a document (such as a Word memo or Excel spreadsheet), a digital photo or music track, or the executable code for a software program.

Every file has its own unique name. A defined structure exists for naming files, and you must follow the naming conventions for Windows to understand exactly what file you want when you try to access one. Each filename must consist of two parts, separated by a period—the *name* (to the left of the period) and the *extension* (to the right of the period). A filename can consist of letters, numbers, spaces, and characters and looks something like this: filename.ext.

Windows stores files in *folders*. A folder is like a master file; each folder can contain both files and additional folders. The exact location of a file is called its *path* and contains all the folders leading to the file. For example, a file named filename. doc that exists in the system folder, that is itself contained in the windows folder on your C: drive, has a path that looks like this: C:\windows\system\filename.doc.

Learning how to use files and folders is a necessary skill for all computer users. You might need to copy files from one folder to another or from your hard disk to a floppy disk. You certainly need to delete files every now and then.

TIP By default, Windows hides the extensions when it displays filenames. To display extensions in Windows 8, open the Control Panel, select Appearance and Personalization, and then select Folder Options. When the Folder Options dialog box appears, select the View tab; then, in the Advanced Settings list, *uncheck* the Hide Extensions for Known File Types option. Click OK when you're finished.

Using File Explorer

In Windows 8, all the items stored on your computer—including programs, documents, and configuration settings—are accessible from *File Explorer*. This is a window on the traditional desktop that displays all the disk drives, folders, subfolders, and files on your computer system. You use File Explorer to find, copy, delete, and launch programs and documents.

NOTE What Microsoft calls File Explorer in Windows 8 it called Windows Explorer in previous versions of Windows. Users may also know File/Windows Explorer as the My Computer or My Documents folder.

Launching File Explorer

You launch File Explorer from the traditional desktop. Follow these steps:

1. From the Start screen, click or tap the Desktop tile to open the desktop.

2. Click the File Explorer icon on the taskbar, as shown in Figure 6.1.

FIGURE 6.1

Launching File Explorer from the desktop taskbar.

Exploring the File Explorer Window

When you open File Explorer, you see four icons, as shown in Figure 6.2. These icons let you go directly to the documents, music, pictures, and videos stored on your hard drive. Double-click or tap an icon to view the subfolders and files of that type.

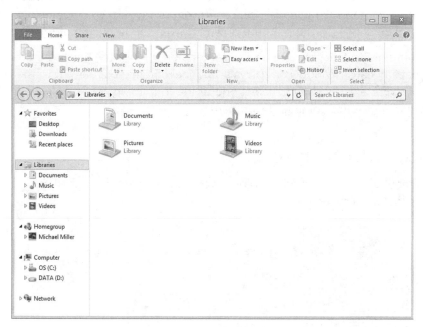

FIGURE 6.2

Navigating through your folders and subfolders with File Explorer.

On the left side of the File Explorer window is a Navigation pane, divided into several sections. The top section, Favorites, lists your most-used folders—Desktop, Downloads, and Recent Places. Next is the Libraries section, which repeats the four icons in the main window—Documents, Music, Pictures, and Videos. Below that is a Homegroup section, which lets you access other computers on your network HomeGroup. The Computer section lets you access all the disk drives and devices connected to your computer. And the Network section lets you access all of your networked computers. Click any icon in the Navigation pane to view the contents of that item.

Working with Ribbons and Tabs

The Windows 8 version of File Explorer displays what is called a *ribbon* at the top of the window. This ribbon contains all the operations and commands you need to manage your files and folders, organized into four tabs—File, Home, Share, and View.

If the ribbon is minimized, you'll only see the names of the tabs. To view the commands on a given tab, click or tap that tab to expand the tab downward and make visible the tab's commands. You can maximize the entire ribbon (expand it downward) by clicking or tapping the down arrow at the right side of the ribbon bar.

From time to time you see additional tabs on the ribbon, beyond the basic four. That's because Windows displays additional commands relevant to the task at hand. For example, if you select one of the four library icons, you see a Manage tab that includes commands for managing the library.

Navigating the Folders on Your PC

After you've launched File Explorer, you can navigate through all your folders and subfolders in several ways:

 NOTE A subfolder is a folder that is contained within another folder. Multiple subfolders can be nested in this fashion.

 NOTE You don't have to double-tap an item on a touchscreen device; a single tap does the job of a double-click.

- To view the contents of a disk or folder, double-click or tap the selected item.
- To move back to the disk or folder previously selected, click or tap the Back button on the toolbar.

- To choose from the history of disks and folders previously viewed, click or tap the down arrow in the Address bar at the top of the File Explorer window and select a disk or folder.

- If you've moved back through multiple disks or folders, you can move forward to the next folder by clicking or tapping the Forward button on the toolbar.

- Go directly to any disk or folder by entering the path in the Address bar (in the format x:\folder\subfolder) and pressing Enter.

- Move backward through the "bread crumb" path in the Address bar. Click or tap any previous folder location (separated by arrows) to display that particular folder.

 TIP Click or tap any arrow between locations in the Address bar to view additional paths from that location.

You can also go directly to key locations by using the list of locations in the Navigation pane on the left side of the File Explorer window. This pane displays the most common locations for files on your system. The top part of the pane displays your Favorite Links, whereas the Computer section on the bottom of the pane displays all the contents of your system in a treelike outline. Click or tap any section of the tree to display that item's contents.

Viewing Files and Folders

There's no set way to view the files and folders stored on your computer. In fact, File Explorer has several options to change the way your files and folders are displayed.

Changing the Way Files Are Displayed

You can choose to view the contents of a folder in a variety of ways. To change the file view, select the View tab in the ribbon bar, shown in Figure 6.3. From here you can select from eight available views:

- Extra large icons

- Large icons

- Medium icons

- Small icons

- List

- Details

- Tiles

- Content

FIGURE 6.3

Use the View tab to change how files are displayed.

 TIP Any of the Icon views are good for working with graphics files or for getting a quick thumbnail glance at a file's contents. The Details view is better if you're looking for files by date or size.

Sorting Files and Folders

When viewing files in File Explorer, you can sort your files and folders in a number of ways. To do this, select the Views tab in the ribbon bar then click or tap the Sort By button. You can then choose to sort by Name, Date Modified, Type, Size, Date Created, Folder Path, Authors, Categories, Tags, or Title. You can also choose to sort the items in either ascending or descending order.

If you want to view your files in alphabetical order, choose to sort by Name. If you want to see all similar files grouped together, choose to sort by Type. If you want to sort your files by the date and time you last edited them, choose the Date Modified option. And if you want to sort by a user-applied file tag (assuming you've done this in the file's host program), choose the Tags option.

Grouping Files and Folders

You can also configure File Explorer to group the files in your folder, which can make it easier to identify particular files. For example, if you sort your files by time and date modified, they're grouped by date (Today, Yesterday, Last Week, and so on). If you sort your files by type, they're grouped by file extension, and so on.

To turn on grouping, click or tap the Group By button on the View tab of the ribbon bar. You can then choose to group by any of the same parameters available for sorting. File Explorer groups your files and folders by the selected criteria.

Working with Libraries

Then there's the concept of *libraries*, which is a different way to manage your files. A library is kind of a virtual folder; it doesn't physically exist on your hard disk; instead it points to the subfolders and files you place within it.

If you've opened File Explorer, you've already seen four libraries. That's because the Documents, Music, Pictures, and Videos icons don't point to specific folders, but rather to libraries of files of a given type, wherever they're located on your hard disk. That's right—double-clicking or double-tapping doesn't open the Documents folder itself (although that folder does exist); it opens a virtual collection of documents.

So Windows 8 displays all your documents, no matter which folder they're really stored in, in the Documents library. All your digital music files are displayed in the Music library, all your digital photos in the Pictures library, and all your digital video files in the Videos library.

Searching for Files

As organized as you might be, you might not always be able to find the specific files you want. Fortunately, Windows 8 offers an easy way to locate difficult-to-find files, via the Instant Search function. Instant Search indexes all the files stored on your hard disk (including email messages) by type, title, and contents. So you can search for a file by extension, filename, or keywords within the document.

To use the Instant Search feature, follow these steps:

1. From within File Explorer, locate the search box at the top right of the window, as shown in Figure 6.4.

2. Enter one or more keywords into the search box.

3. Press Enter.

FIGURE 6.4

The search box in File Explorer.

Windows displays a list of files that match your search criteria. Double-click or double-tap any icon to open that file.

TIP You can also search for files from the Instant Search box on the Windows Start screen.

Performing Basic File and Folder Operations

In Windows 8, you accomplish most of the file and folder operations you want to do via the Home tab on the ribbon bar, shown in Figure 6.5. You use the buttons on this tab to move, copy, and delete items—as well as perform other key operations.

FIGURE 6.5

Use the Home tab to perform essential file and folder operations.

Creating New Folders

The more files you create, the harder it is to organize and find things on your hard disk. When the number of files you have becomes unmanageable, you need to create more folders—and subfolders—to better categorize your files.

To create a new folder, follow these steps:

1. Navigate to the drive or folder where you want to place the new folder.

2. Select the Home tab on the toolbar.

3. Click or tap the New Folder button.

4. A new, empty folder appears within the File Explorer window, with the filename New Folder highlighted.

5. Type a name for your folder (which overwrites the New Folder name), and press Enter.

 CAUTION Folder and filenames can include up to 255 characters—including many special characters. Some special characters, however, are "illegal," meaning that you *can't* use them in folder or filenames. Illegal characters include the following: \ / : * ? " < > |.

CAUTION   The one part of the filename you should never change is the extension—the part that comes after the "dot." That's because Windows and other software programs recognize different types of program files and documents by their extension. This is why, by default, Windows hides these file extensions—so you can't change them by mistake.

Renaming Files and Folders

When you create a new file or folder, it helps to give it a name that somehow describes its contents. Sometimes, however, you might need to change a file's name. Fortunately, Windows makes it relatively easy to rename an item.

To rename a file (or folder), follow these steps:

1. Click the file or folder you want to rename.

2. Select the Home tab on the ribbon bar.

3. Click or tap the Rename button to highlight the filename.

4. Type a new name for your file or folder (which overwrites the current name) and press Enter.

Copying Files

Copying a file lets you re-create that file in a different location, either on your computer's hard drive or on some sort of external media. Here's how to do it:

NOTE   It's important to remember that copying is different from moving. When you *copy* an item, the item remains in its original location—plus you have the new copy. When you *move* an item, the file is no longer present in the original location—all you have is the item in the new location.

1. Select the item you want to copy.

2. Select the Home tab on the ribbon bar.

3. Click or tap the Copy To button; this displays a pull-down menu of popular and recently visited locations.

4. To copy directly to one of the listed locations, click or tap that location from the list.

5. To copy to another location, click or tap Choose Location from the pull-down menu to display the Copy Items dialog box, shown in Figure 6.6. Navigate to the new location for the item then click or tap the Copy button.

FIGURE 6.6

Selecting the location to copy to.

That's it. You've just copied the file from one location to another.

Moving Files

Moving a file (or folder) is different from copying it. Moving cuts the item from its previous location and places it in a new location. Copying leaves the original item where it was *and* creates a copy of the item elsewhere.

In other words, when you copy something you end up with two of it. When you move something, you only have the one instance.

To move a file, follow these steps:

1. Select the item you want to move.

2. Select the Home tab on the ribbon bar.

3. Click or tap the Move To button; this displays a list of popular and recently visited locations.

4. To move an item to one of the listed locations, click or tap that location from the list.

5. To move the item to another location, click or tap Choose Location on the pull-down menu to display the Move Items dialog box. Navigate to the new location for the item then click or tap the Move button.

Deleting Files

Too many files eat up too much hard disk space—which is a bad thing because you only have so much disk space. (Music and video files, in particular, can chew up big chunks of your hard drive.) Because you don't want to waste disk space, you should periodically delete the files (and folders) you no longer need.

Deleting a file is as easy as following these simple steps:

1. Select the file or files you want to delete.

2. Select the Home tab on the ribbon bar.

3. Click or tap the Delete button.

This simple operation sends the file to the Windows Recycle Bin, which is kind of a trash can for deleted files. (It's also a trash can that periodically needs to be dumped—as we discuss momentarily.)

 TIP You can also delete a file by selecting it and then pressing the Del key on your computer keyboard.

Working with the Recycle Bin

As just discussed, all recently deleted files are stored in what Windows calls the Recycle Bin. This is a special folder on your hard disc that temporarily stores all deleted items—which is a good thing.

Restoring Deleted Files

Have you ever accidentally deleted the wrong file? If so, you're in luck, thanks to the Recycle Bin. As you now know, Windows stores all the files you delete in the Recycle Bin, at least temporarily. If you've recently deleted a file, it should still be in the Recycle Bin folder.

To "undelete" a file from the Recycle Bin, follow these steps:

1. From the Windows desktop, double-click or tap the Recycle Bin icon (shown in Figure 6.7) to open the Recycle Bin folder.

FIGURE 6.7

The Recycle Bin, where all your deleted files end up.

2. Click or tap the file(s) you want to restore.

3. Select the Manage tab on the ribbon bar, shown in Figure 6.8.

4. Click or tap the Restore the Selected Items button.

FIGURE 6.8

Managing deleted files in the Recycle Bin.

The deleted file is copied back to its original location, ready for continued use.

Managing the Recycle Bin

Deleted files do not stay in the Recycle Bin indefinitely. When you've deleted enough files to exceed the space allocated for these files, the oldest files in the Recycle Bin are automatically and permanently deleted from your hard disk.

If you'd rather dump the Recycle Bin manually (and thus free up some hard disk space), follow these steps:

1. Double-click or tap the Recycle Bin icon on your desktop to open the Recycle Bin folder.

2. Select the Manage tab on the ribbon bar.

3. Click or tap the Empty the Recycle Bin button.

4. When the confirmation dialog box appears, click or tap Yes to completely erase the files; click or tap No to continue storing the files in the Recycle Bin.

Working with Compressed Folders

Really big files can be difficult to move or copy. They're especially difficult to transfer to other users, whether by email or USB drive.

Fortunately, Windows includes a way to make big files smaller. *Compressed folders* (sometimes called *zip files*) take big files and compress their size, which makes them easier to copy or move. After you've transferred the file, you can uncompress the file to its original state.

Compressing a File

Compressing one or more files is a relatively easy task from within any Windows folder. Just follow these steps:

1. Select the file(s) you want to compress.

2. Select the Share tab on the ribbon bar, shown in Figure 6.9.

3. Click or tap the Zip button.

FIGURE 6.9

Use the Share tab to compress large files to a zip file.

Windows now creates a new folder that contains compressed versions of the file(s) you selected. (This folder is distinguished by a little zipper on the folder icon.) You can now copy, move, or email this folder, which is a lot smaller than the original file(s).

 NOTE The compressed folder is actually a file with a .ZIP extension, so you can use it with other compression/decompression programs, such as WinZip.

Extracting Files from a Compressed Folder

The process of decompressing a file is actually an *extraction* process. That's because you *extract* the original file(s) from the compressed folder. Follow these steps:

1. Select the compressed folder.

2. Select the Extract tab on the ribbon bar, shown in Figure 6.10.

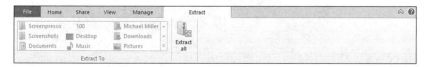

FIGURE 6.10

Use the Extract tab to extract files from a compressed folder.

3. Pull down the Extract To list and select a location for the extracted files.

4. Click or tap the Extract All button.

Copying Files to Another Computer

Of course, you're not limited to copying and moving files from one location to another on a single PC. You can also copy files to other PCs via either a network connection or some sort of portable disk drive.

Copying Files over a Network

We talk more about network operations in Chapter 10, "Setting Up a Home Network." For now, it's important to know that if your PC is connected to a network and has file sharing activated, you can copy and move files from one network computer to another just as you can within folders on a single computer.

Copying Files with a Portable Drive

If you're not on a network, you can use a portable drive to transport files from one computer to another. The most popular type of portable drive today is the *USB drive* (sometimes called a *flash drive* or *thumb drive*), such as the one shown in Figure 6.11, which stores computer data in flash memory. You can find USB drives with capacities up to 32GB—more than big enough to hold even your biggest files.

FIGURE 6.11

Use a USB drive to transport files from one computer to another.

To use a USB drive, simply insert the device into an open USB port on your computer. After you've inserted it, the drive appears as a new drive in the Computer section of the File Explorer navigation pane. Double-click or double-tap the USB drive icon to view the contents of the drive; you can then copy and paste files from your hard drive to the USB drive and vice versa. When you're finished copying files, just remove the USB device. It's that simple.

Copying Files via Email

Another popular way to send files from one computer to another is via email. You can send any file as an email *attachment*; a file is literally attached to an email message. When the message is sent, the recipient can open or save the attached file when reading the message.

To learn how to send files as email attachments, turn to Chapter 16, "Sending and Receiving Email."

THE ABSOLUTE MINIMUM

Here are the key points to remember from this chapter:

- You manage your files and folders from File Explorer, which runs on the traditional Windows desktop.

- Most common file and folder operations are found on the Home tab of the File Explorer ribbon bar.

- If you accidentally delete a file, you might be able to recover it by opening the Recycle Bin window.

- If you need to share a really big file, consider compressing it into a compressed folder (also known as a zip file).

- To copy a file to another PC, you can copy the file over a network, send the file as an email attachment, or copy the file to a portable USB drive.

7

CONNECTING OTHER DEVICES TO YOUR PC— AND YOUR PC TO OTHER DEVICES

If you just purchased a brand-new, right-out-of-the-box personal computer, it probably came equipped with all the components you could ever want— or so you think. At some point in the future, however, you might want to expand your system by adding a printer, a scanner, an external hard drive, better speakers, a different mouse or keyboard, or something equally new and exciting.

Adding new hardware to your system is relatively easy if you know what you're doing. That's where this chapter comes in.

Most Popular Peripherals

When it comes to adding stuff to your PC, what are the most popular peripherals? Here's a list of hardware you can add to or upgrade on your system:

- **Hard drive**—Adds more storage capacity to your system or performs periodic backups from your main hard disk. The easiest type of hard drive to add is an external unit, which typically connects via USB and costs just a hundred bucks or so. If you have a traditional desktop PC, you might also be able to add a second internal drive inside your system unit, but that's a lot more work.

 NOTE Learn more about adding a hard drive to your system in Chapter 9, "Adding Storage and Backup."

- **Memory card reader**—Enables you to read data from devices (such as digital cameras) that use various types of flash memory cards.

- **USB memory device**—Provides gigabytes of removable storage; you can transport the USB memory device from one computer to another, connecting to each PC's USB port.

- **Monitor**—Replaces or supplements the built-in display on a notebook computer, or replaces the existing monitor on a desktop system (typically with a larger screen).

- **Video card**—On traditional desktop PCs, upgrades your system's video playback and graphics, typically for video editing or playing visually demanding PC games.

- **Sound card**—On traditional desktop PCs, improves the audio capabilities of your systems; this is particularly important if you're playing state-of-the-art PC games, watching surround-sound DVD movies, or mixing and recording your own digital audio.

- **Speakers**—Upgrades the quality of your computer's sound system. (Surround-sound speaker systems with subwoofers are particularly popular, especially with PC gamers.)

- **Keyboard**—Replaces a notebook's built-in keyboard with a larger, more fully featured model, or upgrades the capabilities of a desktop's included keyboard.

- **Mouse**—Provides a more traditional input in place of a notebook PC's touchpad, or upgrades the capabilities of a desktop system's mouse. (For example, many users like to upgrade from wired to wireless mice.)

- **Joystick or other game controller**—Enables you to get better action with your favorite games.

- **CD/DVD drive (burner)**—Adds recordable/rewritable capabilities to a netbook or ultrabook that doesn't have a built-in CD/DVD drive.

- **Printer**—Improves the quality of your printouts, adds color to your printouts, or adds photo-quality printing to your system.

 NOTE Learn more about adding a printer or scanner to your system in Chapter 8, "Working with Printers and Scanners."

- **Scanner**—Enables you to scan photographs and documents into a digital format to store on your computer's hard drive.

- **Webcam**—Enables you to send real-time video to friends and family.

- **Wireless router**—Enables you to create a wireless network in your home—and share your broadband Internet connection among multiple computers.

- **Wireless network adapter**—Enables you to connect a desktop computer to any wireless network.

Adding New Hardware to Your System

Everything that's hooked to your PC is connected via some type of *port*. A port is simply an interface between your PC and another device—either internally (inside your PC's system unit) or externally (via a connector on the back of the system unit).

Given the choice, the easiest way to add a new device to your system is to connect it externally. In fact, if you have an all-in-one desktop, notebook, or tablet computer, it's the *only* way to add new hardware; you can't get inside the case to add anything else. And even if you have a traditional desktop PC with a separate system unit, it's still a whole lot easier to add a new device via an external USB port than it is to open the case and add it that way.

 NOTE No matter how you're connecting a new device, make sure to read the installation instructions for the new hardware and follow the manufacturer's instructions and advice.

The most common external connector today is the USB port, like the one shown in Figure 7.1. USB is a great concept (and truly "universal") in that virtually every type of new peripheral comes in a USB version. Want to add a second hard disk? Don't open the PC case; connect an external drive via USB. Want to add a new printer? Connect a USB printer. Want to connect to a home network? Don't bother with Ethernet cards; get a USB-compatible wireless adapter.

FIGURE 7.1

A USB port on a notebook PC. (Photograph courtesy Aidan C. Siegel via the Creative Commons Attribution-Share Alike 3.0 Unported license.)

Not that there aren't other types of ports that you might occasionally run into or need to use. For example, if you want to connect your PC to your TV (which we discuss later in this chapter), you'll probably connect a cable to your PC's HDMI port. (HDMI is a special kind of connection for transmitting high-definition audio/video.) And some high-speed devices (such as really big and expensive hard drives) might connect via FireWire, which is kind of a faster version of USB. But for most purposes, USB is all you need to know about and use.

USB is popular because it's so easy to use. When you're connecting a USB device, not only do you not have to open your PC's case, but you don't even have to turn off your system when you add the new device. That's because USB devices are *hot swappable*. That means you can just plug the new device into the port, and Windows automatically recognizes it in real time.

TIP If you connect too many USB devices, it's possible to run out of USB connectors on your PC. If that happens to you, buy an add-on USB hub, which lets you plug multiple USB peripherals into a single USB port.

To connect a new USB device, follow these steps:

1. Find a free USB port on your system unit and connect the new peripheral.

2. Windows should automatically recognize the new peripheral and install the proper device driver automatically.

That's it! The only variation on this procedure is if the peripheral's manufacturer recommends using its own installation program, typically provided on an installation CD. If this is the case, follow the manufacturer's instructions to perform the installation and setup.

 NOTE   A device driver is a small software program that enables your PC to communicate with and control a specific device. Windows includes built-in device drivers for many popular peripherals. If Windows doesn't include a particular driver, you typically can find the driver on the peripheral's installation disk or on the peripheral manufacturer's website.

Connecting Portable Devices to Your PC

These days, a lot of the devices you connect to your PC really aren't computer peripherals. Instead, they are gadgets that you use on their own but plug into your PC to share files.

What kinds of portable devices are we talking about? Here's a short list:

*   Portable music players, such as Apple's popular iPod and iPhone
*   Digital cameras
*   Digital camcorders
*   USB memory devices

All of these devices connect to a USB port on your PC, which makes for an easy hookup. As mentioned earlier, USB ports are hot-swappable, which means that all you have to do is connect the device to the proper port—no major configuration necessary. In some cases, the first time you connect your device to your PC, you need to run some sort of installation utility to install the device's software on your PC's hard drive. Each subsequent time you connect the device, your PC should recognize it automatically and launch the appropriate software program.

After your portable device is connected to your PC, what you do next is up to you. Most of the time, you'll be transferring files either from your PC to the portable device, or vice versa. Use the device's software program to perform these operations, or use File Explorer to copy files back and forth.

For example, you can use a USB memory device as a removable and portable memory storage system. One of these USB drives is smaller than a pack of chewing gum and can hold several gigabytes' worth of data in electronic flash memory. Plug a USB memory device into your PC's USB port, and your PC recognizes it just as if it were another disk drive. You can then copy files from your PC to the USB drive to take your work (or your digital music or photo files) with you.

For more detailed information, see the instructions that came with your portable device.

Connecting Your PC to Your Living Room TV

As you'll no doubt soon discover, there are a lot of good movies and TV shows on the Internet that you can watch on your PC—often for free. Although you can watch this programming on your computer screen, that might be a little small for those of us more familiar with the large screen experience.

 NOTE   Learn more about finding movies and TV shows on the Internet in Chapter 30, "Watching TV and Movies Online."

Fortunately, there might be a way to connect your computer to your living room TV and watch your Internet-based programming in full big-screen glory. It's all a matter of which ports you have on the back (or side) of your PC and whether you have similar connectors on your flat-screen television.

The most common way to connect a computer to a flat-screen TV is via HDMI. You might already be familiar with HDMI, which is used to connect many Blu-ray players, cable boxes, and the like to high-definition television sets. (Figure 7.2 shows an HDMI port on a typical notebook PC.) HDMI is nice because it feeds both video and audio via a single cable, in full 1080p high def.

FIGURE 7.2

An HDMI port on a notebook PC.

NOTE Some PCs, especially tablets and notebooks, feature mini-HDMI connectors. In this instance, you need a special HDMI cable with a mini-connector on one end (to connect to your PC) and a standard-sized connector on the other (to connect to your TV). You should be able to find such cables at your local electronics store.

If your computer has an HDMI connector, it's easy to connect an HDMI cable between your PC and an HDMI input on your TV. Connect that single cable and the picture and sound (in full 5.1-channel surround!) from whatever you're watching on your computer is fed to your flat-screen TV.

If your PC doesn't have an HDMI port, you might still be able to connect it to your TV. Here's what to look for:

- Some TVs have a standard VGA connector (typically labeled "PC") that can connect (via a standard VGA cable) to the VGA or monitor output found on almost all PCs.

- If your computer has a DVI output, you can connect a DVI-to-HDMI adapter to this port and then use an HDMI cable to connect to your TV. Because DVI is video only, you also need to run an audio cable from your PC's audio output to your TV's audio inputs.

NOTE DVI (short for *digital video interface*) is a digital connection for transmitting video signals and is often used to connect computers to LCD monitors. Both DVI and HDMI are digital formats, which is why you can convert DVI to HDMI.

- If your computer has an S-Video or single composite video output, you can connect a cable from this port to the similar input on your TV. (Know, however, that S-Video and composite video are standard resolution only; they do not transmit a high-definition video signal.)

After you've connected your computer to your TV, you can see and hear everything your PC is doing through your TV. Just connect to the movie or TV website of choice, switch your TV to the appropriate video input, and get out the popcorn!

THE ABSOLUTE MINIMUM

Here's what you need to know if you're adding new equipment to your computer system:

- The easiest way to connect a new peripheral is via an external USB connection.

- In most cases, Windows automatically recognizes your new hardware and automatically installs all the necessary drivers.

- Connecting a portable device, such as a portable music player or digital camera, is also done via an external USB port.

- You can connect your PC to your TV, typically via HDMI, to watch web-based programming on the bigger display.

8

WORKING WITH PRINTERS AND SCANNERS

Your computer monitor displays images in real time, but they're fleeting. To conveniently create permanent visual records of your work, you need to add a printer to your system. Printers create hard copy output from your software programs—or just make prints of your favorite pictures.

Selecting the Right Printer for Your Needs

You can choose from various types of printers for your system, depending on your exact printing needs. The two main types of printers today are inkjet and laser printers. Both are suitable for home use.

Understanding Inkjet Printers

The most popular type of printer for home use is the *inkjet* printer, like the one shown in Figure 8.1. An inkjet printer works by shooting jets of ink to the paper's surface to create the printed image.

FIGURE 8.1

A typical color inkjet printer. (Photo courtesy HP.)

To work, an inkjet printer needs to be filled with one or more replaceable ink cartridges. The typical inkjet printer has two cartridges—one that contains red, yellow, and blue ink (for color printing) and another with just black ink. You'll probably use up the black ink cartridge first because you'll probably print more single-color text documents than full-color pictures. Your printer should display a message on its front panel when a cartridge is running low; replacement ink cartridges are available at most home office stores.

Inkjet printers are typically lower-priced than laser printers. That's because they're not quite as heavy duty as laser printers, which are more suited for larger print jobs. An inkjet printer is fine for typical home use, but it might not hold up as well in a busy office environment.

Understanding Laser Printers

Laser printers work a little differently than inkjet models. Instead of shooting liquid ink at the paper, a laser printer works much like a traditional copying machine, applying powdered ink (toner) to paper by using a small laser.

As such, laser printers (like the one in Figure 8.2) typically work a little faster than similar inkjets, and they produce slightly sharper results. This makes laser printers better suited for heavy duty use, such as what you might get in an office environment.

FIGURE 8.2

A typical laser printer. (Photo courtesy HP.)

Of course, everything comes at a cost, and laser printers tend to be a little bigger and more expensive than comparable inkjet models. In addition, where most inkjets offer full-color printing, not all laser printers do; you can find both black-and-white and color laser printers for home and office use.

Black and White or Color?

Especially when considering a laser printer, you'll have your choice of either black-and-white or color printers. (Almost all consumer inkjet printers today are full color.) Black-and-white printers are faster than color printers and better if you're printing memos, letters, and other single-color documents. Color printers, however, are great if you have kids, and they're essential if you want to print pictures taken with a digital camera.

As such, most home users tend to choose color printers—they're just more versatile.

Understanding Multifunction Printers

You also have the option of purchasing what is called a "multifunction" printer. This combines a traditional desktop printer with a scanner, a fax machine, and a copier—all in one multifunction unit. As you can see in Figure 8.3, multifunction printers are slightly larger than single-function printers. You can find multifunction printers of both the inkjet and laser varieties; these printers can be either black and white or color.

FIGURE 8.3

A multifunction color laser printer. (Photo courtesy Brother.)

If you need all these functions, by all means consider such a multifunction printer. Know, however, that you'll pay extra to get all this functionality; single-function printers are going to be more affordable than multifunction units.

Adding a Printer to Your System

Most printers connect directly to your computer, typically via USB. Some printers, however, can connect to your home network, typically via Wi-Fi, without being connected to a single PC.

Connecting a Printer Directly to Your Computer

In most instances, connecting a USB printer to your computer is a simple process:

1. Connect one end of a USB cable to the USB output on your printer.

2. Connect the other end of the USB cable to a USB port on your computer.

3. Connect the printer to a power outlet.

4. Turn on the printer.

Windows should automatically recognize the new printer and install the proper device driver automatically. Follow the onscreen instructions to finish the installation.

 NOTE It's possible that your printer might offer additional functionality, such as scanning, which is common in multifunction units. If so, you might need to install the printer and any neces-sary software from the accompanying installation CD or DVD. As always, follow the manufacturer's instructions for best results.

Connecting a Printer to Your Network

If you're sharing a printer between multiple computers on your home network, you might want to go with a network printer—one that connects to your wireless network, but doesn't physically connect to any single computer. The primary ben-efit of a network printer is that you can place it anywhere in your home; because it's not tethered to a given PC, it doesn't have to sit next to any computer. In fact, most network printers can connect to your network wirelessly or via Ethernet.

In general, the setup goes something like this:

1. Turn on your printer.

2. Connect the printer to your wireless router, either via Wi-Fi or Ethernet. In most instances the printer automatically detects and connects to your network.

3. If your wireless network has a security password (and it should) enter that password on your printer's keypad.

Follow any additional instructions in your printer's installation manual. When the printer is properly configured, it should appear as an printing option for all computers connected to your network.

Printing to Your System's Printer

Printing from a given app is typically as easy as clicking or tapping the Print button. In some instances the print function might be contained within a pull-down File or Print menu.

In any case, one-click printing is typically the norm. That is, you click the Print button and printing ensues. In most programs, however, you can fine-tune your printing options by selecting the File menu and clicking Print. This typically displays a Print Options dialog box or page, like the one shown in Figure 8.4. From here you can select which printer to print to, which pages to print, how many copies to print, whether to print in portrait (vertical paper) or landscape (horizontal paper) modes, and so forth.

FIGURE 8.4

The print options page in Microsoft Word.

Know, however, that print functionality does differ from program to program. Make sure you consult a given app's help files if you need assistance in configuring various print options.

Making Digital Copies with a Scanner

Just as a printer makes a hard copy of a digital file, a scanner makes a digital copy of a printed document or picture. You can use a scanner to scan legal and other documents or to scan your favorite digital photographs. The process is similar, no matter the source.

A scanner, like the one in Figure 8.5, works by running an image sensor across the face of the document, which is placed face-down on the scanner's glass bed. This image sensor digitizes the elements of the document, which are then converted into the appropriate file format. In most instances, it's as easy as pressing a button and letting the scanner do its thing.

FIGURE 8.5

A typical flatbed scanner. (Photo courtesy Canon.)

Most scanners cost about $100 and connect to your computer via USB, the same way you connect a printer. This is an affordable way to create digital copies of old photo prints, letters, and the like—which you can then store along with your more-recent digital photo files.

Scanning is typically as simple as placing a document on the scanner's bed and pressing the scanner's Scan button. This activates scanning software installed on your computer, and the resulting scanned image is stored as a digital file on your PC.

THE ABSOLUTE MINIMUM

Here are the key points to remember when connecting and configuring your new computer:

- There are two types of consumer printers in use today—inkjet and laser.

- An inkjet printer is typically the lowest cost option; it works by shooting liquid ink onto sheets of paper.

- Laser printers are typically faster, more durable, and more expensive than inkjet models; laser printers work by applying solid ink (toner) to sheets of paper via laser.

- Both inkjet and laser printers are available in black-and-white and color models.

- Multifunction printers add scanning, copying, and faxing functionality to a basic printer.

- A printer can connect directly to a PC via USB or (in some models) wirelessly to your home network.

- Scanners let you digitize photos and other documents to store in digital files.

ADDING STORAGE AND BACKUP

Most desktop and traditional notebook computers these days come with a fairly large amount of internal storage, typically 320GB (for a basic notebook) up to 2TB (that's two *terabytes*—one of which is equivalent to one thousand gigabytes) or even more. That's plenty of storage for most people, even if you download a lot of music and videos or store a ton of digital photos.

However, today's ultrabook and tablet PCs don't have that much internal storage because they don't have hard drives. (These lightweight computers use solid state flash storage that typically provides no more than 128GB to 256GB storage capacity.) And tablet PCs have even less onboard storage.

What do you do, then, if you need more storage space for your valuable files? The solution is to add more capacity with an external hard drive. (And you can use that same external drive to back up your data, as well.)

Understanding External Storage

Most traditional computers use internal hard drives to store digital data—software applications, documents, photos, music, and so forth. This same hard disk technology is available in external drives that connect to your computer via USB.

When it's been connected, an external hard disk appears as another drive in the Computer section of File Explorer. You can access it just like your internal hard drive, and you can use it to store files or software programs.

You can find external hard drives in a variety of capacities, starting at 320GB or so and going all the way up to 3TB. Most manufacturers offer traditional desktop hard drives, like the one in Figure 9.1, as well as smaller portable drives, like the one in Figure 9.2. As you might suspect, the portable drives are designed to work better with portable notebook PCs.

FIGURE 9.1

A typical desktop external hard drive. (Photo courtesy Seagate.)

FIGURE 9.2

A small portable external drive. (Photo courtesy Western Digital.)

Connecting an External Hard Drive

In most instances, connecting an external hard drive is a simple two-step process:

1. Connect the external hard drive to a power source.

2. Use a USB cable to connect the external hard drive to a USB port on your computer.

Some desktop hard drives have power switches. If yours does, you need to turn it on, as well.

When the hard drive is powered up and connected to your computer, it should appear in the Computer section of File Explorer as a new drive. It should take the next available letter; for example, if your internal hard drive is drive C: and your CD/DVD drive is drive D: then the new external drive should be labeled as drive E:.

Backing Up Your Important Files

Protecting your valuable data—including all your music and personal photos—is something you need to do. After all, what would you do if your computer crashes or your hard disk dies? Do you really want to lose all your valuable documents and files?

Of course you don't—which is why you need to back up your key files on a regular basis.

Backing Up to an External Hard Drive

The easiest way to back up your files is with an external hard drive. Get a big enough external drive (about the same size as your main hard disk), and you can copy your entire hard disk to the external drive. Then, if your system ever crashes, you can restore your backed-up files from the external drive to your computer's system unit.

Most external hard drives come with some sort of backup software installed, or you can use a third-party backup program. The backup process can be automated, so that it occurs once a day or once a week, and only backs up those new or changed files since your last backup.

Whichever program you use, you should back up your data at least weekly—if not daily. That way you won't lose much fresh data if the worst happens.

 TIP Given the affordability of external hard drives and how easy most backup programs make the process, there's no excuse not to back up your data on a regular basis. It's cheap protection in case something bad happens to your computer.

Using Windows 8's File History Utility

In Windows 8, you can back up all your important files with the File History utility. By default, File History saves copies of files every hour, and it keeps all saved versions forever. (You can change these settings by clicking Advanced Settings in the navigation bar of the File History window.)

To activate File History on your computer, follow these steps:

1. From the Windows desktop, open the Control Panel.

2. Go to the System and Security section and click Save Backup Copies of Your Files with File History.

3. When the File History screen appears, as shown in Figure 9.3, click the Turn On button.

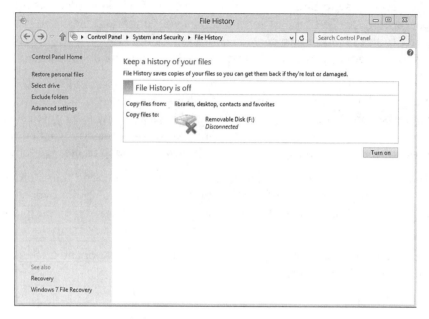

FIGURE 9.3

Backing up important files with Windows' File History utility.

 TIP File History automatically uses the first external drive on your system for its backup. If you want to use a different backup drive, click Select Drive in the navigation pane and, when the next screen appears, select a different drive or network location.

To restore any or all files you've backed up, open the File History utility and click Restore Personal Files from the navigation pane. When the Home screen appears, navigate to and select those files you want to restore, and then click the blue Restore button.

 TIP You can also use File History to restore a given file to an earlier state. This is useful if you're editing a document, for example, and want to use an earlier version of the document before more recent editing.

Backing Up Online

The newest way to back up your data is to do it over the Internet, using an online backup service. This type of service copies your important files from your computer to the service's own servers, over the Internet. This way, if your local data is lost or damaged, you can then restore the files from the online backup service's servers.

The benefit of using an online backup service is that the backup copy of your library is stored offsite, so you're protected in case of any local physical catastrophe, such as fire or flood. Most online backup services also work in the background, so they're constantly backing up new and changed files in real time.

The downside of an online backup service comes if you need to restore your files. It takes a long time to transfer lots of big files to your computer over an Internet connection. Plus, you have to pay for the backup service—on an ongoing basis. Most online backup services run $50 or more per year, per computer.

If online backup appeals to you, check out these popular online backup services designed for home users:

- Carbonite (www.carbonite.com)
- IDrive (www.idrive.com)
- Mozy (www.mozy.com)
- Norton Online Backup (us.norton.com/online-backup/)
- SOS Online Backup (www.sosonlinebackup.com)

THE ABSOLUTE MINIMUM

Here are the key points to remember when connecting and configuring your new computer:

- External hard drives let you add extra storage capacity to your system—up to 3TB extra.

- You can find both desktop-type external drives and smaller, portable drives for use with notebook PCs.

- Connecting an external drive is typically as easy as connecting it to one of your PC's USB ports.

- An external drive shows up in File Explorer as just another drive on your system.

- You can also use an external hard drive to back up valuable data from your main hard drive.

- Windows 8 includes a File History utility that automates the backup process for files on your computer.

- Also available are online backup services, which back up your data over the Internet.

10

SETTING UP A HOME NETWORK

When you need to connect two or more computers, you need to create a computer *network*.

Why would you want to connect two computers? Maybe you want to transfer files or digital photos from one computer to another. Maybe you want to share an expensive piece of hardware (such as a printer) instead of buying one for each PC. Maybe you want to connect all your computers to the same Internet connection. Whatever your reasons, it's easy to set up and configure a simple home network. Read on to learn how!

How Networks Work

When it comes to physically connecting your network, you have two ways to go—wired or wireless. A wireless network is more convenient (no wires to run), but a wired network is faster. Which you choose depends on how you use the computers you network.

If you use your network primarily to share an Internet connection or a printer or to transfer the occasional word processing file, wireless should work just fine. However, if you plan on transferring a lot of big files from one PC to another or using your network for multiplayer gaming, you should stick to a faster wired network. (For that matter, if you watch a lot of streaming video over the network, wired can be more reliable than wireless.)

Wired Networks

A *wired network* is the kind that requires you to run a bunch of cables from each PC to a central hub or router. In a wired network, all your PCs are connected together through a central *network router*, via an Ethernet cable. (Most new PCs come with built-in Ethernet capability, so you don't have to purchase anything additional—other than the router, that is.) Although this type of network is fast and easy enough to set up, you still have to deal with all those cables—which can be a hassle if your computers are in different areas of your house.

The speed you get from a wired network depends on the type of Ethernet technology used by each piece of equipment. The oldest Ethernet technology transfers data at just 10Mbps; Fast Ethernet transfers data at 100Mbps; and the newer Gigabit Ethernet transfers data at 1 *gigabit* per second (that's 1,000Mbps). Either Fast Ethernet or Gigabit Ethernet are fine for transferring really big files between computers or for playing real-time PC games.

 NOTE How quickly data is transferred across a network is measured in megabits per second, or Mbps. The bigger the Mbps number, the faster the network—and faster is always better than slower.

Wireless Networks

The alternative to a wired network is a *wireless network*. Wireless networks use radio frequency (RF) signals to connect one computer to another. The advantage of wireless, of course, is that you don't have to run cables. This is a big plus if you have a large house with computers on either end or on different floors.

The most popular wireless networks use the Wi-Fi standard. The original Wi-Fi standard, known as 802.11b, transferred data at 11Mbps—slower than Fast Ethernet, but fast enough for most practical purposes. Next up was 802.11g, which transferred data at 54Mbps—more than fast enough for most home-networking needs.

 NOTE Wi-Fi is short for *wireless fidelity.*

Even faster is the new 802.11n standard, which delivers a blazing 600Mbps data transmission with a substantially longer range than older equipment. Current 802.11b and g equipment has a range of about 100 feet between transmitter and receiver; 802.11n gives you a 160-foot range, with less interference from other wireless household devices. You'll need the higher speeds if you plan on watching TV shows or movies on a wireless PC.

 NOTE The 600Mbps rate for 802.11n networks is the theoretical maximum. In practice, expect rates between 200Mbps and 300Mbps.

In addition, you can combine wired and wireless technologies into a single network. Some PCs can connect directly to a wireless router via Ethernet, whereas others can connect via wireless Wi-Fi signals. This type of mixed network is quite common.

Connecting and Configuring

Whether you're going wired or wireless, the setup is surprisingly easy. You have to assemble the appropriate cables, along with a network router, and then install and connect it all together. After everything is hooked up properly, you then have to configure all the PCs on your network. The configuration can be made from within Windows or via the configuration utility provided with your network router or wireless adapter. You run this utility on each computer you connect to your network and then configure the network within Windows.

Setting Up a Wireless Network in Your Home

Connecting multiple computers in a home network is actually fairly simple. Just make sure that you do the proper planning beforehand and buy the appropriate hardware and cables; everything else is a matter of connecting and configuration.

NOTE For the purposes of this chapter the assumption is that you're setting up a wireless network, as that's what most people today use. Connecting a wired network is equally easy, the big difference is that you have to connect Ethernet cables between your router and each computer instead of making a wireless connection.

How It Works

A wireless network revolves around a device called a *wireless router*. This device functions like the hub of a wheel and serves as the central point in your network; each computer on your network connects through the wireless router.

NOTE Most wireless routers can make both wireless and wired connections. A typical wireless router includes four or more Ethernet ports in addition to wireless capabilities.

Every computer in a wireless network can connect to the router wirelessly—assuming, that is, that each computer contains wireless functionality. Almost all notebook and tablet PCs have built-in wireless connectivity, but many desktop PCs don't. (Although some do, of course.) You can add wireless functionality to a desktop PC via a wireless adapter, which is a small device that connects to your PC via USB.

When complete, your network should look something like the one in Figure 10.1.

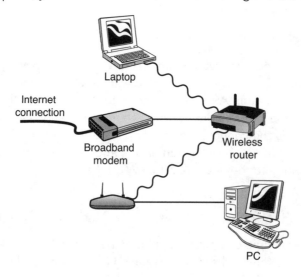

FIGURE 10.1

A typical wireless network.

What You Need

Here's the specific hardware you need to set up your network:

- Wireless router (one for the entire network)

- Broadband modem (typically supplied by your Internet service provider; either cable modem or DSL modem, depending on your service)

 NOTE   Some Internet service providers supply combination broadband modem/wireless router boxes.

- Wireless network adapters (one for each desktop PC; these are already built into notebook and tablet PCs, and are sometimes built into desktops, as well)

If you're connecting only notebook or tablet PCs to your network, you don't need any wireless adapters (they're built into all portable computers)—you only need the wireless router and broadband modem. In addition, some desktop PCs have built-in wireless connectivity; if your desktops are so enabled, you don't need wireless adapters for them, either.

Making the Connections

Naturally, you should follow the instructions that come with your networking hardware to properly set up your network. In general, however, here are the steps to take:

1. Run an Ethernet cable from your broadband modem to your wireless router and connect it to the port on your router labeled Internet or WAN. (If your router doesn't have a dedicated Internet port then you can connect it to any port.)

2. Connect your wireless router to a power source.

3. Power on your broadband modem and wireless router.

4. Connect the first PC in your network to the router, as discussed in the "Connecting Your Computer to Your New Network" section, later in this chapter.

5. Follow the instructions provided by the router's manufacturer to create and configure a new wireless network. Make sure you configure your network to use wireless security, which requires a password (sometimes called a *network key*) before a device can connect to the network.

6. Configure the first PC for your new network.

7. Connect and configure all your remaining PCs for your new network.

 TIP   When you first connect a new router to your network, you should configure the router using the software that came with the device. Follow the manufacturer's directions to configure the network and wireless security.

After you've connected all the computers on your network, you can proceed to configure any devices (such as printers) you want to share over the network. For example, if you want to share a single printer over the network, you can connect it to one of the network PCs and then share it through that PC. (You can also install network printers that connect directly to your wireless router, not to any specific PC.)

Connecting Your Computer to Your New Network

After your network hardware is all set up, you have to configure Windows to recognize and work with your new network. With Windows 8, this is a relatively painless and practically transparent step.

Connecting via Ethernet

If you're connecting to your network via Ethernet, you don't have to do a thing. After you connect an Ethernet cable between your PC and your router, Windows recognizes your new network and starts using it automatically.

Connecting Wirelessly

If you're connecting via a wireless connection, configuration is only slightly more involved. All you have to do is select which wireless network to connect to. Follow these steps:

1. Display the Charms Bar and click or tap Settings to display the Settings panel, shown in Figure 10.2.

2. Click or tap the Wi-Fi icon (typically labeled "Available" if you're not yet connected to a network) to display a list of available networks, as shown in Figure 10.3.

3. Click or tap your wireless network.

4. If prompted, enter the password (or network key) for your network.

Click to select Wi-Fi network

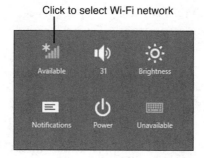

FIGURE 10.2

Click or tap the Wi-Fi icon to display available wireless networks.

FIGURE 10.3

Select your wireless network from the list.

Adding Your Computer to a HomeGroup

The easiest way to network multiple home computers is to create a HomeGroup for your network. A HomeGroup is kind of a simplified network that enables you to automatically share files and printers between connected computers.

NOTE   Only PCs running Windows 7 or Windows 8 can be part of a HomeGroup. PCs running older versions of Windows do not have the HomeGroup feature and must use the normal networking functions instead.

To create a new HomeGroup, follow these steps:

1. Display the Charms Bar and click or tap Settings to display the Settings panel.

2. Click or tap Change PC Settings to display the PC Settings screen.

3. Scroll down the list on the left and select HomeGroup, as shown in Figure 10.4.

FIGURE 10.4

Creating a new HomeGroup.

4. Click or tap the Create button.

5. When the next screen appears, as shown in Figure 10.5, go to the Library and Devices section and click or tap "on" those items you want to share with other computers. You can choose to share your Documents, Music, Pictures, Videos, or Printers and Devices.

6. If you want non-computers, such as network-connected TVs or video game consoles, to be able to access the content on this computer, scroll to the Media Devices section, shown in Figure 10.6, and click or tap "on" this option.

7. Scroll to the Membership section, shown in Figure 10.7, and write down the password. You need to provide this to users of other computers on your network who want to join your HomeGroup.

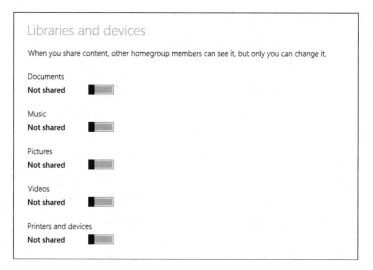

FIGURE 10.5

Configuring HomeGroup sharing.

FIGURE 10.6

Granting non-PC devices access to your computer's content.

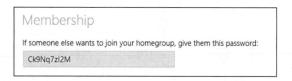

FIGURE 10.7

Viewing the HomeGroup password.

Accessing Computers on Your Network

After you have your home network set up, you can access shared content stored on other computers on your network. How you do so depends on whether the other computer is part of your HomeGroup or not.

Accessing HomeGroup Computers

You access the content of other computers connected to your HomeGroup via File Explorer. Follow these steps:

1. Open the Windows desktop and click the File Explorer icon on the taskbar.

2. When File Explorer opens, go to the HomeGroup section of the navigation pane.

3. Click or tap the name of the user who's computer you want to access.

4. Windows displays the shared libraries on the selected computer, as shown in Figure 10.8; double-click or tap a library to access that particular content.

FIGURE 10.8

Viewing shared libraries on a HomeGroup computer.

Accessing Other Computers on Your Network

A computer doesn't have to be connected to your HomeGroup for you to access its content. Windows enables you to access any computer connected to your home network—although you can only share content the computer's owner has configured as sharable.

To access other computers on your network, follow these steps:

1. Open the Windows desktop and click the File Explorer icon on the taskbar.

2. Go to the Network section of the navigation pane.

3. Click or tap the computer you want to access.

4. Windows displays the shared folders on the selected computer; double-click or tap a folder to view that folder's content.

  TIP   On most older computers, shared files are stored in the Public folder. Look in this folder first for the files you want.

Managing Your Network

In Windows 8, all network functions can be monitored and managed via the Network and Sharing Center, shown in Figure 10.9.

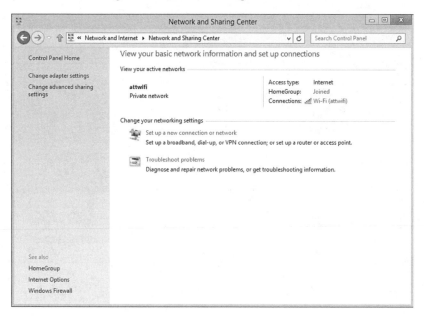

FIGURE 10.9

The Windows 8 Network and Sharing Center.

To open the Network and Sharing Center, follow these steps:

1. Open the Windows Control panel and click or tap Network and Internet.

2. Click or tap Network and Sharing Center.

You can use the Network and Sharing Center to configure all manner of network-related settings, including network discovery (to see other PCs on your network), file sharing, public folder sharing, printer sharing, password-protected sharing, and media sharing (for music, video, and picture files).

THE ABSOLUTE MINIMUM

Here are the key things to remember about creating a home network:

- To share information or hardware between two or more computers, as well as to share an Internet connection, you have to connect your computers in a network.

- There are two basic types of networks: wired and wireless (Wi-Fi).

- A wireless network uses a wireless router to serve as the hub for all connected devices.

- The easiest way to share content between connected computers is to create a HomeGroup.

- After you've connected your computers in a network, you can access other connected computers via File Explorer.

11

CONNECTING TO THE INTERNET—AT HOME AND ON THE ROAD

It used to be that most people bought personal computers to do serious work—word processing, spreadsheets, databases, the sort of programs that still make up the core of Microsoft Office. But today, people also buy PCs to access the Internet—to send and receive email, surf the Web, watch movies and listen to music, and socialize with other users.

To do this, of course, you first have to connect your computer to the Internet. Fortunately, Windows makes this easy to do.

Different Types of Connections in the Home

The first step in going online is establishing a connection between your computer and the Internet. When you're connecting from home, you need to sign up with an Internet service provider (ISP). This is a company that, as the name implies, provides your home with a connection to the Internet.

Most ISPs today offer some form of *broadband* access. Broadband is the fastest type of Internet connection available to homes today, and it comes in many flavors—cable, digital subscriber line (DSL), Fiber Optic Service (FiOS), and even satellite. Whichever type of broadband connection you choose, the Internet comes into your home via a wire or cable and connects to a device called a *modem*, which then connects either directly to your computer or to a wireless modem, so you can share the connection with all the computers and wireless devices in your home.

 NOTE In some rural areas, broadband access might not be available. If you don't have access to broadband Internet, you have to connect via a *dial-up connection*—that is, by dialing in through your normal telephone line. Unfortunately, dial-up connections are much, much slower than broadband connections, which means it takes longer to download music and photos—and makes watching video online problematic.

Broadband DSL

DSL is a phone line-based technology that operates at broadband speeds. DSL service piggybacks onto your existing phone line, turning it into a high-speed digital connection (384Kbps to 10Mbps, depending on your ISP). With DSL, you don't have to surrender your normal phone line when you want to surf, as you do with traditional dial-up service; DSL connections are "always on." Most providers offer DSL service for $30–$50 per month. Look for package deals that offer a discount when you subscribe to both Internet and phone services.

 CAUTION Many ISPs provide slower speeds for data uploaded from your computer. So you may see, for example, an offer of 50Mbps downstream but just 8Mbps upstream. In addition, some ISPs employ "speed caps" for customers who download too much data, effectively throttling their use or charging extra for excessive data usage. It pays to check the fine print on these items before you sign up.

Broadband Cable

Another popular type of broadband connection is available from your local cable company. Broadband cable Internet piggybacks on your normal cable television line, providing speeds in the 500Kbps to 50Mbps range, depending on the provider. Most cable companies offer broadband cable Internet for $30–$50 per month, which is about the same as you pay for a similar DSL connection. As with DSL, look for package deals from your cable company, offering some sort of discount on a combination of Internet, cable, and (sometimes) digital phone service.

FiOS Broadband

The newest type of broadband connection is FiOS. As the name implies, this type of service delivers an Internet connection over a fiber optic network.

FiOS connection speeds are similar to those of broadband cable, with different speeds available at different pricing tiers. Most ISPs offer download speeds between 3Mbps and 50Mbps. Pricing is also similar to broadband cable, in the $30/month to $50/month range.

In the home, the FiOS line connects to a modem-like device called an optical network terminal (ONT) that can split the signal to provide a combination of Internet, television, and telephone services. You typically connect the ONT to your wireless router or PC via Ethernet. In the U.S., FiOS Internet service is available in limited areas through AT&T and Verizon.

Broadband Satellite

If you can't get DSL, cable, or FiOS Internet in your area, you have another option—connecting to the Internet via satellite. Any household or business with a clear line of sight to the southern sky can receive digital data signals from a geosynchronous satellite at speeds between 1Mbps and 52Mbps.

The largest provider of satellite Internet access is HughesNet. (Hughes also developed and markets the popular DIRECTV digital satellite system.) The HughesNet system (www.hughesnet.com) enables you to receive Internet signals via a small dish that you mount outside your house or on your roof. Fees range from $50 to $110 per month.

Sharing an Internet Connection

If you have more than one PC in your home, you can connect them to share a single high-speed Internet connection. That is, you don't have to bring in separate lines and modems for each of your PCs, nor do you have to pay for more than one connection.

You share an Internet connection by connecting your broadband modem to your home network. It doesn't matter whether you have a wired or a wireless network; the connection is similar in both instances. All you have to do is run an Ethernet cable from your broadband modem to your network router, and then Windows does the rest, connecting your modem to the network so that all your computers can access the connection.

To work through all the details of this type of connection, turn to Chapter 10, "Setting Up a Home Network." It's really quite easy!

Connecting to a Public Wi-Fi Hotspot

If you have a notebook or tablet PC, you also have the option to connect to the Internet when you're away from home. Many coffeehouses, restaurants, hotels, and public spaces offer wireless Wi-Fi Internet service, either free or for an hourly or daily fee. Assuming that your notebook has a built-in Wi-Fi adapter (which almost all do), connecting to a public Wi-Fi hotspot is a snap.

 NOTE A *hotspot* is a public place that offers wireless access to the Internet using Wi-Fi technology. Some hotspots are free for all to access; others require some sort of payment.

When you're near a Wi-Fi hotspot, your PC should automatically pick up the Wi-Fi signal. Make sure that your PC's Wi-Fi adapter is turned on (some notebooks have a switch for this, either on the front or on the side of the unit), and then follow these steps:

1. From the Windows Start screen, display the Charms Bar and click or tap Settings to display the Settings panel, shown in Figure 11.1.

FIGURE 11.1

Click or tap the Wi-Fi icon to display available wireless networks.

2. If there's a hotspot nearby, the Wi-Fi icon should be labeled "Available." Click or tap this icon to display a list of available networks, as shown in Figure 11.2.

 TIP Most public networks do *not* have wireless security engaged. They'll display on the Settings panel with a little warning shield next to the wireless icon.

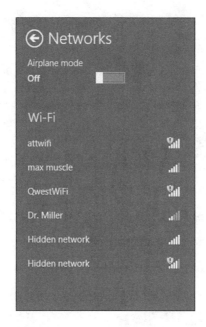

FIGURE 11.2

Select your wireless network from the list.

3. Click or tap the wireless network to which you want to connect.

After Windows connects to the selected hotspot, you can log on to the wireless network. Windows may do this automatically, prompting you that further input is required and displaying the hotspot's logon screen. You may also have to do this manually, by opening the Internet Explorer web browser and trying to go to a website—any website. If the hotspot has free public access, you can surf normally. If the hotspot requires a password, payment, or other logon procedure, it intercepts the request for your normal home page and instead displays its own login page. Enter the appropriate information, and you'll be surfing in no time!

TIP If your notebook or tablet is configured to connect to your mobile phone carrier's data network, you see additional mobile broadband connection options within Windows. By default, Windows connects to available Wi-Fi networks first, as they're typically free or lower cost; if no Wi-Fi networks are available, then it connects to the data network you select.

Activating Airplane Mode

If you're using your notebook or tablet computer on an airplane, you can switch to Window's special Airplane Mode, which suspends all of your PC's signal transmitting and receiving functions. It's just like the airplane mode you find on many smartphones, and it enables you to use your computer while you're in the air without fear of interfering with the plane's electronics.

To switch into Airplane Mode, follow these steps:

1. Display the Charms Bar and click or tap Settings to display the Settings panel.

2. Click or tap Change PC Settings to display the PC Settings page.

3. Select Wireless from the left column.

4. Click or tap "off" the Airplane Mode option.

You can switch off Airplane Mode when your plane lands.

THE ABSOLUTE MINIMUM

When you're configuring your new PC system to connect to the Internet, remember these important points:

- You connect to the Internet through an Internet service provider, or ISP; you need to set up an account with an ISP before you can connect.

- There are three common types of broadband service available today: DSL, cable, and FiOS, and the more expensive satellite service is an option for rural areas.

- If you have more than one computer at home, you can share your Internet connection by connecting your broadband modem to your home network.

- If you have a notebook PC, you can connect to the Internet wirelessly at any public Wi-Fi hotspot, such as those offered by Starbucks, Caribou Coffee, and similar establishments.

USING INTERNET EXPLORER TO SURF THE WEB

Now that you've connected to the Internet, either at home or via a public wireless hotspot, it's time to get surfing. The World Wide Web is a particular part of the Internet with all sorts of cool content and useful services, and you surf the Web with a piece of software called a *web browser*.

The most popular web browser today is Microsoft's Internet Explorer. There's a new version of Internet Explorer in Windows 8 that's fully integrated into the full-screen touch-enabled experience, which makes it fun and cool to use. This chapter shows you how to use the new Internet Explorer and then takes you on a quick trip around the Web—just enough to get your online feet wet!

Understanding the Web

Before you can surf the Web, you need to understand a little bit about how it works.

Information on the World Wide Web is presented in *pages*. A web page is similar to a page in a book, made up of text and graphics. A web page differs from a book page, however, in that it can include other elements, such as audio and video, and links to other web pages.

It's this linking to other web pages that makes the Web such a dynamic way to present information. A *link* on a web page can point to another web page on the same site or to another site. Most links are included as part of a web page's text and are called *hypertext links*, or just *hyperlinks*. (If a link is part of a graphic, it's called a *graphic link*.) These links are usually in a different color from the rest of the text and often are underlined; when you click a link, you're taken directly to the linked page.

Web pages reside at a *website*. A website is nothing more than a collection of web pages (each in its own computer file) residing on a host computer. The host computer is connected full-time to the Internet so that you can access the site—and its web pages—anytime you access the Internet. The main page at a website is called the *home page*, and it often serves as an opening screen that provides a brief overview and menu of everything you can find at that site. The address of a web page is called a *URL*, which stands for *uniform resource locator*. Most URLs start with http://, add a www., continue with the name of the site, and end with a .com, .org, or .net.

 TIP You can normally leave off the http:// when you enter an address into your web browser. In most cases, you can even leave off the www. and just start with the domain part of the address.

Using Internet Explorer

The web browser included in Microsoft Windows is Internet Explorer (IE). In Windows 8, there are actually two versions of Internet Explorer. There's a full-screen version, accessible from the Start screen, that's designed to take full advantage of Windows 8's interface. Then there's another, more traditional, windowed version of IE that runs on the Windows desktop.

We'll focus our attention on the Windows 8 version of Internet Explorer—the version you launch from the Start screen. To launch this web browser, all you have to do is click or tap the Internet Explorer tile on the Start screen, as shown in Figure 12.1.

FIGURE 12.1

Launching Internet Explorer from the Windows Start screen.

As you can see in Figure 12.2, Internet Explorer launches full screen. By default, the only thing you see is the current web page you're viewing; all the other controls and command bars (sometimes called the "chrome") are hidden so you can concentrate on the web page at hand.

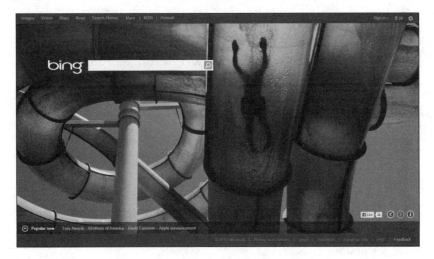

FIGURE 12.2

The Internet Explorer web browser in Windows 8.

When you want to go to another web page, or revisit one you've viewed previously, all you have to do is right-click your mouse anywhere in the browser or swipe up from the bottom of the screen on a touchscreen display. This displays the Address Bar at the bottom of the screen and the Tab Bar at the top, as shown in Figure 12.3.

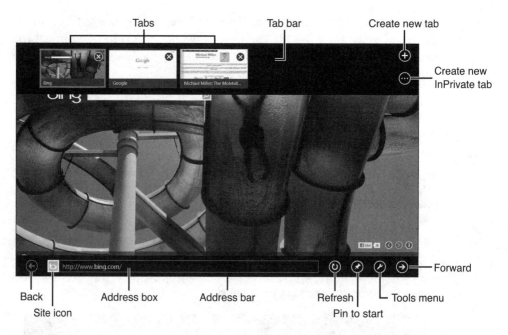

FIGURE 12.3

Internet Explorer with Address bar (bottom) and Tab bar (top) displayed.

The Address bar is where you enter new web page addresses (also called URLs) and access other controls, such as the following:

- **Back**—Click to move back to the last-viewed web page.

- **Address box**—Enter the address of the web page you want to view.

- **Refresh**—Click to reload the current web page.

- **Pin to Start**—When you find a web page you think you'll be visiting frequently, click this button to "pin" that page to the Start screen by creating a tile for that web page.

- **Tools**—Click if you want to search the content of the current web page or view this page in the traditional desktop version of Internet Explorer.

- **Forward**—If you've moved back through one or more web pages, click this button to move forward to the next page.

The Tab bar is where you can view other open tabs, switch between tabs, and open new tabs. That's right, Internet Explorer lets you open multiple web pages at the same time, one on each tab, and then easily switch from one tab (web page) to another. We discuss how to use tabs later in this chapter.

Basic Web Surfing

Internet Explorer enables you to quickly and easily browse the World Wide Web—just by clicking your mouse or tapping your touchscreen display. Here's a step-by-step tour of IE's basic functions:

1. When you launch Internet Explorer, it loads the last page you visited.

2. Enter a new web address in the Address box, and press Enter. Internet Explorer loads the new page.

3. Click or tap any link on the current web page. Internet Explorer loads the new page.

4. To return to the previous page, click or tap the Back button (or press the Backspace key on your keyboard). If you've backed up several pages and want to return to the page you were on last, click or tap the Forward button.

Revisiting Your Favorite Web Pages

Most traditional web browsers (and the desktop version of IE) let you set a "home" page that always opens when you launch the browser. The Windows 8 version of Internet Explorer doesn't let you set a home page, but does display your favorite and recently visited pages as tiles on a special panel, shown in Figure 12.4. You can then click or tap a tile to revisit that page.

FIGURE 12.4

Revisiting frequent and pinned pages.

To display the favorites and pinned panel, all you have to do is click or tap in the Address box. A panel with two sections of tiles—Frequent and Pinned—opens. The Frequent tiles display those web pages you've visited most often. The Pinned tiles display those pages you've pinned to the Start screen. (Pinned pages also appear on the Start screen itself, of course.)

To pin a page, follow these steps:

1. Navigate to the web page you want to pin.

2. Right-click or press and hold the page to display the Address bar.

3. Click or tap the Pin to Start button; this displays the Pin panel, shown in Figure 12.5.

4. Confirm or edit the name of the page.

5. Click or tap the Pin to Start button.

FIGURE 12.5

Pinning a web page to the Start page.

Using Tabbed Browsing

Internet Explorer utilizes a multidocument interface that lets you display multiple web pages on separate tabs within a single browser screen. This use of tabs enables you to keep multiple web pages open simultaneously—which is great when you want to keep previous pages open for reference or want to run web-based applications in the background.

To open a web page on a new tab, follow these steps:

1. Right-click or press and hold within the browser to display the Tab bar, shown in Figure 12.6.

2. Click or tap the New Tab (+) button to display the frequent and pinned panel.

FIGURE 12.6

The Tab bar.

3. Click or tap a tile on this panel. Alternatively, you can enter a new web page address in the Address box.

You switch between tabs by displaying the Tab bar and then clicking or tapping the tab you want to view. You can close a tab by clicking or tapping the X by the tab.

InPrivate Browsing

On occasion you might want to visit a website that you don't want others to know you've visited. When you don't want a specific browsing session tracked, you can use Internet Explorer's InPrivate Browsing feature to browse completely anonymously. With InPrivate Browsing, no record of the pages you visit is kept via any means on your computer; no one need know where you've been on the Web.

You enable this anonymous browsing by opening a separate InPrivate Browsing tab. Follow these steps:

1. Right-click or press and hold within the browser to display the Tab bar.

2. Click the ellipsis (…) button to display the pop-up menu.

3. Click or tap New InPrivate Tab.

A new tab opens, with a blue InPrivate box next to the normal Address box, as shown in Figure 12.7. Enter the URL you want to browse to then press Enter. Any browsing you do on this screen is not recorded.

FIGURE 12.7

Internet Explorer, ready for InPrivate Browsing.

Searching from the Browser

If you search the Web a lot, and you probably do, you might frequently go to your favorite search site. Fortunately, Internet Explorer lets you speed up your searches by searching from the Address box of the browser. This lets you perform web searches without having to first navigate to a separate search site.

To conduct a search from within Internet Explorer, just enter your query into the Address box and press the Enter key on your keyboard. Your query is sent via IE over the Internet to Microsoft's Bing search engine—which receives the query, searches its own previously compiled index of web pages, and returns a page of search results, which is displayed in the Internet Explorer window. It's that easy.

Using the Desktop Version of Internet Explorer

The Windows 8 version of Internet Explorer is easy to use and more than sufficient for most users. Some power users, however, might prefer the additional functionality found in the traditional version of Internet Explorer, which runs on the Windows 8 desktop.

To launch the desktop version of Internet Explorer, follow these steps:

1. From the Windows Start screen, click or tap the Desktop icon.

2. When the Windows Desktop appears, as shown in Figure 12.8, click or tap the Internet Explorer icon on the task bar at the bottom of the screen.

FIGURE 12.8

Click the Internet Explorer icon to launch the desktop version of Internet Explorer.

Figure 12.9 shows the desktop version of Internet Explorer. This version of IE looks and acts more like a traditional web browser, and features additional functionality. Use the desktop version of IE when you need to keep large lists of favorite pages, print pages, manage downloaded files, and perform other advanced operations.

FIGURE 12.9

The traditional desktop version of the Internet Explorer web browser.

THE ABSOLUTE MINIMUM

Here are the key things to remember about surfing the Web:

- You surf the Web with the Internet Explorer web browser.

- Windows 8 includes two versions of Internet Explorer—a full-screen Windows 8 version and a traditional desktop version.

- The Windows 8 version of Internet Explorer displays web pages full screen without any "chrome," menus, or bars.

- To display the Address Bar, right-click within a web page or swipe up from the bottom of the page (on a touchscreen display).

- To go to a particular web page, enter the page's address in the Address box and then press Enter. (You can also click or tap a hyperlink on a web page to jump to the linked page.)

- Internet Explorer offers tabbed browsing, where you can open new web pages in additional tabs; click or tap a tab to switch to that web page.

- IE8 lets you search the Web from within the browser by entering your query into the Address box.

13

SEARCHING AND RESEARCHING ONLINE

Now that you know how to surf the Web, how do you find the precise information you're looking for? Fortunately, there are numerous sites that help you search the Web for the specific information you want. Not surprisingly, these are among the most popular sites on the Internet.

This chapter is all about searching the Web, and using the Internet for research. It covers the best places to search and research the information you need. I even help you cheat a little by listing some of the most popular sites for different types of information.

So pull up a chair, launch Internet Explorer, and loosen up those fingers—it's time to start searching!

How to Search the Web

Internet *search engines* are sites that employ special software programs (called *spiders* or *crawlers*) to roam the Web automatically, feeding what they find back to a massive bank of computers. These computers then build giant *indexes* of the Web.

When you perform a search at a search engine site, your query is sent to the search engine's index. (You never actually search the Web itself; you only search the index that was created by the spiders crawling the Web.) The search engine then creates a list of pages in its index that match, to one degree or another, the query you entered.

Constructing a Query

Almost every search site on the Web contains two basic components—a *search box* and a *Search button*. You enter your query—one or more *keywords* that describe what you're looking for—into the search box and then click the Search button (or press the Enter key) to start the search. The search site then returns a list of web pages that match your query; click any link to go directly to one of the pages.

How you construct your query determines how relevant the results you receive will be. It's important to focus on the keywords you use because the search sites look for these words when they process your query. Your keywords are compared to the web pages the search site knows about; the more keywords found on a web page, the better the match.

Choose keywords that best describe the information you're looking for—using as many keywords as you need. Don't be afraid of using too many keywords; in fact, using too *few* keywords is a common fault of many novice searchers. The more words you use, the better idea the search engine has of what you're looking for.

Searching for an Exact Phrase

Normally, a multiple-word query searches for web pages that include all the words in the query, in any order. There is a way, however, to search for an exact phrase. All you have to do is enclose the phrase in quotation marks.

For example, to search for **Monty Python**, the comic troupe, *don't* enter Monty Python as your query. Instead, enter **"Monty Python"**—with the two keywords surrounded by quotation marks. Putting the phrase between quotation marks returns results about the comedy troupe, whereas entering the words individually also returns pages about snakes and guys named Monty.

Where to Search

Now that you know *how* to search, *where* should you search? There's one obvious choice, and a few alternatives.

Google—The Most Popular Search Site on the Web

The most popular search engine today is Google (www.google.com). Google is easy to use, extremely fast, and returns highly relevant results. That's because it indexes more pages than any other site—billions and billions of pages, if you're counting.

Most users search Google several times a week, if not several times a day. The Google home page, shown in Figure 13.1, is a marvel of simplicity and elegant web page design. All you have to do to start a search is to enter one or more key-words into the search box and then click the Google Search button. This returns a list of results ranked in order of relevance, such as the one shown in Figure 13.2. Click a results link to view that page.

FIGURE 13.1

Searching the Web with Google.

Google also offers a variety of advanced search options to help you fine-tune your search. Some of these options are displayed in the Search Options section of the left-hand sidebar. These options let you filter your results by type (Web, Images, Maps, Videos, News, Shopping, and more), time (Past 24 Hours, Past Week, and so on), and other factors. It's a nice way to narrow down what you're looking for.

Additional options are found on the Advanced Search page, which you get to by clicking the Options (gear) button on any search results page and then selecting Advanced Search. To narrow your search results, all you have to do is make the appropriate selections from the options present.

Search | About 12,000,000 results (0.29 seconds)

Everything | **Que**: Computing & Technology Books, Video, Articles for Home ...
www.quepublishing.com/
Learn Office, Windows, Mac OS X, Facebook, Twitter, iPhone, iPad, and more with **Que** books, articles, web editions, eBooks, video, podcasts, blogs, ...

Images
Maps
Videos
News
Shopping
More

About
The Que series of products are all about helping you learn about ...

Register your Product
Register the Que Publishing products you own to unlock ...

Using Series
Que is excited to announce one of our newest publishing series ...

Contact Us
Contact Us. Please Select Your Query. Please select the ...

Chicago, IL
Change location

Books
Pottermore.com Secrets and Mysteries Revealed: The ...

Gadgets & Hardware ...
Gadgets & Hardware Resource Center. Upgrading & Repairing ...

More results from quepublishing.com »

Any time
Past hour
Past 24 hours
Past week
Past month
Past year
Custom range...
More search tools

Que Publishing | InformIT
www.informit.com/imprint/index.aspx?st=61090
Que Publishing is excited to announce our new web site, **quepublishing**.com. We gathered our consumer products in one easy place—look for books, eBooks, ...

Welcome to **Que Publishing** (Pearson Technology Group Canada)
www.quepublishing.ca/
Every day, **Que Publishing** works to produce superior books designed to make people's lives easier, more dynamic, and more enriched. With over 20 years ...

FIGURE 13.2

The results of a Google search.

TIP You can also use Google to display stock quotes (enter the stock ticker), answers to mathematical calculations (enter the equation), and measurement conversions (enter what you want to convert). Google can also track USPS, UPS, and FedEx packages (enter the tracking number), as well as the progress of airline flights (enter the airline and flight number).

Bing—Microsoft's Answer to Google

Google's a great search site, but it has serious competition in the form of Bing (www.bing.com). Bing is Microsoft's search site; not surprisingly, it's designed to integrate well with Windows 8.

As you can see in Figure 13.3, Bing looks and feels a little like a Windows 8-style app. Its design fits in well with Windows 8's full screen approach. And, also not surprisingly, it's the default search engine when you search from Internet Explorer's Address box.

FIGURE 13.3

Searching the Web with Bing.

You search Bing the same way you search Google. Enter your query into the search box and press Enter on your keyboard. Bing displays its results on a separate page, like the one shown in Figure 13.4; click a result to see that web page.

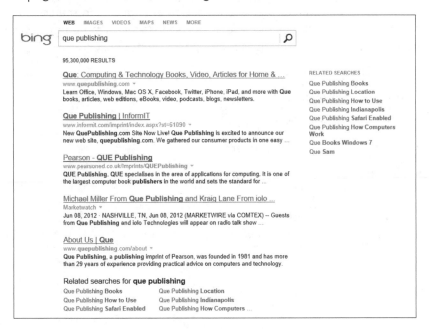

FIGURE 13.4

The results of a Bing search.

Other Search Sites

Although Google and Bing are far and away the most popular search engines today, many other search engines provide excellent (and sometimes different) results. These search engines include

- AltaVista (www.altavista.com)

- Ask.com (www.ask.com)

- Open Directory (www.dmoz.org)

- Yahoo! (www.yahoo.com)

Searching for People and Businesses

As good as Google and other search sites are for finding specific web pages, they're not always that great for finding people. When there's a person (or an address or a phone number) you want to find, you need to use a site that specializes in people searches.

People listings on the Web go by the common name of *white pages directories*, the same as traditional white pages phone books. These directories typically enable you to enter all or part of a person's name and then search for his address and phone number. Many of these sites also let you search for personal email addresses and business addresses and phone numbers.

The best of these directories include

- AnyWho (www.anywho.com)

- InfoSpace (www.infospace.com)

- Switchboard (www.switchboard.com)

- WhitePages.com (www.whitepages.com)

 TIP All of these white pages directories also serve as yellow pages directories for looking up businesses. They're one-stop search sites for any individual or business you want to look up!

Using Wikipedia for Research

Although many people use Google or Bing for research, searching the Web for just the right information can sometimes be like looking for a needle in a haystack; the information you get is totally unfiltered and not always accurate. A better way to research is to use a site designed primarily for research.

Such a site is Wikipedia (www.wikipedia.com), which is fast becoming the primary information site on the Web.

Understanding Wikipedia

Wikipedia is like a giant online encyclopedia—but with a twist. Unlike a traditional encyclopedia, Wikipedia's content is created solely by the site's users, resulting in the world's largest online collaboration.

At present, Wikipedia hosts close to 4 million English-language articles, with at least that many articles available in more than 250 different languages. The articles are written and revised by tens of thousands of individual contributors. These users volunteer their time and knowledge at no charge, for the good of the Wikipedia project.

You don't have to be an academic type to contribute to Wikipedia, and you don't have to be a student to use it. Anyone with specialized knowledge can write an article, and regular people like you and me can read them.

Searching Wikipedia

Information on the Wikipedia site is compiled into a series of articles. You search Wikipedia to find the exact articles you need.

To find an article on a given topic, go to the Wikipedia home page, shown in Figure 13.5, enter your query into the search box, and then click the right-arrow button. If an article directly matches your query, Wikipedia now displays that article. If a number of articles might match your query, Wikipedia displays the list of articles, organized by type or topic. Click the article name to display the specific article.

For example, if you search Wikipedia for **john adams**, it displays the article on founding father John Adams. If, instead, you search only for **adams**, it displays a disambiguation page with sections for matching people and places bearing the name of "Adams," as shown in Figure 13.6. From there you can find the article on the second president, as well as lots of other articles.

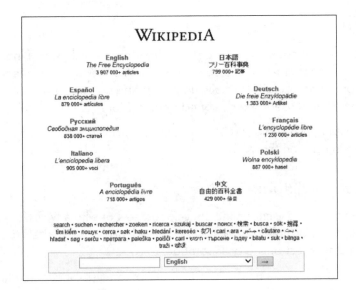

FIGURE 13.5

The Wikipedia home page.

FIGURE 13.6

A disambiguation page—resulting from too wide a search.

Reading Wikipedia Articles

As you can see in Figure 13.7, each Wikipedia article is organized into a summary and subsidiary sections. Longer articles have a table of contents, located beneath the summary. Key information is sometimes presented in a sidebar at the top right of the article.

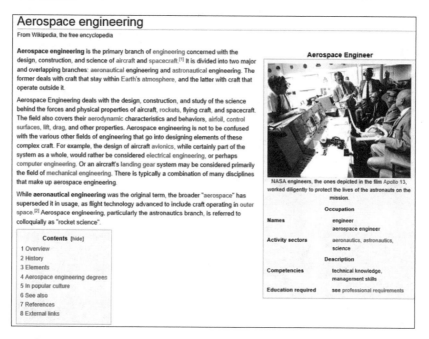

FIGURE 13.7

A typical Wikipedia article.

One of the things I liked about reading the encyclopedia when I was a kid was jumping around from article to article. This is easier than ever in Wikipedia, as the text of each article contains blue hypertext that links to related articles in the Wikipedia database. Click one of these links to jump to that article.

If you want to know the source for the information in an article, scroll to the bottom of the page, where the sources for key facts within the article are footnoted. Additional references and information about the topic also appear at the bottom of the page.

And, because Wikipedia articles are continually updated by users, it's often useful to view the history of an article's updates. This way you can see how an article looked before its most recent revisions. Click the History tab; to see a list of edits and who made those edits. You can also use the View History tab to read previous versions of an article.

TIP Some articles feature discussions from users, which can sometimes provide additional insight. Click the Discussion tab to read and participate in ongoing discussions.

THE ABSOLUTE MINIMUM

Here are the key points to remember from this chapter:

- When you need to search for specific information on the Internet, you can use one of the Web's many search engine sites.

- The most popular Internet search engine is Google, which indexes billions of individual web pages.

- Also popular is Microsoft's search engine, Bing.

- It's better to search for people (and their phone numbers and addresses) at specific people-search sites, such as InfoSpace and Switchboard.

- When you need to research specific topics, Wikipedia is a good source; it contains information written and edited by its large user base.

14

SHOPPING AND SELLING ONLINE

Many users have discovered that the Internet is a great place to buy things—all kinds of things. All manner of online merchants make it easy to buy books, CDs, and other merchandise with the click of a mouse.

The Web isn't just for shopping, however. You can also use sites such as eBay and craigslist to sell your own stuff online. It's a great way to get rid of all that old stuff cluttering your attic—or a few unwanted Christmas presents!

How to Shop Online

If you've never shopped online before, you're probably wondering just what to expect. Shopping over the Web is actually easy; all you need is your computer and a credit card—and a fast connection to the Internet!

Online shopping is pretty much the same, no matter which retailer website you visit. You proceed through a multiple-step process that goes like this:

1. **Find an online store** that sells the item you're shopping for.

2. **Find a product**, either by browsing or searching through the retailer's site.

3. **Examine the product** by viewing the photos and information on a product listing page.

4. **Order the product** by clicking a "buy it now" button on the product listing page that puts the item in your online shopping cart.

5. **Check out** by entering your payment (credit card) and shipping information.

6. **Confirm the order** and wait for the merchant to ship your merchandise.

Let's look at each of these steps separately.

Step 1: Find an Online Store

The first step in online shopping is finding where you want to shop. Most major retailers, such as Target and Walmart, have their own websites you can use to shop online, as do most catalog merchants. In addition, there are a good number of online-only retailers that offer a variety of merchandise, such as Amazon.com. You should find no shortage of places to shop online.

You can also use a price comparison site to help find the best merchandise and pricing online. These sites let you search for specific products and then sort and filter the results in a number of different ways. Many of these sites include customer reviews of both the products and the available merchants; some even let you perform side-by-side comparisons of multiple products, which is great if you haven't yet made up your mind as to what you want to buy.

The most popular (and useful) of these price comparison sites include

- BizRate (www.bizrate.com)

- Google Shopping

- mySimon (www.mysimon.com)

- NexTag (www.nextag.com)

- PriceGrabber (www.pricegrabber.com), shown in Figure 14.1

- Shopping.com (www.shopping.com)

- Yahoo! Shopping (shopping.yahoo.com)

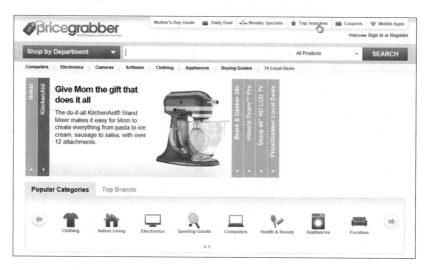

FIGURE 14.1

Comparing prices at PriceGrabber.

Step 2: Find a Product

After you've determined where to shop, you need to browse through different product categories on that site or use the site's search feature to find a specific product.

Browsing product categories online is similar to browsing through the departments of a retail store. You typically click a link to access a major product category, and then click further links to view subcategories within the main category. For example, the main category might be Clothing; the subcategories might be Men's, Women's, and Children's clothing. If you click the Men's link, you might see a list of further subcategories: outerwear, shirts, pants, and the like. Just keep clicking until you reach the type of item that you're looking for.

Searching for products is often a faster way to find what you're looking for if you have something specific in mind. For example, if you're looking for a men's silk jacket, you can enter the words **men's silk jacket** into the site's search box and get a list of specific items that match those criteria. The only problem with searching is that you might not know exactly what it is you're looking for; if this describes your situation, you're probably better off browsing. But if you *do* know what you want—and you don't want to deal with lots of irrelevant items—then searching is the faster option.

 TIP When searching for items at an online retailer, you can use the same general search guidelines I discussed in Chapter 13, "Searching and Researching Online."

Step 3: Examine the Product

Whether you browse or search, you'll probably end up looking at a list of different products on a web page. These listings typically feature one-line descriptions of each item—in most cases, not near enough information for you to make an informed purchase.

The thing to do now is to click the link for the item you're particularly interested in. This should display a dedicated product page, complete with a picture and full description of the item. This is where you can read more about the item you selected. Some product pages include different views of the item, pictures of the item in different colors, links to additional information, and maybe even a list of optional accessories that go along with the item.

If you like what you see, you can proceed to the ordering stage. If you want to look at other items, just click your browser's Back button to return to the larger product listing.

Step 4: Order the Product

Somewhere on each product description page should be a button labeled Purchase, Buy Now, Add to Cart, or something similar. This is how you make the actual purchase: by clicking that "buy" button. You don't order the product just by looking at the product description; you have to manually click the "buy" button to place your order. (Figure 14.2 shows a product page on Amazon.com; click the Add to Cart button to purchase this item.)

When you click the "buy" button, that particular item is added to your *shopping cart*. That's right, the online retailer provides you with a virtual shopping cart that functions just like a real-world shopping cart. Each item you choose to purchase is added to your virtual shopping cart.

After you've ordered a product and placed it in your shopping cart, you can choose to shop for other products on that site or proceed to the site's checkout. It's important to note that when you place an item in your shopping cart, you haven't actually completed the purchase yet. You can keep shopping (and adding more items to your shopping cart) as long as you want.

FIGURE 14.2

Getting ready to purchase a book on Amazon.com.

You can even decide to abandon your shopping cart and not purchase anything at this time. All you have to do is leave the website, and you won't be charged for anything. It's the equivalent of leaving your shopping cart at a real-world retailer and walking out the front door; you don't actually buy anything until you walk through the checkout line. (Although, with some sites, the items remain in your shopping cart—so they'll be there waiting for you the next time you shop!)

Step 5: Check Out

To finalize your purchase, you have to visit the store's *checkout*. This is like the checkout line at a traditional retail store; you take your virtual shopping cart through the checkout, get your purchases totaled, and then pay for what you're buying.

The checkout at an online retailer typically consists of one or more web pages with forms you have to fill out. If you've visited the retailer before, the site might remember some of your personal information from your previous visit. Otherwise, you have to enter your name, address, and phone number, as well as the address you want to ship the merchandise to (if that's different from your billing address). You also have to pay for the merchandise, typically by entering a credit card number.

The checkout provides one last opportunity for you to change your order. You can delete items you decide not to buy or change quantities on any item. At some merchants you can even opt to have your items gift-wrapped and sent to some-one as a present. You should be able to find all these options somewhere in the checkout process.

You might also have the option of selecting different types of shipping for your order. Many merchants offer both regular and expedited shipping—the latter for an additional charge.

Another option at some retailers is to group all items for reduced shipping cost (the alternative is to ship items individually as they become available). Grouping items is attractive cost-wise, but you can get burned if one of the items is out of stock or not yet available; you could end up waiting weeks or months for those items that could have been shipped immediately.

 TIP The better online retailers tell you either on the product description page or during the checkout process whether or not an item is in stock. Look for this information to help you decide how to group your items for shipment.

Step 6: Confirm the Order

After you've entered all the appropriate information, you're asked to place your order. This typically means clicking a button that says Place Your Order or something similar. You might even see a second screen asking you whether you *really* want to place your order, just in case you had second thoughts.

After you place your order, you see a confirmation screen, typically displaying your order number. Write down this number or print this page; you need to refer to this number if you have to contact customer service. Most online merchants also send you a confirmation message, including this same information, via email.

That's all there is to it. You shop, examine the product, place an order, proceed to checkout, and then confirm your purchase. It's that easy!

How to Shop Safely

Shopping online is every bit as safe as shopping at a traditional brick-and-mortar retailer. The big online retailers are just as reputable as traditional retailers, offering safe payment, fast shipping, and responsive service.

How do you know that you're shopping at a reputable online retailer? Simple— look for the following features:

- Payment by major credit card. (Smaller merchants might accept credit cards via PayPal or a similar online payment service; this is also acceptable.)

- A *secure server* that encrypts your credit card information—and keeps online thieves from stealing your credit card numbers. (You know that you're using a secure site when the little lock icon appears in the lower-right corner of your web browser.)

- Good contact information—email address, street address, phone number, fax number, and so on. (You want to be able to physically contact the retailer if something goes wrong.)

- A stated returns policy and satisfaction guarantee. (You want to be assured that you'll be taken care of if you don't like whatever you ordered.)

- A stated privacy policy that protects your personal information. (You don't want the online retailer sharing your email address and purchasing information with other merchants—and potential spammers.)

- Information *before you finalize your order* that tells you whether the item is in stock and how long it will take to ship. (More feedback is better.)

 TIP Credit card purchases are protected by the Fair Credit Billing Act, which gives you the right to dispute certain charges and limits your liability for unauthorized transactions to $50. In addition, some card issuers offer a supplemental guarantee that says you're not responsible for *any* unauthorized charges made online. (Make sure that you read your card's statement of terms to determine the company's exact liability policy.)

Buying and Selling on eBay

Some of the best bargains on the Web come from other consumers, just like you, selling their own items online. The most popular website for individual sales is eBay, which is an online marketplace that facilitates transactions between people and businesses that have things to sell and customers who want to buy those things.

Most transactions on eBay are in the form of *online auctions*. An online auction is, quite simply, a Web-based version of a traditional auction. You find an item you'd like to own and then place a bid on the item. Other users also place bids, and at the end of the auction—typically a seven-day period—the highest bidder wins.

Not every transaction on eBay is an auction transaction, however. An increasing number of eBay sales are at a fixed price, no bidding involved, through eBay's Buy It Now feature and through merchants who run their own eBay Stores. With more than 36 million items listed for sale on any given day, you're bound to find something you want to buy; eBay has it all, from rare collectibles and vintage sports memorabilia to trendy clothing and the latest electronics equipment.

Who Sells on eBay?

eBay started out as a pure online auction site. eBay's job was to host the auction listings and facilitate the transactions between buyers and sellers. (Note that eBay doesn't actually sell anything itself, nor does it hold inventory; all the transactions are between individual buyers and sellers, with eBay functioning solely as the middleman.)

In the beginning, eBay sellers were almost exclusively individuals—people like you and me with items they wanted to sell. In this way, eBay functioned like a giant garage sale or yard sale. An individual had something to sell, he listed it on eBay, and another individual decided to buy it. The second individual paid the first individual, who then shipped the item to the buyer. It was pretty simple.

Today, however, eBay is more than just person-to-person transactions. Many of eBay's original sellers have gotten quite big, listing hundreds of auctions every week and turning their eBay sales into real businesses. In addition, many existing businesses have turned to eBay as a way to make additional sales. So when you buy on eBay today, you might be buying from an individual selling just a few items, an individual running a small business out of her home, or a large business selling eBay items on the side.

Whomever you buy from, the process for the buyer is the same—as are the protections. The eBay marketplace is a level one, where all buyers and sellers follow the same rules and regulations. And the process for bidding and buying is the same no matter who you're buying from; just remember, you're buying from an independent seller, not from eBay itself.

 NOTE There is no cost to register with eBay, although if you want to sell items, you have to provide your credit card and checking account numbers. (eBay uses this information to help weed out potential scammers and to provide a billing option for the seller's eBay fees.)

How Does an eBay Auction Work?

If you've never used eBay before, you might be a little curious about what might be involved. Never fear; participating in an online auction is a piece of cake—something hundreds of millions of other users have done before you. That means you don't have to reinvent any wheels; the procedures you follow are well established and well documented.

An eBay auction is an Internet-based version of a traditional auction—you know, the type where a fast-talking auctioneer stands in the front of the room, trying to coax potential buyers into bidding *just a little bit more* for the piece of merchandise up for bid. The only difference is that there's no fast-talking auctioneer online (the bidding process is executed by special auction software on the auction site), and your fellow bidders aren't in the same room with you—in fact, they might be located anywhere in the world. Anyone can be a bidder, as long as he or she has Internet access—and is registered with eBay. You do this from eBay's home page (www.ebay.com), shown in Figure 14.3.

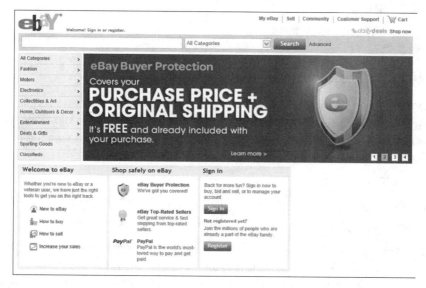

FIGURE 14.3

Where all the auction action starts—eBay's home page.

A potential buyer reads the item listing and makes a bid, specifying the maximum amount he or she will pay; this amount has to be equal to or greater than the seller's minimum bid, or higher than any other existing bids.

At this point, eBay's built-in bidding software automatically places a bid for the bidder that bests the current bid by a specified amount—but doesn't reveal the bidder's maximum bid. For example, the current bid on an item might be $25. A bidder is willing to pay up to $40 for the item, and enters a maximum bid of $40. eBay's "proxy" software places a bid for the new bidder in the amount of $26—higher than the current bid, but less than the specified maximum bid. If there are no other bids, this bidder will win the auction with a $26 bid. Other potential buyers, however, can place additional bids; unless their maximum bids are more than the current bidder's $40 maximum, they are informed (by email) that they have been outbid—and the first bidder's current bid is automatically raised to match the new bids (up to the specified maximum bid price).

At the conclusion of an auction, eBay informs the high bidder of his or her winning bid. When the seller receives the buyer's payment (typically via PayPal), the seller then ships the merchandise directly to the buyer. eBay also bills the seller a small percentage of the final bid price (8.75% or so).

 NOTE Learn even more about eBay auctions in my companion book, *Sams Teach Yourself eBay in 10 Minutes* (Sams, 2011), available in bookstores everywhere.

eBay Bidding, Step-by-Step

Bidding in an online auction is kind of like shopping at an online retailer—except that you don't flat-out make a purchase. Instead, you make a bid—and you only get to purchase the item at the end of the auction if your bid was the highest bid made.

Here's how it works:

1. You look for items using eBay's search function (via the Search box on eBay's home page) or by browsing through the product categories.

2. When you find an item you're interested in, take a moment to examine all the details. A typical item listing (like the one shown in Figure 14.4) includes a photo of the item, a brief product description, shipping and payment information, and instructions on how to place a bid.

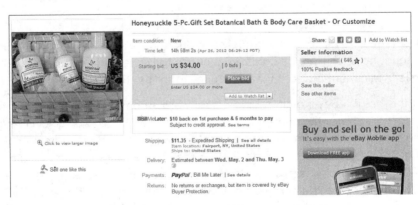

FIGURE 14.4

An eBay item listing—ready to bid?

NOTE Some auctions have a *reserve price*. The high bid must be greater than this price (which is hidden) to actually win the auction. If bids don't reach the reserve, the seller is not obligated to sell the item.

3. Now it's time to place your bid, which you do by clicking the Place Bid button. Remember, you're not buying the item at this point; you're just telling eBay how much you're willing to pay. Your bid must be at or above the current bid amount. My recommendation is to determine the maximum amount you'd be willing to pay for that item, and bid that amount—regardless of what the current bid level is.

 NOTE If an item is listed at a fixed price, you'll see a Buy It Now button instead of or in addition to the Place Bid button. Click the Buy It Now button to purchase the item for that fixed price, as described in the "Buy It Quick with Buy It Now" section later in this chapter.

4. eBay uses automatic proxy bidding software to automatically handle the bidding process from here. You bid the maximum amount you're willing to pay, and eBay's proxy software enters the minimum bid necessary—without revealing your maximum bid amount. Your bid will be automatically raised (to no more than your maximum amount) when other users bid.

5. The auction proceeds. Most auctions run for seven days, although sellers have the option of running 1-, 3-, 5-, 7-, and 10-day auctions. (The 10-day listing costs $0.40 extra.)

6. If you're the high bidder at the end of the auction, eBay informs you (via email) that you're the winner.

7. You can pay immediately (via the PayPal service) by clicking the Pay Now button in this end-of-auction notice. Your payment should include both the cost of the item (the winning bid amount) and a reasonable shipping/handling charge, as determined by the seller.

8. The seller ships the item to you.

It's important to note that even though you've been using the services of the eBay site, the ultimate transaction is between you and the individual seller. You don't pay eBay; eBay is just the middleman.

NOTE PayPal is an online payment service (owned by eBay) that lets sellers accept credit card payments in their auctions. (Many small online retailers also use PayPal to handle their credit card transactions.) PayPal functions as a middleman; the buyer pays PayPal (via credit card), and then PayPal deposits the funds in the seller's bank account.

TIP To increase your chances of winning an auction, use a technique called *sniping*. When you snipe, you hold your bid until the very last seconds of the auction. If you bid high enough and late enough, other bidders won't have time to respond to your bid—and your high bid will win!

Buy It Quick with Buy It Now

Tired of waiting around for the end of an auction, only to find out you didn't have the winning bid? Well, there's a way to actually *buy* some items you see for auction without going through the bidding process. All you have to do is look for those item listings that have a Buy It Now option.

Buy It Now is an option that some (but not all) sellers add to their auctions. With Buy It Now, the item is sold (and the auction ended) if the first bidder places a bid for a specified price. (For this reason, some refer to Buy It Now auctions as "fixed-price" auctions—even though they're slightly different from eBay's *real* fixed-priced listings.)

Other eBay sellers choose to skip the auction process entirely and sell their items at a fixed price. These listings also display the Buy It Now button but without a bidding option. Fixed-priced listings are common in eBay Stores, where larger sellers offer a constant supply of fixed-priced merchandise for sale all year round.

Buying an item with Buy It Now is really simple. If you see an item identified with a Buy It Now price, just click the Buy It Now button. You are immediately notified that you've purchased the item, and are instructed to pay—typically via PayPal.

TIP Even if a seller offers the Buy It Now option in an auction, you don't have to bid at the Buy It Now price. You can bid at a lower price and hope that you win the auction, which then proceeds normally. (The Buy It Now option disappears when the first bid is made—or, in a reserve price auction, when the reserve price is met.)

Protecting Yourself Against Fraudulent Sellers

When you're bidding for and buying items on eBay, you're pretty much in "buyer beware" territory. You agree to buy an item, almost sight unseen, from someone whom you know practically nothing about. You send that person a check and hope and pray that you get something shipped back in return—and that the thing that's shipped is the thing you thought you were buying, in good condition. If you don't like what you got—or if you received nothing at all—the seller has your money. And what recourse do you have?

The first line of defense against frauds and cheats is to intelligently choose the people you deal with. On eBay, the best way to do this is via the Feedback system.

Next to every seller's name is a number and percentage, which represents that seller's Feedback rating. You should always check a seller's Feedback rating before you bid. If the number is high with an overwhelmingly positive percentage, you can feel safer than if the seller has a lot of negative feedback. For even better protection, click the seller's name in the item listing to view his Member Profile, where you can read individual feedback comments. Be smart and avoid those sellers who have a history of delivering less than what was promised.

 TIP   If you're new to eBay, you can build up your feedback fast by purchasing a few low-cost items—preferably using the Buy It Now feature, so you get the transaction over quickly. It's good to have a Feedback rating of 20 or better before you start selling!

What do you do if you follow all this advice and still end up receiving unacceptable merchandise—or no merchandise at all? Fortunately, eBay offers a Buyer Protection plan for any auction transaction gone bad.

To file for a claim under Buyer Protection plan, go to eBay's Resolution Center (resolutioncenter.ebay.com). Follow the onscreen instructions from there. (You have 45 days to file a claim after you've paid for the item.)

eBay Selling, Step-by-Step

Have some old stuff in your garage or attic that you want to get rid of? Consider selling it on eBay. Selling on eBay is a little more involved than bidding but can generate big bucks if you do it right. Here's how it works:

 NOTE   eBay makes its money by charging sellers two types of fees. (Buyers don't pay fees to eBay.) *Insertion fees* are based on the minimum bid or reserve price of the item listed. *Final value fees* are charged when you sell an item, based on the item's final selling price. Fees are typically charged directly to the seller's credit card account.

1. If you haven't registered for an eBay seller account yet, do so now. You need to provide eBay with your credit card and checking account number, for verification and billing purposes.

2. Before you list your first item, you need to do a little homework. That means determining what you're going to sell and for how much, as well as how you're going to describe the item. You need to prepare the information you need to write a full item description, as well as take a few digital photos of the item to include with the listing.

3. Homework out of the way, it's time to create the auction listing. Start by clicking the Sell button on eBay's home page. As you can see in Figure 14.5, eBay displays a series of forms for you to complete; the information you enter into these forms is used to create your item listing. You need to select a category for your item; enter a title and description; determine how long you want your auction to run and what kind of payments you'll accept; insert a photo of the item, if you have one; and enter the amount of the desired minimum (starting) bid.

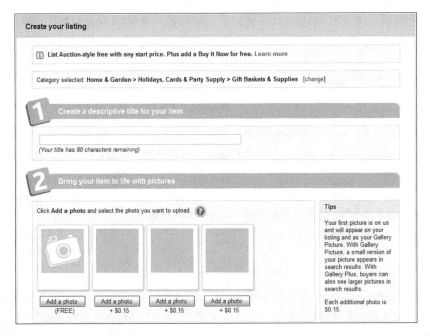

FIGURE 14.5

Creating a new eBay item listing.

4. After you enter all the information, eBay creates and displays a preliminary version of your auction listing. If you like what you see, click OK to start the auction.

5. Sit back and wait for the auction to progress.

6. When the auction is over, eBay notifies you (via email) of the high bid and provides the email address of the winning bidder.

7. Many winning bidders pay via credit card (using the PayPal service) as soon as the auction is over, by clicking the Pay Now link in the end-of-auction notice they receive. If the high bidder doesn't pay immediately, email him an invoice containing the final bid price and the shipping/handling charges.

8. After you've been paid, pack the item and ship it out.

 TIP You can monitor the progress of all your current auctions with the My eBay page. Just click the My eBay link at the top of eBay's home page.

That's it—you've just completed a successful eBay auction!

Buying and Selling on Craigslist

eBay isn't the only place to buy and sell items on the Web. When you want to buy or sell something locally, craigslist is the place.

Craigslist is a network of local online classifieds sites. On craigslist you pick your local site and then create a classified ad for what you're selling; potential buyers browse the ads, contact the seller, and pay for and pick up the items locally.

Understanding Online Classifieds

Like eBay, craigslist is just a middleman, facilitating sales between individual buyers and sellers. Unlike eBay's online auctions, however, items on craigslist are typically listed at a fixed cost; there is no bidding process. As with traditional print-based classified ads, some sellers might accept lower prices than listed if you make an offer, or they might list an item at a fixed price "or best offer." All negotiations are between the seller and the buyer. Most sales are paid for with cash.

Another big difference between eBay and craigslist is that eBay is a fairly full-featured marketplace; eBay offers a number of tools for both buyers and sellers that help to automate and take the guesswork out of the process. Not so with craigslist, which resembles what eBay was like about 10 years ago, before it became more sophisticated. Creating an ad is pretty much filling in a blank text box, with little help from craigslist on how to do it. Craigslist doesn't even get involved in the selling process; buyers pay sellers directly, often in cash. There's no PayPal to deal with, and no way to pay via credit card.

For that matter, craigslist doesn't offer the buyer and seller protection plans that you find on eBay—which makes buying via classified ad that much more risky. If a buyer pays with a bad check, there's not much the seller can do about it; if a seller gets an item home and finds out it doesn't work as promised, *caveat emptor.*

Browsing the Listings

As noted previously, craigslist is actually a network of individual local sites. In fact, the craigslist home page, shown in Figure 14.6, is nothing more than a listing of these local sites. So to use craigslist, you first have to navigate to your specific local site; you do this by going to the national craigslist home page and then clicking your city or state from the list.

FIGURE 14.6

The global craigslist site.

After you're on your local craigslist site, you see links to all the product and service categories offered by craigslist in your area. As you can see in Figure 14.7, the categories available mirror those in a typical newspaper classifieds section, including the following major categories:

- Community (musicians wanted, lost and found, local news, and so on)
- Housing
- Jobs
- Personals
- For Sale
- Services
- Gigs
- Resumes
- Discussion forums

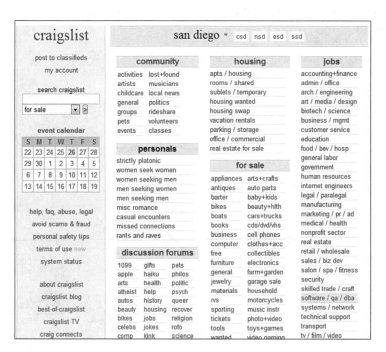

FIGURE 14.7

Category listings on craigslist.

If you're looking for an item for sale, it's probably going to be in the For Sale category. If you're looking for something else, however, then the other categories might hold interest. It might surprise you to know that in many cities craigslist is the largest marketplace for job wanted ads; it's also a big site for home and apartment listings. For that matter, craigslist has a thriving personals section, in case that's what you're looking for.

Buying on Craigslist

If you want to buy a specific type of item, you need to browse craigslist's For Sale listings. Within this major category there are additional subcategories, such as Computers, Furniture, Musical Instruments, Electronics, Tools, and the like. Click through to a subcategory to view the ads within that category.

As you can see in Figure 14.8, a typical craigslist ad includes a title, a description of the item being sold, and one or more pictures of the item. Unlike with eBay, craigslist offers no direct mechanism for contacting the seller or for purchasing directly from the listing page. Although some ads include the seller's phone number, most don't. Instead, you contact the seller by clicking the email link included in the ad.

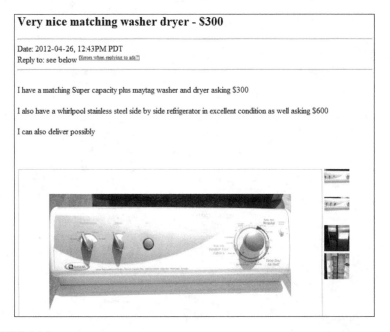

FIGURE 14.8

A typical craigslist For Sale ad.

So if you're interested in the item, contact the seller via email and express your interest. You can then arrange a time to view the item; if you like what you see, you can pay for it then and take it with you.

Listing an Item for Sale

If you're a seller, the big difference between eBay and craigslist is that craigslist is absolutely free. The site charges nothing to list an item, and it charges no final value or commission fees. This makes craigslist quite attractive to sellers; you can list anything you want and don't have to pay if it doesn't sell.

 NOTE Although the vast majority of craigslist ads are free, not all are. In particular, craigslist charges for job listings in some major cities, brokered apartment listings in New York City, and all listings in the adult services category.

Listing an item for sale on craigslist is similar to listing a fixed-price item on eBay. The differences are more in what you *don't* have to do; there are fewer "blanks" to fill in—and fewer options for your listing.

 TIP Selling on craigslist is better than eBay when you have a big or bulky item that might be difficult to ship long distances. Local buyers can pick up the items they purchase.

To list an item for sale on the craigslist site, follow these steps:

1. Navigate to the home page for your local craigslist community.

2. Click the Post to Classifieds link on the left side of the page.

3. When the next page appears, click the category in which you want to list— probably the For Sale category.

4. Select an appropriate subcategory.

5. In larger metropolitan areas, you might be prompted to select the area or county nearest you. Do so.

6. You now see the listing creation page, as shown in Figure 14.9. Enter information into the appropriate fields: Posting Title, Price, Specific Location, Posting Description, and Reply To (your email address).

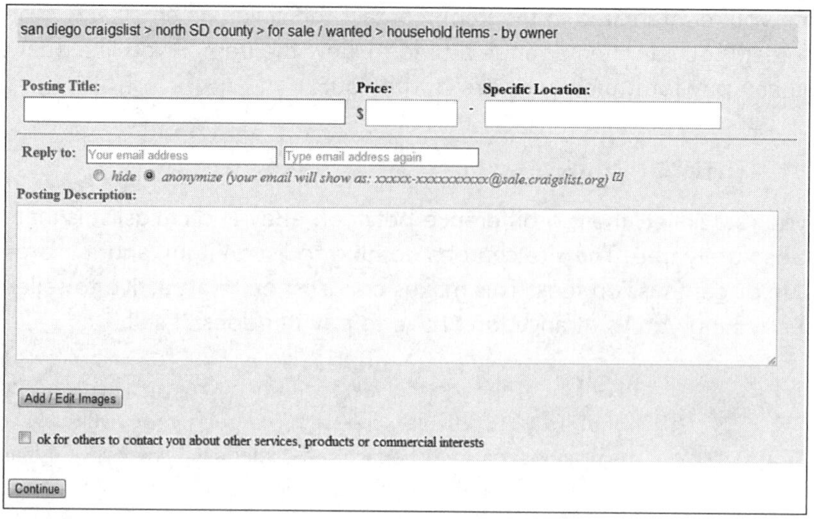

FIGURE 14.9

Creating a new craigslist classified listing.

7. If you want to include digital photos of your item in the listing, click the Add/Edit Images button and select the files you want to upload.

8. After you've entered all the necessary information, click the Continue button.

9. Craigslist now displays a preview of your listing; if you like what you see, click Continue. (If you don't like what you see, click the Edit button and make some changes.) Your listing appears on the Craigslist site within the next 15 minutes or so.

For your protection, craigslist displays an anonymized email address in your item listing. Buyers email this anonymous address and the emails are forwarded to your real email address. That way you won't get email stalkers from your craigslist ads—in fact, no one will know exactly who is doing the posting!

Making the Sale

When someone replies to your listing, craigslist forwards you that message via email. You can then reply to the potential buyer directly; in most instances, that means arranging a time for that person to come to your house to either view or purchase the item of interest.

Unlike eBay, where you have to ship the item to the buyer, craigslist buyers more often than not pick up the items they purchase. That means you have to be at home for the buyer to visit, and you have to be comfortable with strangers visiting.

You also have to be prepared to help the buyer load up whatever it is you're selling into his or her vehicle for the trip home—which can be a major issue if you're selling big stuff and you're a small person.

 CAUTION If you're not comfortable with strangers visiting your house and you're selling something portable, arrange to meet at a neutral location. If you're selling a larger item, make sure another family member or friend is home when the buyer is supposed to visit.

As to payment, the vast majority of craigslist purchases are made with cash. You might want to keep some ones and fives on hand to make change, in case the buyer pays with larger bills.

For higher priced items, you might want to accept payment via cashier's check or money order. Just be sure that the check or money order is made out for the exact amount of the purchase; you don't want to give back cash as change for a money order purchase.

 CAUTION Under no circumstances should you accept payment via personal check. It's far too easy for a shady buyer to write you a check and take off with the merchandise, only for you to discover a few days later that the check bounced. If you *must* accept a personal check, hold onto the merchandise for a full 10 working days to make sure the check clears; it's probably easier for all involved for the buyer to just get the cash.

THE ABSOLUTE MINIMUM

Here are the key points to remember from this chapter:

- You can find just about any type of item you want for sale somewhere on the Internet.

- Shopping online is a lot like shopping in a traditional store; you find the product you want, go through the checkout system, and make your payment.

- Internet shopping is very safe, especially if you buy from a major merchant that offers a secure server and a good returns policy.

- If you want to sell your own items online, try eBay, which lets you list items either at a fixed price or via online auction format.

- Another good place to sell items you own is craigslist, which functions like a local classified advertising site.

15

MANAGING YOUR FINANCES ONLINE

The Internet is a great place to find financial information. Whether you're looking for the latest stock quotes, financial news, or interest rates, what you need is never more than a few clicks away.

You can also use the Internet to manage your finances. That means doing online banking, online bill pay, and more, all from the comfort of your personal computer.

Using Windows 8's Finance App

When it comes to finding the latest financial news, stock quotes, and the like, you need look no further than the Windows Start screen. That's because Windows 8 includes a very nice Finance app that gives you all the financial information you seek.

You launch the Finance app by clicking or tapping the Finance tile on the Start screen, as shown in Figure 15.1. Note that the Finance tile is a "live" tile; it displays the latest financial news and information on the tile itself. If all you need to know is whether the Dow is up or down, you don't even have to launch the app.

FIGURE 15.1

Click or tap the "live" Finance tile to launch the Finance app.

What you see next is the Finance Today screen, shown in Figure 15.2, which details the day's top financial headline and the performance of the major stock indices. If you want to read the story behind the headline, just click or tap it. Otherwise, this screen is just the tip of the Finance iceberg.

FIGURE 15.2

The Finance Today screen.

Scroll or swipe right to see the Indices screen, shown in Figure 15.3. For each of the four major indices (Dow, S&P 500, NASDAQ, and Russell 2000) you see today's performance graph, opening value, previous closing value, day range, and 52-week range. Click or tap an index's name to view the detailed information about that particular index.

FIGURE 15.3

The Finance Indices screen.

Scroll or swipe right again and you see the News screen, shown in Figure 15.4. Here are more of the day's top financial stories; click or tap a headline to view the complete story in Internet Explorer.

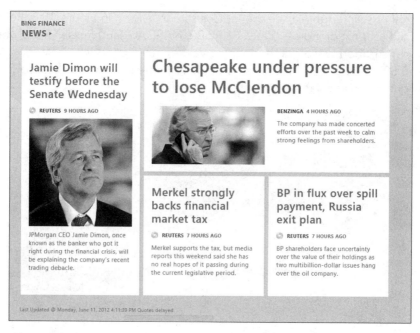

BING FINANCE
NEWS ▸

Jamie Dimon will testify before the Senate Wednesday

REUTERS 9 HOURS AGO

JPMorgan CEO Jamie Dimon, once known as the banker who got it right during the financial crisis, will be explaining the company's recent trading debacle.

Chesapeake under pressure to lose McClendon

BENZINGA 4 HOURS AGO

The company has made concerted efforts over the past week to calm strong feelings from shareholders.

Merkel strongly backs financial market tax

REUTERS 7 HOURS AGO

Merkel supports the tax, but media reports this weekend said she has no real hopes of it passing during the current legislative period.

BP in flux over spill payment, Russia exit plan

REUTERS 7 HOURS AGO

BP shareholders face uncertainty over the value of their holdings as two multibillion-dollar issues hang over the oil company.

Last Updated @ Monday, June 11, 2012 4:11:39 PM Quotes delayed

FIGURE 15.4

The Finance News screen.

Additional screens are displayed when you scroll or swipe further right. These include the following:

- **Watchlist**, your personal list of stocks to watch, shown in Figure 15.5.

- **Market Movers**, the biggest gainers and losers on the market today.

- **Across the Market**, performance data for Currencies, Bonds, Commodities, and Exchange Traded Funds.

- **Rates**, the latest mortgage (30-year fixed and 3/1-year ARM), savings (money market and six-month CD), and credit card rates.

- **Fund Picks**, the top-performing and highest-rated mutual funds.

TIP   To add new stocks and funds to your watchlist, right-click on any Finance screen to display the Options Bar, then click or tap Watchlist. This displays the freestanding Watchlist screen; click or tap the + tile. When the Add to Watchlist panel appears, enter the company name or symbol and then click or tap the Add button.

All in all, a very useful app. If you're at all interested in the financial market, check it out!

FIGURE 15.5

The Finance Watchlist screen.

Doing Your Banking Online

Tired of standing in line at your local bank? Well, if you have a personal computer and an Internet connection, you can do all your normal banking tasks online. No more standing in line; now you can transfer funds, check account balances, and pay your bills from home. It's online banking, either over the Web or with a personal finance service program such as Mint.

How Online Banking Works

There are two basic approaches to online banking. You can use your web browser to access your bank's website from any PC, and from there manage your account and pay bills. Or you can use a service or app such as Mint or Quicken to manage all your personal financial accounts in one place. Each approach has its pros and cons.

Using your bank's website is the easiest type of online banking, and almost all banks offer it. No expensive software is necessary, and many banks offer Web-based access free or at a low monthly cost. Best of all, you can do it from any computer; just open Internet Explorer, go to your bank's website, enter your user-name and password, and you're in. (Initial registration might take a little longer, of course.)

Consolidating all your accounts in a single service is more complicated, but it also offers more functionality. When you go this route, you get all the money-management features built into the app, which typically let you manage not just your bank accounts but also credit cards, loans, IRA/401K accounts, stocks and bonds, and the like.

CAUTION Not all banks offer Quicken or Mint access, pre-ferring that their customers use the bank's website. In addition, some banks charge extra for this type of third-party access.

Which is the best approach for you? Well, if you're just getting started and want the easiest possible approach, stick with using your bank's website. If you're comfortable with more advanced financial management, however, you might prefer the cross-account management capabilities of a third-party financial management app.

TIP Some banks charge either a monthly or per-transaction fee to access their online banking features. Other banks offer Web-based banking (and sometimes third-party access) for free. If you anticipate doing a lot of online banking, it pays to shop around for the best deal.

Using Your Bank's Website

As noted, most banks today have their own websites and thus offer some form of Web-based banking. You probably have to sign up to use your bank's Web-based services; make sure you have all your account numbers (and possibly your ATM PIN) handy when you're signing up. You're then assigned a username and pass-word, and you're ready for future sessions.

Why use Web-based banking? First, it's great to be able to access and manage your checking and savings accounts from home or on the road; you don't have to be physically present to check your account balances or transfer funds between accounts. Second, when compared to third-party financial apps, anyone can go the Web route; you don't need to purchase and learn any particular software program to do your banking. Then there's the fact that you can access a bank's web page from any PC connected to the Internet, so that you can do your banking when you're on the road and away from home. The same can't be said for software programs, such as Quicken, that are installed on specific machines. In addition, setting up your account at a Web-based bank is relatively easy, compared to all the information-entering you have to do with a third-party service. On a website, after you enter your account number and password, your account should be ready to access. Finally, with Web-based banking, all your financial information is stored on the bank's website, so if your computer crashes, your data isn't lost. It's useful, easy, and reliable—what's not to like?

 NOTE Ask your local banker about what online services the bank offers—and to find out the bank's website address.

Accessing a bank's website is simple. After you've signed up for your bank's online service, you log into your bank's website by entering your assigned username and password. From there, you can typically click to view details about any and all accounts you have at that bank, as shown in Figure 15.6. You can view your latest statement online, view your most recent transactions, and perform specific operations—such as transferring funds from one account to another. Even better, many banks offer online bill payment services, so you can use your bank's website to electronically pay all your bills. That's convenient!

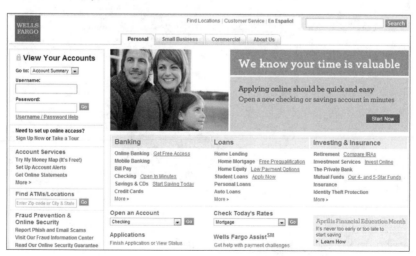

FIGURE 15.6

Wells Fargo's online banking site.

Using Quicken or Mint to Manage Your Finances

The other approach to online banking is to use a software program or service, such as Quicken or Mint. There are several benefits to going this route; the most significant benefit is that you manage *all* your personal finances, from multiple accounts and multiple banks, in a single service. This is in sharp contrast to the website-based approach, where you have to access different websites for each bank and credit card you use. In addition, Quicken and Mint both offer a raft of account management and financial analysis tools, so you can track your budget, see how your investments are performing, and such. There's lots of functionality offered.

Comparing Quicken and Mint is easy. One is a software program that costs money to buy; the other is a web-based service that's free.

Let's start with Quicken, shown in Figure 15.7. Quicken is a traditional software program that you install on the Windows desktop and run whenever you want to view or manage your finances. It comes in several different flavors (Starter Edition, Deluxe, Premier, and Home & Business), priced from $29.99 to $99.99. (Learn more at quicken.intuit.com.)

FIGURE 15.7

Tracking bank accounts and more with Quicken.

Mint, on the other hand, is a Web-based service. As you can see in Figure 15.8, Mint offers much of the same functionality as Quicken, but you don't have to install any software; you can run it at any time from Internet Explorer or from any computer you happen to be using. It's also free, which is always appealing. (Learn more at www.mint.com.)

Whichever program or service you go with, you first have to configure it to work with your bank and other financial accounts—credit cards, loans, and such. After you've entered all your account information, you can use Quicken or Mint to record regularly occurring transactions, analyze expenditures, and such.

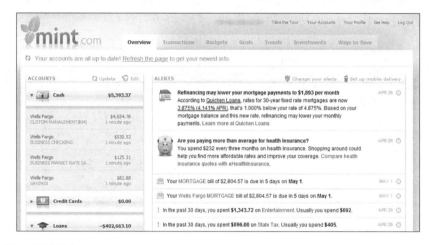

FIGURE 15.8

Managing financial transactions with Mint.

Paying Your Bills Online

One of the primary reasons to participate in online banking is to pay your bills online. Your bank's website should offer online bill pay, as will Quicken, Mint, and other third-party solutions.

How Online Bill Pay Works

How you pay your bills online depends on how you do your online banking.

If you're using your bank's website, online bill paying is handled on that website, by your bank. You need to sign up for your bank's bill-paying service and then enter information about each bill—the payee's mailing address, your account number, the payment amount, that sort of thing. From there it's a simple matter of clicking the appropriate link or button at your bank's website to pay a given bill when it's due. This bill-paying service might be offered free by your bank, although it's more common for a monthly charge to be assessed.

If you're using Quicken or Mint, online bill paying is handled by the app or service itself, not your bank. You enter information about each payee and bill into the app and then click the appropriate button to initiate payments. You might have to pay for this service, too.

 TIP Some payees also let you make payments (via credit card or electronic funds transfer) on their own websites. Check with the billing company to see if online payment of this sort is offered.

Whichever approach you take, you can typically set up a recurring payee list, so that paying a monthly bill is as simple as clicking your mouse or tapping the touchscreen. (You have to set up one-time-only payments as they arise.) You can even instruct your bill payment service to automatically pay selected bills each month, such as your mortgage or car payment. Payment is typically sent electronically from your bank to each payee.

 NOTE In those instances where a payee is not set up to accept electronic payments, your bank or bill-paying service writes a physical check to the payee.

Discovering Online Bill Payment Services

There are also several dedicated companies that offer online bill payment services for a fee. These companies let you pay all your bills electronically for those accounts that accept electronic funds transfers. If an account still requires a physical check, the online bill payment firm cuts and mails a check at your electronic command.

The most popular online bill-payment services include the following:

- MyCheckFree (www.mycheckfree.com)
- MyEZBills (www.myezbills.com)
- Paytrust (www.paytrust.com)
- Xpress Bill Pay (www.xpressbillpay.com)

THE ABSOLUTE MINIMUM

Here are the key points to remember from this chapter:

- Windows 8's Finance app enables you to view the latest financial news and quotes from the Windows Start screen.

- Online banking enables you to check account balances, transfer funds between accounts, and even pay your bills from your PC.

- You can manage your finances by logging into your bank's website or by using a third-party service, such as Quicken or Mint.

- You can also pay your bills from your bank's website or third-party financial management service without writing a single physical check.

16

SENDING AND RECEIVING EMAIL

Email is a modern way to communicate with friends, family, and colleagues. An email message is like a regular letter, except that it's composed electronically and delivered almost immediately via the Internet.

You can use a dedicated email program, such as Microsoft Outlook or Windows 8's Mail app, to send and receive email from your personal computer. Or you can use a web mail service such as Gmail or Hotmail to manage all your email from any web browser on any computer. Either approach is good and enables you to create, send, and read email messages from all your friends, family, and colleagues.

How Email Works

Email—short for "electronic mail"—is like traditional postal mail, except that you compose messages that are delivered electronically, via the Internet. When you send an email message to another Internet user, that message travels from your PC to your recipient's PC through a series of Internet connections and servers, almost instantaneously. Email messages can be of any length and can include file attachments of various types.

To make sure your message goes to the right recipient, you have to use your recipient's *email address.* Every Internet user has a unique email address, composed of three parts:

- The user's name
- The **@** sign
- The user's domain name (usually the name of the Internet service provider)

As an example, if you use Comcast as your Internet provider (with the domain name **comcast.net**) and your login name is **jimbo**, your email address is **jimbo@comcast.net**.

POP Email Versus Web Mail

There are actually two different ways to send and receive email via the Internet.

The traditional way to send and receive email uses a protocol called the Post Office Protocol (POP). POP email requires use of a dedicated email software program and—at the ISP level—separate email servers to send and receive messages.

 NOTE   Many POP email providers also offer web-based access from any web browser.

The other way to send and receive email is via Web-based email services, also known as *web mail.* Unlike straight POP email, you can access web mail from any computer, using any web browser; no special software is required.

POP Email

POP email is the standard type of email account you receive when you sign up with an Internet service provider. You're assigned an email account, given an email address, and provided with the necessary information to configure your email program to access this account.

To use POP email, you have to use a special POP email program, such as Microsoft Outlook (part of the Microsoft Office suite). That email program has to be configured to send email to your ISP's outgoing mail server (called an *SMTP server*) and to receive email from your ISP's incoming mail server (called a *POP3* or *IMAP server*). If you want to access your email account from another computer, you have to use a similar email program and go through the entire configuration process all over again on the second computer.

Web Mail

You're not limited to using the "hard-wired" POP email offered by your ISP; you can also send and receive email from web mail services, such as Google's Gmail and Microsoft's Windows Live Hotmail. These web mail services enable you to access your email from any computer, using any web browser.

If you use a PC in multiple locations—in the office, at home, or on the road—this is a convenient way to check your email at any time of day, no matter where you are. You don't have to go through the same sort of complicated configuration routine that you use with POP email. All you have to do is go to the email service's website, enter your user ID and password, and you're ready to send and receive messages.

 TIP Your ISP might offer web-based access to its traditional POP email, which is convenient when you're away from home and need to check your email.

Most web mail services are completely free to use. Some services offer both free versions and paid versions, with paid subscriptions offering additional message storage and functionality.

The largest web mail services include the following:

- AOL Mail (webmail.aol.com)
- Gmail (mail.google.com)
- Lycos Mail (mail.lycos.com)
- Mail.com (www.mail.com)
- Windows Live Hotmail (www.hotmail.com)
- Yahoo! Mail (mail.yahoo.com)

Using Gmail

One of the largest web mail services today is Google's Gmail. It's the web mail service I use, and one I definitely recommend.

Navigating Gmail

You access the Gmail home page at mail.google.com. If you don't yet have a Google account, you're prompted to sign up for one. Do so now; signing up is free.

After you activate your Gmail account, you're assigned an email address (in the form of *name*@gmail.com), and you get access to the Gmail Inbox page.

The default view of the Gmail page is the Inbox, shown in Figure 16.1, which contains all your received messages. You can switch to other views by clicking the appropriate links on the left side, top, or bottom of the page. For example, to view all your sent mail, simply click the Sent Mail link on the left; to view only unread messages, click the Unread link at the top or bottom.

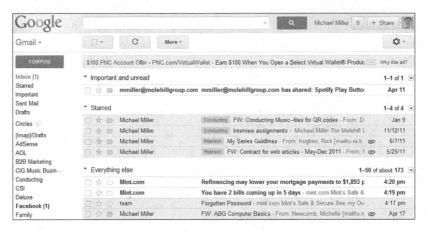

FIGURE 16.1

The Gmail Inbox.

Each message is listed with the message's sender, the message's subject, a snippet from the message, and the date or time the message was sent. (The snippet typically is the first line of the message text.) Unread messages are listed in bold; after a message has been read, it's displayed in normal, nonbold text with a shaded background. And if you've assigned a label to a message, the label appears before the message subject.

To perform an action on a message or group of messages, put a check mark by the message(s), and then click one of the buttons at the top of the list. Alternatively, you can click the More button to display a list of additional actions to perform.

Reading Messages

To read a message, all you have to do is click the message title in the Inbox. This displays the full text of the message on a new page.

If you want to display this message in a new window, click the In New Window icon. To print the message, click the Print All icon. To return to the Inbox, click the Back to Inbox button.

Viewing Conversations

One of the unique things about Gmail is that all related email messages are grouped in what Google calls *conversations*. A conversation might be an initial message and all its replies (and replies to replies). A conversation might also be all the daily emails from a single source with a common subject, such as messages you receive from subscribed-to mailing lists.

A conversation is noted in the Inbox list by a number in parentheses after the sender name(s). If a conversation has replies from more than one person, more than one name is listed.

To view a conversation, simply click the message title; the most recent message displays in full. To view the text of any individual message in a conversation, click that message's subject. To expand *all* the messages in a conversation, click the Expand All link. All the messages in the conversation are stacked on top of each other, with the text of the newest message fully displayed.

Replying to a Message

Whether you're reading a single message or a conversation, it's easy enough to send a reply. In the original message, click the Reply button to expand the message to include a reply box. Or, if a conversation has multiple participants, you can reply to all of them by clicking the down arrow next to the Reply button and then selecting Reply to All.

The text of the original message is already quoted in the reply. Add your new text above the original text. Because the original sender's address is automatically added to the To line, all you have to do to send the message is click the Send button.

Composing a New Message

To compose and send a new message, follow these steps:

1. Click the Compose button at the top of the left column on any Gmail page.

2. When the Compose Mail page appears, as shown in Figure 16.2, enter the recipient's email address in the To box. Separate multiple recipients with commas.

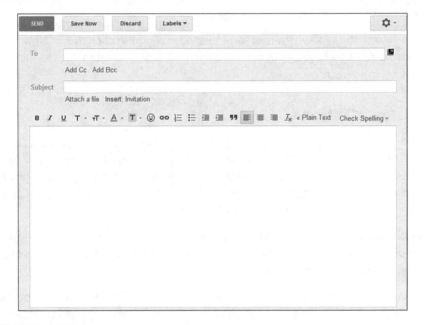

FIGURE 16.2

Composing a new Gmail message.

3. Enter a subject for the message into the Subject box.

4. Enter the text of your message in the large text box. Use the formatting controls (bold, italic, font, and so forth) to enhance your message as desired.

5. When you're done composing your message, click the Send button.

TIP You can also carbon copy and blind carbon copy additional recipients by clicking the Add Cc and Add Bcc links. This expands the message to include Cc or Bcc boxes, into which you enter the recipients' addresses.

Sending Files via Gmail

When you need to send a digital photo or other file to a friend or colleague, you can do so via email. To send a file via email, you attach that file to a standard email message. When the message is sent, the *file attachment* travels along with it; when the message is received, the file is right there, waiting to be opened.

Dangers of File Attachments

It's an unfortunate fact that email file attachments are the biggest sources of computer virus and spyware infection. Malicious users attach viruses and spyware to email messages, oftentimes disguised as legitimate files; when a user clicks to open the file, his computer is infected with the virus or spyware.

 NOTE Learn more about computer viruses and spyware in Chapter 31, "Protecting Against Computer Attacks, Malware, and Spam."

This doesn't mean that all file attachments are dangerous, simply that opening file attachments—especially those you weren't expecting—is risky. As such, you should avoid opening any file sent to you from a user you don't know. You should also avoid opening files that you weren't expecting from friends and colleagues.

The only relatively safe file attachments are those that come from people you know who previously told you they were being sent. So if your boss previously emailed you to tell you he'd be sending you an important Excel file, and you later get an email from him containing an .XLS-format file, that file is probably safe to open. On the other hand, if you receive an email from a complete stranger with an unknown file attached, that's almost definitely a malicious file that you shouldn't open.

What should you do when you receive an unexpected or unwanted file attachment? Fortunately, just receiving an email attachment doesn't activate it; you have to open the file to launch the virus or spyware. What you should do, then, is delete the entire message. Don't open the file attachment; just delete the whole thing—message and attachment together. What's deleted can't harm you or your computer.

Attaching a File in Gmail

It's easy to send file attachments in Gmail. Just follow these steps:

1. Compose a new message and then click the Attach a File link.

2. When the Files screen appears, as shown in Figure 16.3, navigate to and select the file you want to attach, and then click the Open button.

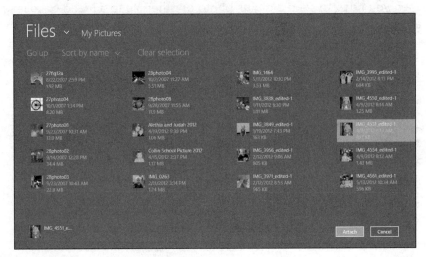

FIGURE 16.3

Selecting a file to attach to a Gmail message.

3. The file you selected now appears under the Subject box on the new message page. Continue to compose, and then send your message as normal.

CAUTION Gmail blocks the transmittal of all executable program files (with an .EXE extension), including those in .ZIP files, in an attempt to prevent potential computer viruses.

Opening an Attachment in Gmail

When you receive a Gmail message with an attachment, you see a paper clip icon next to the message subject/snippet. To view or save an attachment, click the message to open it, and then scroll to the bottom of the message.

If you can view the attachment in Gmail, you see a View link, like the one shown in Figure 16.4. Click this link to view the file in your web browser.

FIGURE 16.4

Viewing and downloading attachments to an email message.

To save the file to your hard disk, click the Download link. When you're asked if you want to open or save the file, as shown in Figure 16.5, click or tap the Save button. After a quick security scan, Windows saves the file and asks if you want to open it. Click the Open button to do so.

Do you want to open or save **The My Series Guidelines.pdf** (895 KB) from **mail-attachment.googleusercontent.com**?   Open   Save   Cancel

FIGURE 16.5

Saving an email file attachment.

Managing Your Email with Windows 8's Mail App

Windows 8 includes a built-in Mail app for sending and receiving email messages. You open the Mail app by clicking or tapping its tile on the Windows Start screen. As you can see in Figure 16.6, this is a "live" tile; your most recent unread messages scroll across the face of the tile, and the number at the bottom left indicates how many unread messages you have.

Michael Miller
Spring schedule
Mike:

Mail   17

FIGURE 16.6

Launching the Mail app; the tile displays the number of unread messages.

By default, the Mail app manages email from the Windows Live Hotmail account linked to your Microsoft Account. This means you see Hotmail messages in your Mail inbox, and you can easily send emails from your Hotmail account.

Checking Your Inbox

As you can see in Figure 16.7, the left panel of the app displays all the folders from the selected email account. Select a folder, such as your inbox, and all the messages from that folder are displayed in the center panel. To read a message, all you have to do is click or tap it; the message content is then displayed in the large right panel.

FIGURE 16.7

Viewing a message from your inbox.

To reply to a message, follow these steps:

1. From an open message, click or tap the Respond button at the top of screen.

2. Select Reply from the pop-up menu to display the Reply screen, shown in Figure 16.8.

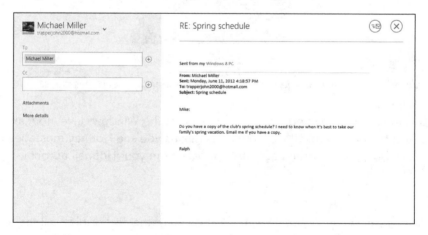

FIGURE 16.8

Replying to a message.

3. Enter your reply at the top of the message; the bottom of the message "quotes" the original message.

4. Click or tap the Send button at the top of the screen when you're ready to send the message.

Sending New Messages

It's equally easy to create and send a new email message. Follow these steps:

1. Click or tap the New (+) button at the top of any Mail screen to display the new message screen, shown in Figure 16.9.

FIGURE 16.9

Creating a new email message.

2. Click or tap within the To box and begin entering the name or email address of the message's recipient. Mail displays a list of matching names from your contact list; select the person you want to email.

3. Click or tap the Add a Subject area and type a subject for this message.

4. Click or tap within the main body of the message area and type your message. Use the Bold, Italic, Underline, Font, Font Color, and other buttons in the bottom bar to format your message.

5. To attach a file to this message, click or tap Attachments in the left column. When the Files screen appears, as shown in Figure 16.10, navigate to and select the file you want to attach, then click or tap the Attach button.

FIGURE 16.10

Attaching a file to an email message.

6. When you're ready to send the email, click or tap the Send button at the top of the message.

That's it. Windows now sends your message, using your default email account.

Adding Another Email Account

By default, the Mail app sends and receives messages from the email account associated with your Microsoft account. You can, however, configure Mail to work with other email accounts, if you have them. Follow these steps:

1. From within the Mail app, display the Charms Bar and then click or tap Settings.

2. When the Settings pane appears, click or tap Accounts.

3. When the Accounts pane appears, click or tap Add an Account.

4. When the next pane appears, as shown in Figure 16.11, click the type of account you wish to add.

5. When the Add Your Account pane appears, enter your email address and password, then click the Connect button.

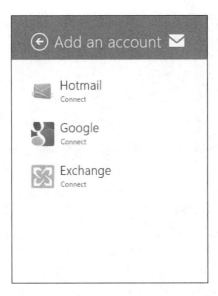

FIGURE 16.11

Attaching a new email account to the Mail app.

The Mail app lets you add Hotmail, Gmail, and Microsoft Exchange email accounts. To view the Inbox of another email account, right-click to display the Options bar, then click Accounts. When the Accounts pane appears, click or tap the email account you wish to view.

THE ABSOLUTE MINIMUM

Here are the key points to remember from this chapter:

- Email is a fast and easy way to send electronic letters over the Internet.

- There are two types of email: POP email, which requires a separate email program, and web mail, which can be sent and received from any web browser.

- The most popular web mail services include Google's Gmail, Microsoft's Windows Live Hotmail, and Yahoo! Mail.

- You can use the Mail app in Windows 8 to send and receive email from your default email account; the app also consolidates messages from other services you've connected to your account.

- Don't open unexpected files attached to incoming email messages; they might contain computer viruses!

SOCIAL NETWORKING WITH FACEBOOK

Want to find out what your friends, family, and colleagues are up to? Want to let them know what you're doing today? Then you need to hop onboard the social networking trend; it's how savvy online users are connecting today.

Social networking enables people to share experiences and opinions with each other via community-based websites; it's a great way to keep up-to-date on what your friends and family are doing. The biggest social network today is a site called Facebook. Chances are all your friends are already using it!

How Social Networking Works

In practice, a social network isn't a network at all; it's just a large website that aims to create a community of users. Each user of the community posts his or her own personal profile on the site, in the form of a *profile page*. There's enough personal information in each profile to enable other users with similar interests to connect as "friends;" one's growing collection of friends helps to build a succession of personal communities.

When you have something new or interesting to share, you post it to the social networking site. All your online friends read your posts, as well as posts from other friends, in a continuously updated *news feed*. The news feed is the one place where you can read updates from all your online friends and family; it's where you find out what's really happening.

Connecting via Social Networks

Social networks are all about connecting with other people, and sharing with them. Most users spend a fair amount of time cruising through the profiles and news feeds, finding out what their friends are doing today. They read articles, play music, and even play games that their friends have shared. They see who's online, and they chat and send emails to each other.

In addition, people use social networks to share family pictures and videos with their friends. All you have to do is upload a photo or video, and all your online friends can view it from your news feed. It's a very efficient way to "pass around" your latest vacation photos!

Finding Friends

Social networks are all about connecting to new and existing friends. The process of finding new friends is called *friending*, and some specific rules are involved.

First, it's important to be connected to all your real-world friends and acquaintances. Second, you want to be connected to people whom you might not personally know, but whom you've heard of and respect. Third, although it's important to have a lot of friends, the coolness of your friends matters more than the number of them. In other words, it's better to have 10 good friends than 100 nobodies. (Although it's hard to convince some social butterflies of that last point...)

Know, however, that when you add someone as a friend, that doesn't imply he or she is a friend in the traditional use of the word. It doesn't even mean that you know that person or want to know that person—only that you've added him or her to your friends list.

After a time, linking from one friend to a friend of that friend to a friend of a friend of a friend leads to a kind of "six degrees of separation" thing. It's fun to see how many friends it takes to connect you to various people. And you get to find new friends by seeing who your friends are friends with.

Getting to Know Facebook

No question about it, the number-one social network today is Facebook (www.facebook.com). Facebook has more than 800 million active users worldwide; chances are, most of your friends and family are already on Facebook, just waiting for you to join up and join in the fun.

 NOTE   Learn more about Facebook in my companion books, *Easy Facebook* and *Facebook for Grown-Ups*, both published by Que.

Signing Up for a Facebook Account

Here are two nice things about using Facebook: It's easy, and it's free. That's right, even though you have to create an account, it's a free account; you never pay Facebook anything to use the site. That's because Facebook, like most websites these days, is totally advertiser supported. So you see some ads after you get on the site, but you aren't out a single penny.

Here's how you sign up for your (free) Facebook account:

1. Launch Internet Explorer and go to the Facebook home page at www.facebook.com.

2. Go to the Sign Up section, shown in Figure 17.1, and enter your first name into the First Name box.

3. Enter your last name into the Last Name box.

4. Enter your email address into the Your Email box and then enter it again into the Re-enter Email box.

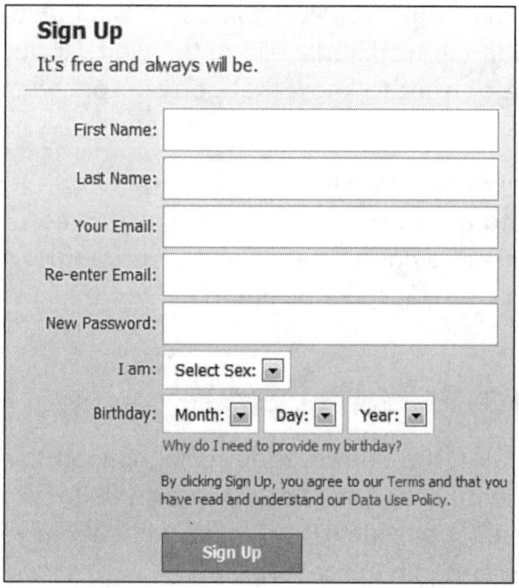

Sign Up

It's free and always will be.

First Name:	
Last Name:	
Your Email:	
Re-enter Email:	
New Password:	

I am: Select Sex: ▼

Birthday: Month: ▼ Day: ▼ Year: ▼

Why do I need to provide my birthday?

By clicking Sign Up, you agree to our Terms and that you have read and understand our Data Use Policy.

Sign Up

FIGURE 17.1

Getting ready to create a new account from the Facebook home page.

NOTE You use your email address to sign into Facebook each time you enter the site.

5. Enter your desired password into the New Password box. Your password should be at least six characters long.

TIP To make your password more secure (harder for someone else to guess, that is), include a mix of alphabetic, numeric, and special characters (like punctuation marks). Longer passwords are also more secure.

6. Select your gender from the I Am (Select Sex) list.

7. Select your date of birth from the Birthday (Month/Day/Year) list.

8. Click the Sign Up button.

9. When prompted to complete the Security Check page, enter the "secret words" from the *CAPTCHA* into the Text in the Box box and then click the Sign Up button on this page.

NOTE A CAPTCHA is a type of challenge-response test to ensure that you're actually a human being, rather than a computer program. You've seen lots of these things on the Web already; they typically consist of warped or otherwise distorted text that cannot be read by a machine or software program. Websites use CAPTCHAs to cut down on the amount of computer-generated spam they receive.

10. Facebook now sends you an email message asking you to confirm your new Facebook account; when you receive this email, click the link to proceed.

That's it—you now have a Facebook account. But Facebook isn't done with you quite yet. You'll also be prompted to find friends who are already on Facebook, and to fill in a few personal details for your profile page. Both activities are worth doing, although you don't have to do them right now if you don't want; you can always come back at a later time and hunt for friends and complete your profile.

Signing In to Your Facebook Account

To sign into Facebook, launch Internet Explorer and go to www.facebook.com. The page you used to register for Facebook displays, but this is the page you use to sign in, too. Signing in is as easy as entering your email address and password into the two boxes in the top right of the page (see Figure 17.2) and then clicking the Log In button.

FIGURE 17.2

Signing into Facebook—enter your email address and password.

 TIP If you don't want to be prompted to enter your login information every time you access the site, check the Keep Me Logged In option.

Understanding Facebook's Home Page

After you've signed in, Facebook drops you right onto the Home page. This is as good a place as any to start your exploration of the Facebook site. It's also where you keep up to date on what your friends are doing.

NOTE   Facebook is constantly upgrading its feature set, so what you see might differ somewhat from what is described here. (That's the case with any website, of course.)

As you can see in Figure 17.3, the Home page consists of four columns. We'll start on the left and work our way across the page.

Facebook toolbar   Ticker

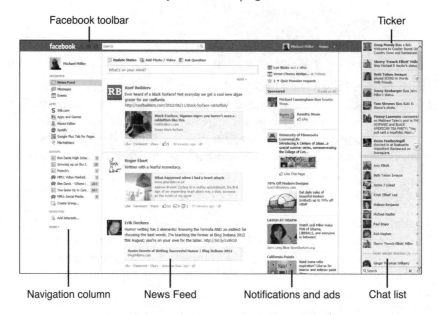

Navigation column   News Feed   Notifications and ads   Chat list

FIGURE 17.3

The Facebook Home page—complete with News Feed of your friends' status updates.

 NOTE   You see all four columns on most widescreen displays. If your computer display is narrower, you only see three columns, with the two right-most columns condensed into a single column.

The left column is one of your primary navigation aids to content on the Facebook site. Click a link here to navigate to a different section of the site.

What do you find in this navigation column? It differs a bit from user to user, but here are the most common elements:

- **Welcome**—This handy page for new users helps you enter profile information, find new friends, and the like.

- **News Feed**—This is the default view on the Home page and where you view all your friends' status updates.

- **Messages**—All the messages you've received from other Facebook members, public or private, are displayed in this area. It's also the place you go to send new messages to other users.

- **Events**—This area displays any Facebook events you've signed up for and upcoming birthdays of your Facebook friends. You can also click here to create new events.

- **Groups**—This lists any Facebook groups that you're a member of.

- **Apps**—Click the Apps link to display all the applications and games you and your friends are using. These are little widget-like utilities and games that add more fun and functionality to the Facebook site.

- **Lists**—This section displays links to various friends lists you've created or Facebook has created for you.

- **Interests**—This lists things you've told Facebook you're interested in.

- **More**—Click this link to display links to Groups, Pages, Questions, Photos, Notes, Deals, and Links.

- **Friends on Chat**—This area is simply a list of all your Facebook friends who are currently online and available to chat. Click a friend's name to start an instant messaging-like chat with that person.

That's the left column. Now we get to the big column in the middle of the page, which contains the *News Feed*. The News Feed is, in essence, a scrolling list of status updates from your Facebook friends. At the top of this list are your Top Stories, those updates that Facebook feels you should be most interested in. These Top Stories are indicated by a blue triangle in the left corner. Other updates (what Facebook calls Recent Stories) are just below the Top Stories section; scroll or swipe down to view them.

 NOTE If there are new non-Top Stories since your last visit, Facebook displays a More Recent Story link at the top of the Top Stories list. (That's so you know they're there, in case you don't scroll down automatically.) Click this link to view the new Recent Stories.

The next column contains a mix of notifications and promotions. For example, you might find a list of friends who have birthdays today; a list of upcoming events you're attending; a list of "people you may know" (and thus might want to add to your friends list); and some blatant advertisements (in the "Sponsored" section). Feel free to ignore most of what you see here.

The top part of the far right column contains something called the Ticker. This Ticker is a scrolling list of what your friends are doing, updated in real time. This list includes more than just status updates; it also includes comments your friends make on other updates, photos uploaded, songs listened to on Spotify and other music services, you name it. Just about anything Facebook knows about, however unimportant, is scrolled here.

Below the Ticker is the Chat panel which lists all your Facebook friends who are online and available to chat in real time. Double-click a name to initiate a chat session.

And that, in a nutshell, is the Facebook Home page. It's more than just a gateway into the Facebook site; it's where you go to keep informed of your friends' activities.

Using the Facebook Toolbar

As just discussed, you can access many parts of the Facebook site from the navigation sidebar on the Facebook Home page. The other primary means of navigating the Facebook site is via the Facebook toolbar, as shown in Figure 17.4, that you find at the top of every Facebook page. It's a key way to get around the site.

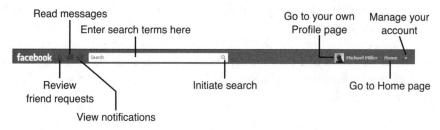

FIGURE 17.4

The Facebook toolbar.

What can you do from the Facebook toolbar? Here's a list, from left to right:

- Click the Facebook logo to go to the Facebook Home page, complete with News Feed.

- View any friend requests you've received. If you have any pending friend requests, you see a white number in a red box—for the number of requests—on top of the icon. Click the icon to view a drop-down list of these requests.

- View your most recent messages. As with the friend requests icon, a white number in a red box displays if you have unread messages. Click the icon to view a drop-down list of messages.

- View notifications from Facebook, such as someone commenting on your status or accepting your friend request. Click the icon to view the most recent notifications.

- Search the Facebook site for people and things. Just enter your query into the Search box, and then click the Search (magnifying glass) button; alternatively, you can press Enter on your computer keyboard (more on searching in just a sec).

- Visit your Profile page by clicking your name or picture.

- Click the Find Friends button (displayed on newer accounts only) to add new people to your Facebook Friends list.

- Click the Home button on the right side of the toolbar for another way to go to the Home page. (Yes, this does exactly the same thing as clicking the Facebook logo; this button was requested by Facebook's Department of Redundancy Department.)

- Access all sorts of account settings, including important privacy settings, by clicking the Account button, and then selecting an option from the drop-down menu. Options are Help Center (if you need help), Account Settings, Privacy Settings, and Log Out.

Keeping Tabs on Friends

Social networking is all about keeping in touch with friends. To get the most out of Facebook, then, you need to find some—friends, that is.

Finding Friends from Your Past

The easiest way to find friends on Facebook is to let Facebook find them for you—based on the information you provided for your personal profile. The more Facebook knows about you, especially in terms of where you've worked and gone to school, the more friends it can find.

To find new friends on Facebook, follow these steps:

1. From the top of any Facebook page, click your name in the toolbar.

2. When your Profile page appears, click the Friends item near the top of the page to display the Friends page.

3. Click the Find Friends button near the top of the page.

4. The next page displays a list of folks that Facebook thinks might be friends, as shown in Figure 17.5. These are typically people who went to the same schools you did, worked at the same companies you did, or are friends of your current friends. To invite any individual to be your friend, click the Add Friend button.

FIGURE 17.5

Viewing potential friends.

You can also search for friends based on a variety of criteria listed in the left column of the Friends page. Just check an item to display people who match that criteria. For example, to search for folks who you went to high school with, check the appropriate High School box.

Finding Friends via Email

Another way to find Facebook friends is to let Facebook look through your email contact lists for people who are also Facebook members, and then you can invite those people to be your friends. Here's how it works:

1. Click the Friend Requests button in the Facebook toolbar and select the Find Friends link in the drop-down menu.

2. When the Friends Step 1 page appears, select the email service you use.

3. If you use a web-based email service, such as Hotmail or Gmail, enter your email address and click the Find Friends button. (If prompted, enter your email password, too.) Facebook now displays a list of your email contacts who are also Facebook members.

4. If you use Microsoft Outlook to check your email, click Other Tools and then select Upload Contact File. When the page changes, click the Find My Windows Contacts button and follow the onscreen instructions to proceed.

5. If you use another software program to manage your email, follow the same instructions in Step 4, except click the Browse or Choose File button then navigate to and select your email contacts file. When you return to the Friends page, click the Upload Contacts button to upload your email contacts list to Facebook and display a list of email contacts who are also Facebook members.

6. When the list of email contacts appears, check the box next to each person with whom you'd like to be friends.

7. Click the Send Invites button to send friend requests to these contacts.

Facebook now sends friend requests to the people you selected. When a person accepts your request, you become friends with that person. If a person does not accept your request, you don't become friends.

Viewing Friends' Profiles

After you've added some folks to your Facebook friends list, you can easily check up on what they've been up to by visiting their profile pages. A Facebook profile page is essentially a person's home page on the Facebook site.

A profile page, like the one shown in Figure 17.6, contains a "timeline" of everything that user has done on Facebook, as well as displays that person's personal information, uploaded photos and videos, upcoming events, and the like.

FIGURE 17.6

A typical Facebook timeline profile.

Keeping in Touch with Status Updates

We've talked a lot about Facebook being the perfect place to update your friends and family on what you're up to—things you're doing, thoughts you're thinking, accomplishments you're accomplishing, you name it. The easiest way to let people know what's what is to post what Facebook calls a *status update*.

Every status update you make is broadcast to everyone on your friends list, displayed in the News Feed on their Home pages. This way everyone who cares enough about you to make you a friend knows everything you post about. And that can be quite a lot—from simple text posts to photos and videos and even links to other web pages.

Posting Status Updates

Facebook makes it extremely easy to post a status update. You have to be signed into Facebook, of course, but then you follow these simple steps:

1. Navigate to the Facebook Home page and go to the Publisher box, shown in Figure 17.7. (This is the text box at the top of the page that initially has the words "What's on your mind?" inside.)

FIGURE 17.7

Enter status updates into the Publisher box.

2. If it's not already selected, click Update Status.

3. Type your message into the What's On Your Mind? box. As you do this, the box expands to contain your text.

4. If you're with someone else and want to mention them in the post, click the Who Are You With? button on the bottom left and enter that person's name.

5. If you want to include your current location in your post, click the Where Are You? button (second from the left) and enter the city or place where you are.

6. To determine who can read this post, click the second blue button from the right (Public, by default), and make a selection. You can opt to make the post Public (anyone on Facebook can read it), visible only to your Friends, or Custom (you select individuals who can and can't view it). Alternatively, you can select which friends list can view the update, or make a post visible only to yourself (Only Me).

7. When you're ready to post your update, click the Post button.

So far, so good. But what if you'd like to attach a photo or video to a status update? All you have to do is click Upload Photo/Video in the Publisher box. When the panel changes, click the Browse or Choose Button; when the Open dialog box appears, navigate to and select the file you want and then click the Open button.

You can also include a link to another web page in a status update. All you have to do is include that web page's URL in your status update. Facebook should recognize the link and display a Link panel, as shown in Figure 17.8. Select a thumbnail image from the web page to accompany the link, or check the No Thumbnail box.

FIGURE 17.8

Adding a web link to a status update.

Commenting On and Liking Posts

Sometimes you read a friend's post, and you want to say something about it. To this end, Facebook enables you to comment on just about any post your friends make. These comments then appear under the post in your News Feed.

To comment on a friend's status update, simply click the Comment link under that post. A text box now displays, like the one shown in Figure 17.9. Enter your comment, and then press Enter; your comment now appears underneath the original post, along with comments from any other people.

FIGURE 17.9

Adding a comment under a friend's status update.

You can also "like" a post without having to enter a comment about it. In this instance, you can simply click the Like link under a status update. This puts a little "thumbs up" icon under the post, along with a message that you "like this."

 NOTE You can both like and comment on a post; they're not mutually exclusive.

Sharing Photos

Facebook is a social network, and one of the ways we connect socially is through pictures. We track our progress through life as a series of pictures, documenting events small and large, from picnics in the backyard to family vacations to births, graduations, and weddings and everything else that transpires.

Uploading Photos to Facebook

Facebook lets you upload and store photos in virtual photo albums. You can upload new photos to an existing album or create a new album for newly uploaded photos.

To upload photos and create a new photo album at the same time, follow these steps:

1. Click your name on the Facebook toolbar to go to your profile page.

2. From your profile page, click the Photos graphic near the top of the page.

3. When the Photos page appears, click the Add Photos button.

4. When the next screen appears, as shown in Figure 17.10, enter a name for the new album and where the photos were taken, select who you want to share the album with, then click the Select Photos to Upload button.

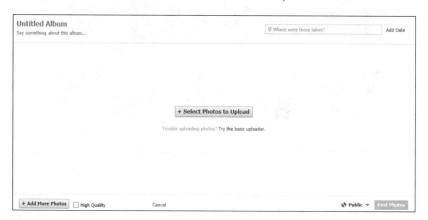

FIGURE 17.10

Entering information about your new photo album.

TIP   Select the High Quality option if you want your friends to be able to download print-quality photos—but know that it takes longer for you to upload these high-resolution pictures.

5. When the Files screen appears, click or tap the photos you want to upload, then click or tap Open.

6. If there are people in the photo you've uploaded, Facebook displays the album page with boxes around the faces. To "tag" that person in Facebook, click a face and then enter that person's name. You can also upload photos to an existing photo album. Follow Steps 1 and 2 and when the Photos page appears, click the photo album you want to upload to. Follow the rest of the steps as normal.

Viewing Photos

Viewing a friend's photos is as easy as going to that person's profile page and clicking the Photos graphic in the information section. As you can see in Figure 17.11, the top part of the next page displays your friend's photo albums; the bottom part of the page displays photos where your friend is tagged. Click the See All link to view additional albums and photos.

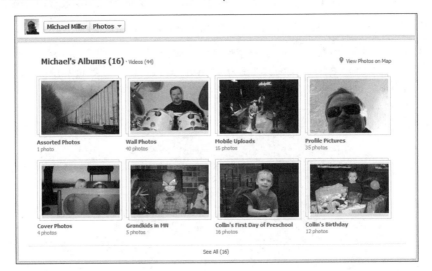

FIGURE 17.11

Viewing a friend's photo albums.

To view the pictures in an album, click that album's name or thumbnail. This displays a page full of pictures. To return to your friend's Photos tab, click the Albums link at the top of the page.

To view a given picture, click that photo's thumbnail. The photo viewer (some-times called the *lightbox*) appears on top of the current page, as shown in Figure 17.12. Mouse over the picture to display the navigation arrows and menu.

FIGURE 17.12

Viewing photos on Facebook.

You move to the next photo in the album by clicking the right arrow; there's no need to close the photo before moving to the next one. Keep clicking the right arrow to move through all the photos in the album; click the left arrow to go back through the previously viewed photos. To close the viewer and get back to the photo album, just click the X (close) button at the top right of the lightbox.

Understanding Facebook Privacy

Facebook is all about connecting users to one another. That's how the site functions, after all, by encouraging "friends" and all sorts of public sharing of information.

The problem is that Facebook, by default, shares all your information with just about everybody. Not just your friends or friends of your friends, but the entire membership of the site. And not just with Facebook members, either; Facebook also shares your information with third-party applications and games and with other sites on the Web.

Fortunately, you can configure Facebook to be much less public than it is by default. If you value your privacy, this might be worth doing.

Controlling Your Default Privacy

You can access most of Facebook's privacy settings from a single gateway page. Not all settings are on this page, but you can get to them from here.

To display the Privacy Settings page, as shown in Figure 17.13, click the down arrow on the Facebook toolbar and select Privacy Settings. The page you see leads you to pretty much everything privacy-related on the site.

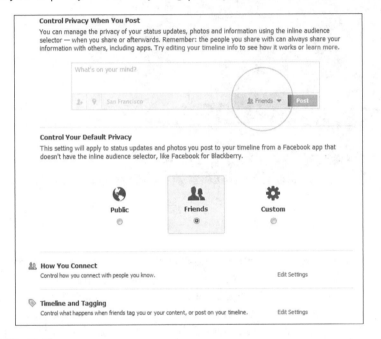

FIGURE 17.13

Facebook's Privacy Settings gateway page.

The most important part of this page is the Control Your Default Privacy section. Here you have three options for how everything you post and share on Facebook is viewed by default. This setting applies to those status updates and photos you post and upload; this is the default setting you see.

You have three options:

- **Public**—In Facebook parlance, public means "everybody." Select this option and everything you post is visible to everyone on Facebook.

- **Friends**—This one's easy to understand. Select this option and everything you post is visible to everyone on your friends list—but to no one else.

- **Custom**—Select this option to select specific people who can view your content or specific people who can't view it. You can also use the Custom option to forbid sharing with anyone except yourself.

Check the sharing option you want, and it is applied throughout the Facebook site.

 TIP   You can also determine who sees your status updates on a post-by-post basis. When you enter a new status update, click the Sharing button (down arrow) beneath the text box; click this to display the privacy menu of Public, Friends, or Custom. Make your selection and this particular post is only viewable by the group you select.

Setting Custom Sharing Options

The Public and Friends options are easy enough to understand, but what about that Custom option?

The Custom option is great for when you really want to fine-tune your sharing options on a very granular basis. Don't want to share your photos with all your friends? Don't want to share your contact information with *anyone*? That's what the Custom option is for.

When you select the Custom option for any privacy setting (including the default setting just discussed), you see the Custom Privacy dialog box. From here you can do the following:

- To hide an item from everyone, pull down the Make This Visible To list and select Only Me.

- To make an item visible only to specific people, pull down the Make This Visible To list, select Specific People or Lists, and then enter the names of those Facebook users (or the name of a custom friends list) you want to see the info.

- To hide an item only from specific people, enter their names into the Hide This From These People box. (This is a good way to hide specific info from your boss or spouse—or your kids.)

Remember to click the Save Setting button when done.

THE ABSOLUTE MINIMUM

Here are the key points to remember from this chapter:

- Social networking sites let you keep in touch with what your friends and family are doing.

- The largest social networking site today is Facebook, with more than 800 million users.

- You view your friends' activity from the Facebook Home page, in the News Feed.

- You let others know what you're doing by posting status updates, which appear in your friends' News Feeds.

- You can also use Facebook to share photos with your friends.

- Facebook enables you to control who sees specific things you post.

18

MORE SOCIAL NETWORKING WITH GOOGLE+, PINTEREST, LINKEDIN, AND TWITTER

Facebook might be the biggest social network on the Web today, but it's not the only one. There are several other social networks that help you keep in touch with friends and family—and, in some cases, focus on specific types of users or interests.

The most popular of these social networks are Google+, Pinterest, LinkedIn, and Twitter. We'll look at each in this chapter.

Using Google+

Google+ is a relatively new social network run by the folks at Google. Like Facebook, Google+ lets you post status updates for your friends to read, and enables you to read all your friends' posts in a unified news feed, called the *stream*. Also like Facebook, membership in Google+ is free.

Who Uses Google+?

Even though Google+ has more than 100 million users, they're not as active as the users on Facebook. That is, Facebook users spend a lot of time on the Facebook site, and post a lot of status updates; Google+ users don't spend as much time onsite, in general, and definitely don't make as many posts.

I've found that Google+ seems to appeal more to sophisticated technical users rather than the general public. As such, you're much more likely to find your friends and family on Facebook than you are on Google+. You might want to check whether any of your friends are using Google+ before you sign up.

Joining Google+

To join Google+, go to plus.google.com. If you already have a Google Account (if you use Gmail, for example), you can log into Google+ with that account. Otherwise, you need to create a new Google Account, which is relatively painless.

Navigating Google+

You navigate Google+ via a series of tabs along the left side of the page. These tabs include the following:

- **Home**, which displays Google+'s stream of posts from your circles of friends.
- **Profile**, where you can view and edit your personal profile information. (Figure 18.1 shows a typical Google+ profile page.)
- **Explore**, which displays new and interesting stuff on Google+.
- **Events**, which lets you create and view online and real-world events with your friends.
- **Photos**, which displays all the photos you've uploaded.
- **Circles**, from which you manage your circles of friends.
- **More**, which leads you to Google+'s online games, video conversations (called *hangouts*), and professional or brand pages.

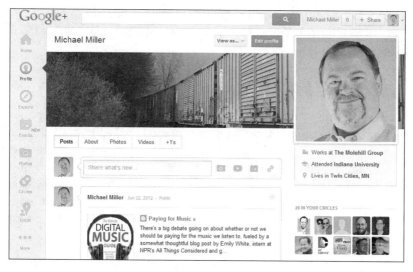

FIGURE 18.1

A typical Google+ profile page; note the tabs along the left side of the page.

Viewing the Stream

For most users, the Google+ Home page is where you want to start. As you can see in Figure 18.2, Google+'s Home page displays the stream of posts from your friends on the social network. All your friends' posts are displayed here.

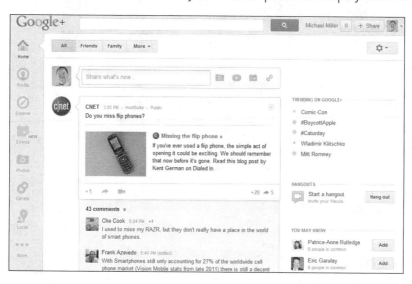

FIGURE 18.2

Viewing posts in the Google+ stream.

You can leave a comment on any post by typing it into the Add a Comment box beneath the post. You can also "like" a post by clicking the +1 button for that post.

Understanding Circles

One unique feature of Google+ is the ease with which you can organize your friends into distinct groups, called *circles*. A circle is just that—a circle of friends that share some common characteristic. For example, you might create one circle for family members, another for people you work with, and a third for old friends from school. You can then send certain posts to your family circle, other posts to your co-workers, and still other posts to your old school friends. By using Google+'s circles feature, you don't have to send everything you post to every single friend on the network.

You manage your friends and circles by clicking the Circle tab on the left side of any page. As you can see in Figure 18.3, all your friends on Google+ are displayed at the top of the page; all your existing circles are at the bottom. To add a friend to a circle, just drag and drop that friend's box onto the given circle.

FIGURE 18.3

Managing friends and circles.

   NOTE   You can add a friend to more than one circle.

This concept of circles also makes it easier for you to manage which posts you read. When you display the Google+ stream, you have the option to display messages from all your circles or just display those from a selected circle. Select a circle in the stream to read only messages from that circle.

Posting to Google+

To make a post on Google+, go to the Home page and start typing into the Share What's New box. The box expands, as shown in Figure 18.4.

FIGURE 18.4

Creating a new Google+ post.

Click the camera icon to attach a photo to the post, click the play icon to attach a video, or click the link icon to add a link to a web page. You should also click one or more of your circles, listed beneath the message box, to determine which circles of friends will be able to see the post.

Press the Enter key on your keyboard when you're ready to post your message. Your post shows up in the streams of those friends in the circles you selected.

Using Pinterest

Pinterest is another up-and-coming social network, but with a twist. This social network is kind of a visual version of Facebook, and as such is becoming increasingly popular among average users.

What Pinterest Is and What It Does

Unlike Facebook, which lets you post text-based status updates, Pinterest is all about images. The site consists of a collection of virtual online "pinboards" that people use to share pictures they find interesting. Users "pin" photos and other images to their personal message boards, and then share their pins with online friends.

Here's how it works. You start by finding an image on a web page that you like and want to share. You then "pin" that image to one of your personal online pinboards, which are like old-fashioned corkboards, except online.

A pinboard becomes a place where you can create and share collections of those things you like or find interesting. You can have as many pinboards as you like, organized by category or topic. Pinterest creates a few default pinboards for you when you first sign up (such as Products I Love and My Style), but you can also create your own custom pinboards, built around your favorite topics and interests.

Friends who follow you see the images you pin, and you see the ones they pin. You can also "like" other people's pins, and repin their items to your pinboards, thus repeating the original pin. It's a very visual way to share things you like, online.

This approach to sharing interesting images has proven extremely popular. Pinterest has more than 20 million users, and they're very active; the average person spends more than 98 minutes per month on the site. (That compares to just 5 minutes per month for Google+ users, 16 minutes/month for LinkedIn users, and 24 minutes/month for Twitter users.)

Pinterest has proven especially interesting to women—anywhere from 60% to 80% of Pinterest users are females. Not surprisingly, the most popular pins on Pinterest are in the clothing/fashion, home décor, crafts, and design categories.

So if you're a woman between the ages of 24 and 44, have a college education, and earn more than $30,000 a year, chances are you're already on Pinterest. And if you're not on yet, you probably want to be.

Joining Pinterest

As of July 2012, Pinterest is still technically in a public testing phase, which means that membership is by invitation only. You can request an invitation from the Pinterest site, or you can ask a current Pinterest to user send you an invitation.

You can request an invitation directly from Pinterest by launching Internet Explorer and going to the Pinterest website, located at www.pinterest.com. Click the red Request an Invite button, enter your email address into the text box, and then click the blue Request Invitation button. You should receive an invitation via email within the next week or so.

When you receive your invitation, click the sign up link in the email message. This opens Internet Explorer and takes you to a congratulations page on the Pinterest site. Follow the instructions there to sign up with either your Facebook or Twitter account.

 NOTE You use your existing Facebook or Twitter account to sign up for Pinterest. If you do not yet have a Facebook or Twitter account, you need to establish one first. (They're free, too.)

Navigating the Pinterest Site

Pinterest is a relatively easy website to get around. After you've logged on, it's a simple matter of displaying certain types of pins from certain users and then knowing how to get back to the main page.

 NOTE You log into Pinterest with the email address and password you created when you signed up, or with your Facebook or Twitter credentials.

The Pinterest home page, shown in Figure 18.5, consists of a two-tier menu bar at the top, with individual pins filling the bulk of the page beneath that. You use the menu bar to navigate around the site.

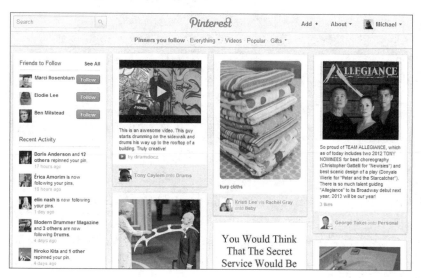

FIGURE 18.5

Pinterest's home page.

Pinning Items to a Pinboard

Pinterest is all about pinning items of interest—hence the name, a combination of "pin" and "interest." To fully participate in the Pinterest community, then, you have to learn how to pin items to your pinboards. There are several ways to do this.

The simplest way to create a pin is from the Pinterest site. To do this, you first need to know the address (URL) of the web page you want to pin. With that URL in hand, follow these steps:

1. Click Add+ on the Pinterest menu bar to display the Add panel.

2. Click Add a Pin to display the Add a Pin panel.

3. Enter the URL of the page you want to pin into the text box and then click the Find Images button.

4. The Add a Pin panel changes to display a slideshow of images found on the selected web page, as shown in Figure 18.6. Click the Next or Prev buttons to cycle through the images until you find the one you want to pin.

FIGURE 18.6

Pinning an item.

5. Pull down the pinboard list and select the board to which you'd like to pin this image.

6. Enter a short (500 characters or less) text description of or comment on this image into the Describe Your Pin box.

7. Click the red Pin It button when done.

Repinning Existing Items

You can also "repin" items that other users have previously pinned. This adds the pinned item to one of your pinboards. To repin an item from its thumbnail image, follow these steps:

1. Mouse over the item you want to repin and then click the Repin button, as shown in Figure 18.7.

FIGURE 18.7

Repinning an item.

2. When the Repin panel appears, pull down the pinboard list and select which board you want to pin this item to.

3. Accept the previous user's description or add your own to the large text box.

4. Click the red Pin it button to repin the item.

Creating New Pinboards

Pinterest creates several default pinboards when you first create your account. You can create additional boards if you like, to better match your own hobbies and interests.

To create a new pinboard, follow these steps:

1. Click Add+ on the Pinterest menu bar to display the Add panel.

2. Click Create a Board to display the Create a Board panel, shown in Figure 18.8.

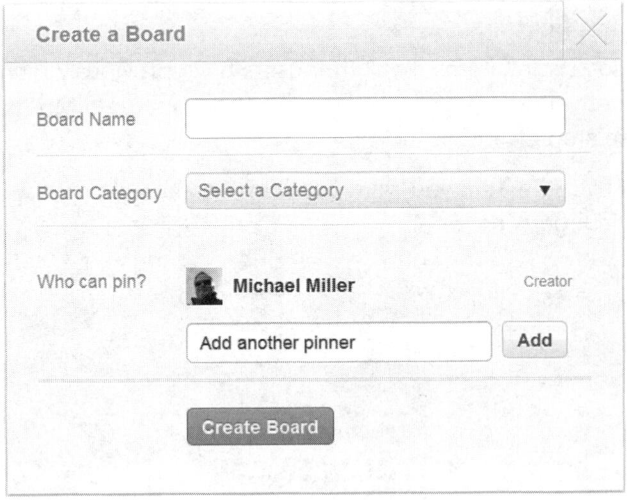

FIGURE 18.8

Creating a new pinboard.

3. Enter the name for the new board into the Board Name box.

4. Pull down the Board Category list and select a category for this board.

5. Go to the Who Can Pin? section and select the Just Me option.

6. Click the red Create Board button.

Pinterest creates the board and displays the page for this board. (It's currently empty.)

Viewing Pinboards and Pins

A user's presence on Pinterest is defined by his or her pinboards and the pins posted there. To view a friend's pinboards and the contents, all you have to do is click that friend's name anywhere on the Pinterest site. Your friend's personal Pinterest page displays with thumbnails of his or her pinboards, as shown in Figure 18.9.

To open a pinboard, click the board's thumbnail image. This displays all the pins for the selected board. Each pin consists of the pinned image, descriptive text (supplied by the user who pinned the item), and the URL for the website where this image was found. To view the web page where the image originally appeared, click the pin.

FIGURE 18.9

Viewing a Pinterest profile page.

Following Other Users

When you find someone who posts a lot of things you're interested in, you can follow that person on Pinterest. When you follow a person, all that person's new pins display on your Pinterest home page.

You can find people to follow by using Pinterest's search box (in the toolbar) to search by name or interest. After you've located a person you want to follow, just go to that person's personal Pinterest page and click the Follow All button.

 TIP Instead of following all of a person's pins, you can opt to follow only selected pinboards. Just go to that person's personal Pinterest page and click the Follow button for the board you want to follow.

Using LinkedIn

LinkedIn is a different kind of social network—not necessarily in how it works, but in who it appeals to. Whereas Facebook, Google+, and Pinterest are aimed at a general audience, LinkedIn is targeted at business professionals. As such, you can use LinkedIn to network with others in your industry or profession, or even to hunt for a new position at another firm. (Figure 18.10 shows the LinkedIn Home page—with a definite business slant.)

FIGURE 18.10

The LinkedIn Home page.

Creating an Account

LinkedIn membership is free. To join the LinkedIn network, go to www.linkedin.com and enter your first and last names, email address, and desired password. Click the Join Now button and you are prompted to enter information to complete your personal profile—employment status, company, title, and so forth. You also are prompted to search your email contacts for people who are already on LinkedIn.

LinkedIn sends a confirmation message to your email address. Click the link in the email to confirm your membership and you're ready to continue building your network and start using the site.

 TIP Use the menu bar at the top of each page to find your way around the LinkedIn site. The menu bar contains links to the LinkedIn Home page, your personal profile, your LinkedIn contacts, groups you belong to, LinkedIn's job search features, and your message inbox.

Personalizing Your Profile

Each LinkedIn member has his or her own personal profile page. This profile page is what other LinkedIn users see when they search for you on the site; it's where you make your initial impression to potential employers and people with whom you want to make contact.

Because your profile page serves as your *de facto* resume on the LinkedIn site, you want to control the information you display to others. Presenting only selected information can help you present yourself in the best possible light.

Fortunately, your LinkedIn profile is fully customizable; you can select which content others see. This content can include a snapshot of your personal information (shown in Figure 18.11), your contact info, summaries of your professional experience and education, recommendations from other users, and more.

FIGURE 18.11

Snapshot information on a LinkedIn profile page.

To edit your profile page, click Profile on the menu bar and then select Edit Profile. When the Edit My Profile page appears, click the Edit button for the section(s) you want to edit.

Finding New Connections

LinkedIn's equivalent of Facebook friends are called *connections*. These are business or professional contacts you know and trust. Anyone on the LinkedIn site can become a connection; you can also invite people who are not yet LinkedIn members to join your connections list.

You can search for LinkedIn members in your email contacts list, or in your Palm, ACT!, or Mac Address contacts. In addition, LinkedIn can search for members who've gone to the same schools or worked for the same employers that you have. You can also invite non-LinkedIn members to be new connections.

To add new connections, pull down the Connections menu and select Add Connections. From there you can search for people you know, or you can invite others (via email) to join your LinkedIn network.

Contacting Other LinkedIn Members

Networking on LinkedIn involves a lot of personal contact, using LinkedIn's own internal email system. This system enables you to send messages to and receive messages from people on your connections list, as well as anyone else who is a member of the LinkedIn site.

To send a new message, pull down the Inbox menu and select Compose New Message. When the Messages page appears, as shown in Figure 18.12, enter the recipient's name or email address into the To box. (Or, to email one of your connections, click the blue graphic next to the To box to display the Choose Connections window.) Type the subject of the message into the Subject box, type your message into the large text box, and then click the Send Message button.

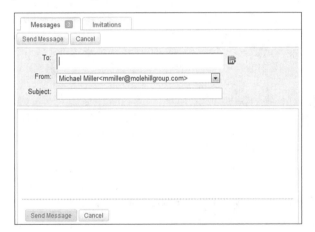

FIGURE 18.12

Sending a new message.

To view messages you've received, click the Inbox menu. This displays all messages you've received. The newest messages are listed first; unread messages are in bold. To read a message, all you have to do is click the message header.

Using Twitter

Then there's Twitter. Unlike Facebook, Pinterest, Google+, and LinkedIn, Twitter isn't a fully featured social network per se. Instead, Twitter is a kind of micro-blogging service that lets you create short (up to 140 characters) text posts—called *tweets*—that your followers receive and read.

 NOTE   Most people use Twitter to follow other users, rather than to tweet themselves. The most popular tweeters include celebrities, companies and brands, and news organizations and reporters.

Joining and Using Twitter

To use Twitter, you first have to register as a user. You can create a free account from the Twitter home page (www.twitter.com).

After you've registered and signed in, you see the Twitter home page, shown in Figure 18.13. The main part of this page, on the right side, displays the most recent tweets, newest first. If a tweet has been shortened, click the Expand link to view it all. You can also click any links in a tweet to go to the mentioned web page or view an embedded photo.

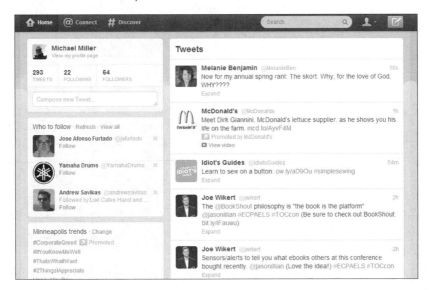

FIGURE 18.13

Twitter's home page.

The left side of the home page displays information about how many tweets you've made, how many people you're following, and how many people are following you. There are also some suggestions on other folks you might want to follow.

Finally, you can navigate to other pages on the Twitter site from the navigation bar at the top of the page. Click @Connect to view tweets that have mentioned you, or click #Discover to view trending topics. You can also search for specific topics using the search box in the navigation bar.

Tweeting with Twitter

To compose and send a tweet, you start on Twitter's home page. All you have to do is enter your text into the Compose New Tweet box on the top-left corner, shown in Figure 18.14. Each tweet can be up to 140 characters long (spaces count as characters); when you're done, click the Tweet button to send your message on its way.

FIGURE 18.14

Composing a new tweet.

 TIP Because space is limited, many tweeters use abbreviations in their tweets. You can mention a hot topic (and make the term searchable) by preceding it with a hashtag (#), like this: **#hottopic**. To mention a given user in a tweet, put an @ sign in front of his username, like this: **@username**.

Following Other Users

If friends or family members are on Twitter, you can follow their activities by "following" their tweets.

To find people to follow, go the #Discover page and click Find Friends in the top-left corner. You can now search for people by email address or name, or you can find out which people in your email contact lists are already on Twitter.

To follow a Twitter user, go to that person's profile page and click the Follow button. All tweets from this user start appearing on your Twitter home page.

CAUTION Some users protect their profiles so that strangers can't follow them without their permission. When you click the Follow button for these users, they have to register their approval before you can follow them.

Customizing Your Profile

Every Twitter use has his or own personal profile page on the site, like the one in Figure 18.15. To customize your profile page, click your name at the top-left corner of the Twitter home page to display your profile and then click the Edit Your Profile button. You can edit any of the information on this page, and you can even change the profile picture that others see. Twitter enables you to choose from several preselected design themes, which can really change the look and feel of your page.

FIGURE 18.15
A typical Twitter profile page.

Using Social Networks—Smartly and Safely

Social networking puts your whole life out there in front of your friends and family—and, in some cases, just about anyone perusing a network's profiles. With so much personal information displayed publicly, how do you protect yourself against those who might want to do harm to you or your children?

Protecting Your Children

Given that social networks are so popular among teenagers and preteens, many parents worry about their children being cyberstalked on these sites. That worry is not ill-founded, especially given the amount of personal information that most users post on their social networking profiles.

It's important to note that all social networking sites try to police themselves, typically by limiting access for younger users. In addition, sites such as Facebook work hard to keep known sex offenders off their sites by monitoring lists of known sex offenders and culling those users from their sites.

That said, the best way to protect your children on social networking sites is to monitor what they do on those sites. As such, it's important that you become "friends" with your children on Facebook, follow their Twitter feeds, and visit their profile pages on a regular basis. You might be surprised what you find there.

It's an unfortunate fact that not all teens and preteens are wise about what they put online. It's not unusual to find provocative pictures posted on their social networking profiles; you probably don't want your children exposing themselves in this fashion.

You also need to warn your kids that not everyone on Facebook or Twitter is truly a "friend." They should be circumspect about the information they make public and with whom they communicate. It's also worth noting that kids shouldn't arrange to meet in person strangers who they're "friends" with online; it's not unheard of for unsavory adults to use social networks as a stalking ground.

In other words, teach your kids to be careful. Hanging out on a site like Facebook is normally no more dangerous than hanging out at the mall, but even malls aren't completely safe. Caution and common sense are always called for.

Protecting Yourself

The advice you give to your children regarding social networks also applies to yourself. Think twice before posting personal information or incriminating photographs, and don't broadcast your every move on your profile page. Also, don't automatically accept friend requests from people you don't know.

Most important, don't view Facebook and similar sites as online dating services. Yes, you might meet new friends on these social networks, but use caution about transferring online friendships into the physical world. If you decide to meet an online friend offline, do so in a public place and perhaps with another friend along. Don't put yourself at risk when meeting strangers—and remember that until you get to know them in person, anyone you correspond with online remains a stranger.

THE ABSOLUTE MINIMUM

Here are the key points to remember from this chapter:

- Google+ is Google's answer to Facebook—although it's nowhere near as popular.

- Pinterest is much more popular, a way to share interesting images with friends.

- LinkedIn is a social network for business professionals.

- Twitter is a way to broadcast short text messages to your followers—and to follow others who tweet.

- Whichever social networking sites you use, be smart about the information you post; some personal information is best not made public.

19

MANAGING YOUR SOCIAL ACTIVITY IN WINDOWS

If you follow a lot of friends on several social networks, it can be quite time consuming to manage them all. Log into Facebook to view your News Feed there, then onto Twitter to view the latest tweets, then onto LinkedIn to see what your contacts are saying there. Wouldn't it be nice if there was a way to follow all your friends' activity in one place?

Well, in Windows 8 there is. The new People app enables you to consolidate tweets and status updates and posts from the people you follow on Facebook, Twitter, LinkedIn, and other networks. Viewing all your friends' activity is just a click (or a tap) away!

Understanding the People App

The Windows 8 People app consolidates messages from several major social networks and your email accounts. You can view the latest updates from your friends in one place—as well as comment on and retweet those updates—without having to visit the social networking sites themselves. It's truly a single hub for all your social networking needs.

What social networks can you connect to from the People app? Here's the list:

- Facebook
- Twitter
- LinkedIn
- Google+ (via your Google Account)

You can also connect the People app to your Microsoft Account, Hotmail account, Microsoft Exchange account, and your Gmail account (again, via your Google Account).

And here's something else: The People app manages and centralizes your contacts for all your Windows applications. So if there's a person who's in your Hotmail contacts list, in your Facebook friends list, and whom you follow on Twitter, he appears as a single contact in the People app. When you want to contact that person, just open the People app, find his name, and email away.

Adding Accounts to the People App

By default, the People app connects to the Microsoft account you used to create your Windows account. You have to manually add all other accounts.

To add a new account to the People app, follow these steps:

1. From the Windows Start screen, click or tap the People tile.

2. From within the People app, click or tap in the upper-right corner of the screen. (This is where logos are displayed for all your currently connected accounts.)

3. When the Accounts pane appears, click or tap Add an Account.

4. When the Add an Account pane appears, as shown in Figure 19.1, click or tap the account you want to add.

5. You see a screen specific to that particular account. Follow the onscreen instructions to connect the two accounts.

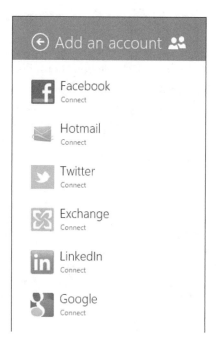

FIGURE 19.1

Adding a new account to the People app.

Using the People App

You launch the People app by clicking or tapping the People tile on the Windows 8 Start screen. As you can see in Figure 19.2, the People tile is a "live" tile that displays a changing selection of profile pictures from your friends, along with the latest status updates.

FIGURE 19.2

Clicking the "live" People tile on the Start screen.

The People app itself has three components: People (consolidates all your contacts from all connected accounts), What's New (displays the latest posts from your friends), and Me (displays information about you). We'll look at each section of the app separately.

Viewing Posts by Person

When you want to access all your contacts, click People at the top of the People app. As you can see in Figure 19.3, all your contacts from all your accounts are listed here, in alphabetical order.

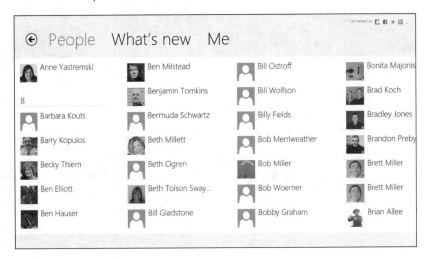

FIGURE 19.3

Viewing all your contacts on the People screen.

TIP Your "favorite" friends will appear first in the People list. To add a contact to your favorites list, open that person's profile page, right-click to display the Options Bar, and then click or tap Favorite.

Scroll right and left through the list by pressing the left and right arrow keys on your keyboard, dragging the scrollbar at the bottom of the window with your mouse, or swiping your finger left or right on a touchscreen display. You can also skip directly to names starting with a given letter by pressing that letter on your keyboard; for example, pressing "G" takes you right to those contacts that start with the letter G.

You can also search for a particular contact. Press Windows+Q to display the Search pane, shown in Figure 19.4. Enter the name of the person you're looking for and press Enter; Windows returns a list of contacts that match your search criteria. Click or tap the contact you want to view.

FIGURE 19.4

Searching for a specific contact.

   NOTE If a person is listed in multiple programs or services, the People app consolidates all that information into a single contact. So, for example, if a contact is listed in your Hotmail, Facebook, and Twitter accounts, information from all those accounts (Hotmail, Facebook, and Twitter) is listed in his single People contact page.

Click or tap a contact name to view full details about this person. There are three screens worth of info for each contact. The first screen, shown in Figure 19.5, is the Contact screen. It shows the person's profile picture (typically the one used for his Facebook or Twitter profile) and contains links to send a message to that person (via whatever social networks and email accounts that person has), map the person's address, and view all info about that person.

   TIP You can also send a person an email message directly from the All screen. Just right-click the person's name and then click or tap Send Email. This opens your default email app with a message addressed to this person.

The second screen, dubbed What's New, scrolls through this person's latest posts on Facebook, Twitter, or LinkedIn. The third screen, Photos, shows photographs uploaded by this person to the various social networks.

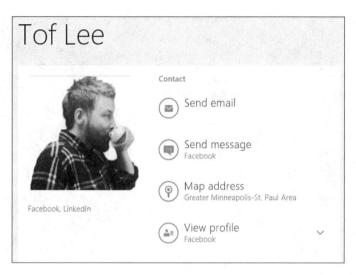

FIGURE 19.5

Viewing information about a contact.

In short, the All screen tells you everything you want to know about everyone you know—and enables you to message them, too.

Viewing What's New

When you want to see what all your friends are posting on Facebook, Twitter, and LinkedIn, click What's New at the top of the People app. Each status update or tweet or other post is displayed in its own panel, as shown in Figure 19.6. Scroll right to view more posts.

To "like," comment on, or retweet a given post, click or tap the corresponding link or icon under the post. This opens the post in a new page with the necessary input box. For example, Figure 19.7 shows a contact's status update from Facebook. The full post is displayed in the left column (along with the contact's name and picture). To "like" this post, click or tap the Likes box at the top of the right column. To comment on this post, enter your comment into the Add a Comment box in the lower right.

FIGURE 19.6

Viewing what's new with your contacts.

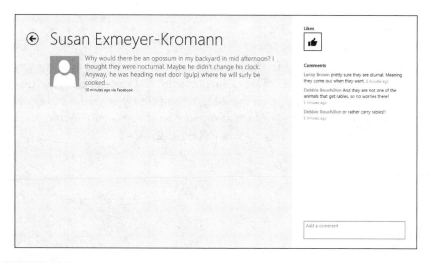

FIGURE 19.7

Viewing and responding to a status update.

Viewing Posts and Information About Yourself

Want to know what others can learn about you online? Then select Me at the top of the People app; the Me pages, shown in Figure 19.8, display information about you, your latest social network posts (What's New), the most recent notifications you've received, and photos you've uploaded to various social networks.

FIGURE 19.8

Viewing what's new about you.

If you'd like to edit the information displayed on your Me page, display the Options Bar and click Edit. This opens Internet Explorer and takes you to your Windows Live profile page on the web. Click Edit by any information you want to change and enter any new information you want displayed. When you return to your Me page, the new information will be displayed.

THE ABSOLUTE MINIMUM

Here are the key points to remember from this chapter:

- The Windows 8 People app consolidates contact information and posts from all your friends across all major social networks.

- You can use the People app to view status updates, tweets, and other posts from friends on Facebook, Twitter, and LinkedIn.

- The People app also functions as a universal contacts list for all your Windows apps.

- Your own personal information is also displayed in the People app—including posts and mentions on your connected social networks.

20

UNDERSTANDING AND USING WINDOWS APPS

When you want to do something on your computer, you need to use the appropriate applications. *Applications*—more commonly called *apps*—are software programs that perform one or more functions. Some apps are work-related; others provide useful information; still others are more entertaining in nature. But whatever it is you want to do, you need to launch the right app.

With Windows 8 there are actually two kinds of apps. Old-style software apps run in windows on the traditional desktop, whereas newer Windows 8 apps (newly developed for Windows 8) run full-screen from the Start screen. Most people will use a mix of traditional and Windows 8 apps in their day-to-day use.

Using Apps in Windows 8

Both traditional and Windows 8 apps have a lot in common, especially in how you find them, launch them, and switch between them. It's a matter of knowing the right commands and operations.

Searching for Apps

When it comes to finding the app you want, you can scroll through the various pages of the Start screen, but not all apps are necessarily tiled there. For example, you may remove little-used apps from the Start screen to make things a little less cluttered. And even if an app is on the Start screen, if there are too many tiles there, you might not be able to quickly find it.

For this reason, Windows 8 enables you to search for apps by name. It's really quite easy to do:

1. From the Windows Start screen, press Windows+Q to display the Search panel, shown in Figure 20.1.

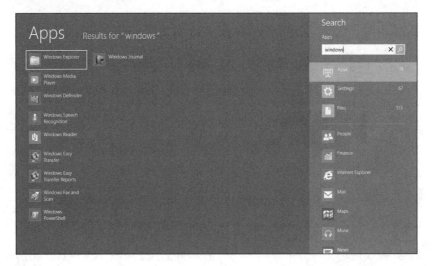

FIGURE 20.1

Searching for apps in Windows 8. (Matching apps are on the left.)

2. If Apps is not selected from the search list, click or tap it now.

3. Enter the name of the app you're looking for into the search box.

4. Press the Enter key or click or tap the magnifying glass button to start the search.

Windows displays all apps that match your query. Click or tap an app to launch it.

Displaying All Apps

You can also display all apps and utilities that are installed on your computer. To do this, follow these steps:

1. From the Windows Start screen, right-click in any open area of the screen (or swipe your finger up from the bottom of the screen on a touchscreen device) to display the Options Bar.

2. Click or tap All Apps.

This displays the Apps screen, shown in Figure 20.2. All installed apps are displayed here, organized as follows:

FIGURE 20.2

Viewing all installed apps.

- Apps
- Windows Accessories
- Windows Ease of Access
- Windows System

Scroll to the right to view additional apps; click or tap an app to launch it.

 NOTE There might be additional sections on the Apps screen, added by specific apps installed on your system.

Pinning Apps to the Start Screen

You might find that it's easier to launch a frequently used app by adding it to the Windows Start screen—what's known as "pinning" the app. When you pin an app to the Start screen you create a tile for the app; you can click or tap the tile to launch the app.

To pin an app to the Start screen, follow these steps:

1. Go to the Apps screen and find the app you'd like to pin.

2. Right-click the app or swipe down on the app (if you have a touchscreen device) to display the Options Bar at the bottom of the screen, as shown in Figure 20.3.

3. Click or tap Pin to Start.

FIGURE 20.3

Pinning an app to the Start menu.

The app you selected is added to the end of the Start screen. You can then drag it to a different position, if you like.

Switching Between Apps

If you have more than one open app, it's easy to switch between them. In fact, there are several ways to do this:

- **Press Alt+Tab**—A box displays in the center of the screen, as shown in Figure 20.4, with the current app highlighted. Continue pressing Tab (while holding down the Alt button) to cycle through all open apps.

- **Press Windows+Tab**—The Switcher panel displays at the left side of the screen, as shown in Figure 20.5, with the current app highlighted. Continue pressing Tab (while holding down the Windows button) to cycle through all open apps.

FIGURE 20.4

Press Alt+Tab to cycle through open apps.

FIGURE 20.5

Press Windows+Tab to display the Switcher panel.

 TIP You can also display the Apps panel by "bumping" your mouse against the top-left corner of the screen. This displays a small thumbnail of the open app; move your mouse downward to display the full Apps panel.

- **With a touchscreen device**—Press and drag from the left edge of the screen inward toward the center. The next open app appears on top of the previous app.

Working with Windows 8 Apps

Most Windows 8 apps are fairly intuitive to use. You seldom find difficult-to-understand elements such as pull-down menus and toolbars; instead, most operations are front and center for you to click or tap.

There are, however, a few common operations you need to familiarize yourself with. We'll look at these next.

Viewing and Configuring App Options

Many Windows 8 apps have options you can or need to configure. For example, the Weather app needs to know where you live so it can deliver the proper weather reports.

To configure an app's options you need to display the Options Bar. Figure 20.6 shows a typical Options Bar from the Calendar app; every app has different options. In fact, some Options bars drop down from the top of the screen instead of pull up from the bottom!

FIGURE 20.6

The Options bar for the Messaging app.

To display the Options bar(s), follow these steps:

1. From within the app, right-click the screen or swipe up from the bottom of the screen (on a touchscreen device) to display the Options bar.

2. Click or tap the options you want to configure.

Closing an Open App

In previous versions of Windows you needed to close open apps when you were done with them. That's not the case in Windows 8; you can leave any Windows 8 app running as long as you like without using valuable system resources. (An open but unused app is essentially paused until you return to it.)

You can still, however, close open apps, if you'd like. There are two ways to do this:

- With a touchscreen device, swipe down from the top of the screen toward the center. This reduces the app to a small window and then closes it.

- With a mouse, "bump" the cursor against the top-left corner of the app. This displays a small thumbnail of the app; right-click the thumbnail and select Close from the pop-up menu.

Working with Traditional Software Apps

Windows 8 apps are newer apps designed specifically for Windows 8, but there are still lots of older software programs available that you might find useful, such as Microsoft Word (and the entire Office suite), Adobe Photoshop Elements, and even Apple's iTunes player. You need to learn how these traditional software programs work.

You launch traditional software apps from the Start screen, the same as Windows 8 apps. These older apps, however, run on the traditional Windows desktop, within their own windows. As such, you can have multiple open apps onscreen at the same time, with the windows stacked on top of or tiled next to each other.

Most traditional apps have different onscreen elements than do newer Windows 8 apps. We'll look at the more common elements next.

Using Menus

Many software apps use a set of pull-down *menus* to store all the commands and operations you can perform. The menus are aligned across the top of the window, just below the title bar, in what is called a *menu bar*.

You open (or pull down) a menu by clicking the menu's name with your mouse. The full menu then appears just below the menu bar, as shown in Figure 20.7. You activate a command or select a menu item by clicking it with your mouse.

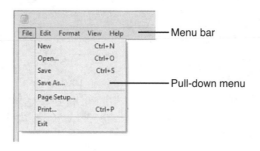

FIGURE 20.7

Navigating the menu system in the Notepad app.

Some menu items have a little black arrow to the right of the label. This indicates that additional choices are available, displayed on a *submenu*. Click the menu item or the arrow to display the submenu.

> **TIP** If an item in a menu, toolbar, or dialog box is dimmed (or grayed), that means it isn't available for the current task.

Other menu items have three little dots (called an ellipsis) to the right of the label. This indicates that additional choices are available, displayed in a dialog box. Click the menu item to display the dialog box.

The nice thing is, after you get the hang of this menu thing in one program, the menus should be similar in all the other programs you use. For example, many apps have a File menu that, when clicked, displays a pull-down menu of common file-oriented operations. Although each program has menus and menu items specific to its own needs, these common menus make it easy to get up and running when you install new software programs on your system.

Using Toolbars and Ribbons

Some apps put the most frequently used operations on one or more *toolbars*, typically located just below the menu bar. (Figure 20.8 shows a typical toolbar.) A toolbar looks like a row of buttons, each with a small picture (called an *icon*) and maybe a bit of text. You activate the associated command or operation by clicking the button with your mouse.

Buttons

 Toolbar

FIGURE 20.8

A typical toolbar, in Adobe Photoshop.

> **TIP** If the toolbar is too long to display fully on your screen, you see a right arrow at the far-right side of the toolbar. Click this arrow to display the buttons that aren't currently visible.

Other programs substitute a *ribbon* for the toolbar. For example, all the apps in Microsoft Office have ribbons that contain buttons or controls for the most-used operations. As you can see in Figure 20.9, each ribbon has different tabs, each containing a unique collection of buttons. Click the tab to see the ribbon buttons for that particular type of operation.

Tabs   Buttons

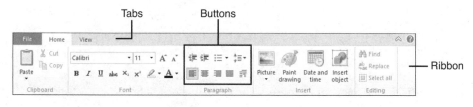

                                                                    Ribbon

FIGURE 20.9

A ribbon with tabs for different types of operations in the WordPad app.

 TIP If you're not sure which button does what on a toolbar or ribbon, you can mouse over the button to display a ToolTip. A *ToolTip* is a small text box that displays the button's label or other useful information.

Closing an Open App

When you're working with a desktop app, you should close it when you're done. The easiest way to do this is to click the X at the top-right corner of the window, as shown in Figure 20.10. You might also be able to pull down the app's File menu and select Exit, or click the File tab and click Exit from there.

FIGURE 20.10

Click the X to close the app.

THE ABSOLUTE MINIMUM

Here are the key points to remember from this chapter:

- An application, or app, is a software program that performs a specific function.

- You can search for Apps by pressing Windows+Q, or view all installed apps by right-clicking the Start screen and then clicking All Apps.

- To switch between apps, press Alt+Tab. Alternatively, press Windows+Tab to display the Switcher panel and display all running apps.

- Many Windows 8 apps have an Options bar you can display by right-clicking within the app.

- Traditional apps run on the desktop and use some combination of pull-down menus, toolbars, and ribbons.

- Windows 8 apps don't have to be officially closed when you're done using them; to close a traditional app, click the X in the top-right corner of the window.

21

EXPLORING WINDOWS 8'S BUILT-IN APPS

Windows 8 comes with a variety of apps and utilities you can start using as soon as you log onto your system. Most of these are Windows 8 apps, but some still run on the traditional desktop.

This chapter describes all the apps and utilities built into Windows 8 and explores how you can use some of the more popular ones.

Discovering Windows 8's Apps and Utilities

Windows 8 is more than just an operating environment; it's also host to a number of useful apps and utilities. Most of these apps are designed specifically for Windows 8's interface, but others run in the traditional desktop environment.

Tables 21.1 details the apps included with Windows 8.

TABLE 21.1   Windows 8 Apps

Name	Description
Calendar	Manages schedules and appointments.
Camera	Controls your PC's webcam (if it has one).
Desktop	Runs old-style software programs as on a traditional Windows desktop.
Finance	Serves as a hub for financial news and information.
Internet Explorer	Microsoft's web browser.
Mail	For sending and receiving email.
Maps	Displays street maps and driving directions.
Messaging	Sends instant messages to users of various IM services.
Music	Plays music stored on your PC and downloads new music from the Web.
News	Displays the latest news headlines; customizable to your personal news preferences.
People	Serves as a contact manager program and consolidates posts from all your friends across multiple social networks.
Photos	Displays digital photos stored on your PC.
SkyDrive	Cloud-based document storage and online apps.
Sports	Displays the latest sports headlines and scores; customizable for your favorite sports and teams.
Store	Accesses the Windows Store so you can purchase and download new Windows apps.
Travel	Displays favorite travel destinations and top travel stories.
Video	Enables you to view movies and TV shows from the Web, or view your own videos stored on your PC.
Weather	Displays local weather conditions and forecasts.
Windows Reader	A Windows 8 reader for PDF- and XPS-format files.
Xbox LIVE Games	Enables you to purchase, download, and play Xbox LIVE games on your PC, as well as interface with fellow gamers.

In addition, Windows 8 includes a number of apps (dubbed *accessories*) that add extra functionality to the basic operating system. Most of these apps run on the traditional desktop; Table 21.2 details these accessory programs.

TABLE 21.2 Windows 8 Accessories

Name	Description
Calculator	A combination standard/scientific/programming/statistics calculator.
Character Map	Enables you to insert all manner of special characters into your word processing and other documents.
Math Input Panel	Enables you to create handwritten equations (on a tablet or touchscreen PC) that are converted into digital format.
Notepad	A very basic word processor.
Paint	A very basic illustration/coloring tool.
Remote Desktop Connection	Enables you to remotely control other PCs as if you were using them directly—great for accessing your home PC when you're on the road.
Snipping Tool	Enables you to take snapshots of the current computer screen.
Sound Recorder	Enables you to record what's currently playing through your computer's speakers.
Steps Recorder	Typically used for troubleshooting system problems; records a series of screenshots used in performing a given operation.
Sticky Notes	Enables you to create virtual sticky notes on the traditional desktop.
Windows Fax and Scan	Enables you to send and receive faxes, as well as scan printed documents into digital files.
Windows Journal	Enables you to create handwritten notes (on a tablet or touchscreen PC) that are converted into digital format.
Windows Media Player	A full-featured music and video player.
WordPad	A slightly more fully featured word processor than Notepad (but still not as fully featured as Microsoft Word).
XPS Viewer	Enables you to view XPS-format files.

If you have difficulty seeing what's on the computer screen or typing on a traditional keyboard, Windows 8 includes four useful utilities for improved ease of access. Table 21.3 details these utility programs.

TABLE 21.3 Windows 8 Ease of Access Utilities

Name	Description
Magnifier	Enlarges all or part of the screen, for the visually impaired.
Narrator	"Reads" onscreen text out loud, for the visually impaired.
On-Screen Keyboard	Displays a fully functioning onscreen keyboard, like the one shown in Figure 21.1—ideal for tablets or other touchscreen devices without a traditional keyboard.
Windows Speech Recognition	Converts speech to digital text, ideal for the visually impaired.

FIGURE 21.1

Windows 8's on-screen keyboard—for when tablet users need to type.

Finally, Windows 8 includes a number of utility programs that help you better manage your computer and the Windows environment. Table 21.4 details these system utilities.

TABLE 21.4 Windows 8 System Utilities

Name	Description
Command Prompt	Opens a "DOS window" with a prompt where you can enter system commands.
Computer	Opens the Computer Explorer, shown in Figure 21.2, which enables you to access the different devices connected to your computer. Also enables you to drill down to individual drives, folders, and subfolders, just like File Explorer.
Control Panel	Enables you to configure various Windows system settings.
Default Programs	Enables you to select which programs Windows uses by default to open specific types of files.
File Explorer	Enables you to manage files on your system.
Help and Support	Accesses Windows 8's help system.

TABLE 21.4 (continued)

Name	Description
Run	Displays the Run box, which you can use to open programs directly (by entering their program name or filename).
Task Manager	Displays the Task Manager, which details current system resource usage and enables you to close frozen programs.
Windows Defender	Installed on PCs that do not have other malware protection options, protects your system against computer viruses and spyware.
Windows Easy Transfer	Enables you to transfer files and settings from an older computer to a newer one.
Windows Easy Transfer Reports	Displays reports associated with use of the Easy Transfer Wizard.
Windows PowerShell	For developers, an environment for creating scripts and batch files.

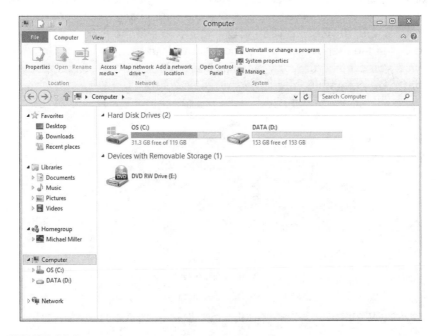

FIGURE 21.2

Viewing the drives of your computer system with Computer Explorer.

To display all available apps and utilities, right-click on the Start screen to display the Apps bar, then click or tap All Apps. This opens the Apps screen, with all apps and utilities displayed there.

Working with Popular Apps

We've already examined some of these apps in the book and examine others when appropriate. With that in mind, let's take a quick look at a few additional apps—what they do and how they work.

Maps

The Windows 8 Maps app lets you create street maps and driving directions. It's based on Bing Maps, which is Microsoft's web-based mapping service.

You launch the Maps app by clicking or tapping the Maps tile on the Start screen. What you see next is a map of the United States, with controls at the top and bottom of the screen.

To display a street map of your current location, display the Options Bar and click or tap My Location. The resulting map is like the one shown in Figure 21.3. You can click and drag your mouse to move the map in any direction—or, if you have a touchscreen device, just drag your finger to move the map. You can zoom in and out of the map by using the zoom controls at the lower left. On a touchscreen device, you can zoom out by pinching the screen with your fingers, or you can zoom in by expanding your fingers on the screen.

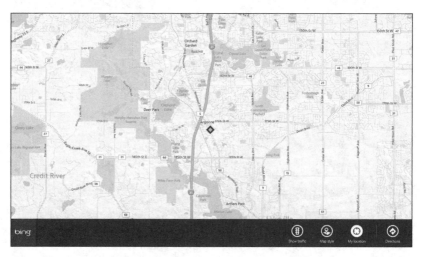

FIGURE 21.3

Viewing a street map with the Maps app.

TIP After a brief time, both command bars on the map disappear. To make them display again, right-click anywhere on the map.

To show current traffic conditions (green is smooth flowing; yellow and red, less so), click or tap Show Traffic in the Options bar. To change from a traditional street map to a satellite map, click or tap Map Style in the Options bar and select Aerial View. To switch back to the traditional map, select Road View.

To generate driving directions, display the Options Bar and click or tap Directions. You can then enter the start and end addresses into the Directions panel. Click or tap the right arrow button to display turn-by-turn directions onscreen, as shown in Figure 21.4.

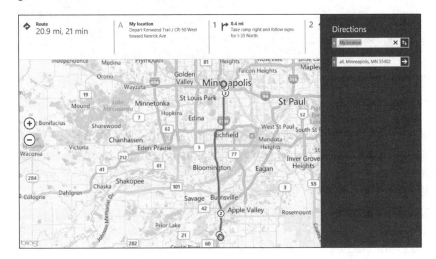

FIGURE 21.4

Generating turn-by-turn driving directions.

News

When you want to read the latest headlines, use Windows 8's News app. It works great "out of the box," but you can also customize it to display news stories from those sources you personally select.

When you launch the app, you see the Top Story page, like the one shown in Figure 21.5. This is indeed the top story of the day, at least as selected by Microsoft's Bing News. Click or tap anywhere on this page to open the full story for in-depth reading.

FIGURE 21.5

Viewing the top story of the day with Windows' News app.

Scroll to the right to view stories organized by topic: U.S., World, Technology, Business, Entertainment, Politics, Sports, and Health. Click or tap any story tile to read that particular story, or click or tap the section header to view more stories about that particular topic.

So far, everything you've seen is under the heading of Bing Daily—today's top daily news. You can also view news trends, by displaying the Options Bar at the top of the page and clicking or tapping Trends.

Then there's your personalized news, which you access by clicking or tapping My News in the Options Bar. As you can see in Figure 21.6, you essentially create your own customized news page by adding specific sections for the news you want to read. To add a new news section, click or tap Add a Section; when the Add a Section panel appears, enter the news topic and click or tap the Add button.

You can also view news gathered by specific news sources, such as BBC News, CNN, Fox News, or Al Jazeera. (Every viewpoint is covered!) Display the Options Bar and click or tap Sources; when the Sources page appears, as shown in Figure 21.7, click the news source you want to read. This displays a screen of stories from that source.

FIGURE 21.6

Viewing your personalized My News page.

FIGURE 21.7

Selecting news sources in the News app.

Weather

Windows 8's Weather app is one of the better looking apps available. It's also quite useful.

The functionality starts before you ever launch the App. The Weather tile displays current weather conditions, "live," right on the Windows Start screen, as you can see in Figure 21.8. Click or tap the tile to launch the app.

FIGURE 21.8

Viewing current conditions "live" on the Weather app tile.

Figure 21.9 shows what the Weather app itself looks like. The background image represents current conditions; for example, a sunny spring day is represented by a beautiful image of fresh leaves in the sunlight. Current conditions are on the left—temperature, wind, humidity, and the like. The rest of the screen is devoted to a five-day forecast.

FIGURE 21.9

Viewing current conditions and a five-day forecast in the Weather app.

Scroll right to view additional weather information, including an hourly forecast, various weather maps (shown in Figure 21.10), and a graph for historical weather in your location. Click any item to view it.

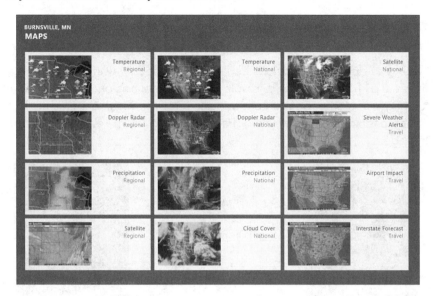

FIGURE 21.10

Viewing available weather maps.

Of course, before the Weather app can deliver your weather, it has to know where you're located. To do this, display the top and bottom Options bars, then click or tap Places in the top bar to see a list of places already added. (The app starts with Seattle as the default city, a conceit from Microsoft's Seattle-based programmers.) Click or tap the + tile, then enter a new location.

 TIP You can switch locations at any point by clicking or tapping Places in the Options bar. You can also view weather around the world by clicking or tapping World Weather in the Options bar.

Windows Reader

Windows Reader enables you to view and read PDF- and XPS-format documents. PDF is a popular format for e-books and other documents because it exactly reproduces the printed page; XPS is Microsoft's attempt to replicate the PDF format, which hasn't been widely adopted.

NOTE Windows Reader is Microsoft's first PDF reader app. In previous versions of Windows, you had to download and use the Adobe Reader program if you wanted to read PDF files.

To open a new document to read, display the Options bar then click or tap Open. Navigate to the file you want to read and then click or tap the Open button.

When you display the Options bar, you see various viewing options, as shown in Figure 21.11. You can opt to display the document as one full page at a time, two full pages at a time, or as a continuously scrolling document (slightly larger, for easier reading). Use the arrow or Page Up/Page Down keys to move from page to page.

FIGURE 21.11

Reading a PDF-format document with Windows Reader.

THE ABSOLUTE MINIMUM

Here are the key points to remember from this chapter:

- Windows 8 contains a variety of apps and utilities that expand the functionality of the basic operating system.

- Most apps included with Windows 8 take full advantage of the Metro environment; most system utilities run on the older desktop.

- The Maps app displays street maps and driving directions.

- The News app delivers a world full of the latest news headlines and stories from a variety of sources.

- The Weather app displays current weather conditions and a five-day forecast.

- The Windows Reader app enables you to read PDF-format files without the need for the separate Adobe Reader program.

22

FINDING AND INSTALLING NEW APPS

Your new computer system probably came with a bunch of programs preinstalled on its hard disk. Some of these are the apps that come with Windows 8, some are preview or limited-use versions provided by the PC manufacturer (included in the hope you'll purchase the full version if you like what you see), and some are real, honest-to-goodness fully functional applications. The more the merrier.

As useful as some of these programs might be, at some point you're going to want to add something new. Maybe you want to install the full version of Microsoft Office, or purchase a full-featured photo editing program, such as Adobe Photoshop Elements. Maybe you want to add some educational apps for the kids or a productivity program for yourself. Maybe you just want to play some new computer games.

Whatever type of app you're considering, installing it on your computer system is easy. In fact, you might find just what you're looking for in Microsoft's Windows Store. Wherever you find a new app, however, installing it on your system is relatively easy—as you'll soon discover.

Finding and Installing Apps from the Windows Store

With Windows 8, Microsoft is plunging headfirst into the app model popularized by Apple's iPhone and Google's Android smartphones. That is, applications are designed specifically for the given operating system and sold through a central "app store." You search or browse the app store for the apps you want and then purchase and download them directly to your device.

This new app model is very consumer friendly, especially when it comes to pricing. A traditional computer software program can cost hundreds of dollars, whereas most apps cost $10 or less—and many don't cost anything. In addition, you can download and install the apps you want without ever leaving home; you install apps directly from the app store to your device.

In the case of Windows 8, Microsoft has created a new Windows Store where Windows 8 apps are available. You access the Windows Store by clicking or tapping the Store tile on the Windows desktop, shown in Figure 22.1.

FIGURE 22.1

Click or tap the Store tile to shop the Windows Store.

As you can see in Figure 22.2, the Windows Store offers all manner of free and paid apps. You see the Spotlighted apps first, but you can then scroll right to view specific app listings.

In particular, tap the following tiles to see

- All stars
- Top paid
- Top free
- New releases
- Picks for you

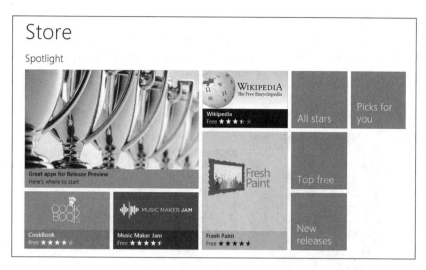

FIGURE 22.2

Shopping for apps in the Windows Store.

Scroll even further right and you can view apps organized by category—Games, Social, Entertainment, Photo, Music & Video, Sports, Books & Reference, News & Weather, Health & Fitness, Food & Dining, Lifestyle, Shopping, Travel, Finance, Productivity, Tools, Security, Business, Education, and Government. Tap a category to view all the apps within.

For example, Figure 22.3 shows the Entertainment category. You can sort the available apps by price, using the first pull-down list, or by other criteria in the second list—Noteworthy, Newest, Highest Rating, Lowest Price, or Highest Price.

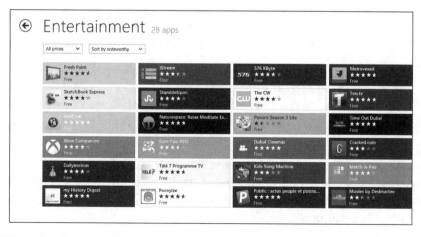

FIGURE 22.3

Entertainment apps in the Windows Store.

When you find an app you want, click or tap it. The app's page opens (see Figure 22.4). Read more about the app here, and then click or tap the Purchase or Install (for free apps) button to download and install the app on your computer. The new app should install at the end of your current Start screens.

FIGURE 22.4

Getting ready to download and install a new app.

Finding and Installing Apps from Your Local Retailer

All the apps in the Windows Store are optimized for use with Windows 8's interface. However, there are a great many more traditional software programs available that work just fine with Windows 8—albeit on the desktop, not in Windows 8 full-screen mode.

You can find these software programs at just about any consumer electronics store, office store, or computer store. Traditional software programs run the gamut from rather generic sub-$10 apps to more sophisticated productivity apps priced several hundred dollars or more.

Most software programs today come on either a CD-ROM or DVD disk; these disks typically come with their own built-in installation utilities. All you have to do is insert the program's disk in your computer's CD/DVD drive. The installation utility should run automatically.

When the installation utility launches, you usually see some sort of notification window asking if you want to install the new software. Assuming you do, click or tap the appropriate install or setup option.

The program's installation program should then proceed apace. All you have to do from here is follow the onscreen instructions—and, if instructed, reboot your computer at the end of the installation process.

Finding and Installing Apps Online

Nowadays, many software publishers make their products available via download from the Internet. Some users like this because they can get their new programs immediately without having to make a trip to the store.

TIP Most software publishers that offer downloadable software also let you order CD or DVD versions of their software—although you might have to pay extra to get a physical copy.

When you download a program from a major software publisher, the process is generally easy to follow. You probably have to read a page of do's and don'ts, agree to the publisher's licensing agreements, and then click a button to start the download. If you're purchasing a commercial program online, you also need to provide your credit card information, of course. Then, after you specify where (which folder on your hard disk) you want to save the downloaded file, the download begins.

When the download is complete, you should be notified via an onscreen dialog box. When prompted, choose to run the program you just downloaded. Follow the onscreen instructions from there.

Sometimes, programs you download from the Internet require the use of something called ActiveX controls—a technology that Internet Explorer normally blocks, for security reasons. If you try to install a program and nothing happens, look for a message at the bottom of the Internet Explorer screen. If you're sure that this is a legitimate part of the program you're installing, click or tap the message and select Install ActiveX Control from the pop-up menu. The installation should proceed normally from this point.

CAUTION Limit your software downloads to reputable download sites and software publisher sites. Programs downloaded from unofficial sites might contain computer viruses or spyware, which can damage your computer. Learn more in Chapter 31, "Protecting Against Computer Attacks, Malware, and Spam."

Understanding Cloud Computing Apps

There is another type of app that's becoming increasingly popular. You don't actually install this type of app on your computer; instead it runs over the Web from what we call the *cloud*.

In essence, the cloud is that nebulous assemblage of computers and servers on the Internet. Cloud-based computing involves storing your files on and running apps from the cloud. The apps aren't located on your PC; they're located in the cloud, and you run them from within Internet Explorer or a similar web browser.

Because of this, cloud apps are sometimes called web-based apps. They're just like traditional software-based apps, except they run over the Internet.

With traditional software applications, you have to install a copy of the application on each computer you own; the more computers you use, the more expensive that gets. Web-based applications, on the other hand, are typically free to use. That's always appealing.

Then there's the issue of the documents you create. With traditional software applications, your documents are stored on the computer on which they were created. If you want to edit a work document at home, you have to transfer that document from one computer to another—and then manage all the different "versions" you create.

 TIP Cloud apps are also great for group collaboration. Multiple users from different locations can access the same document over the Internet, in real time.

Document management is different with a web-based application. That's because your documents aren't stored on your computer; instead, they're stored on the Internet, just like the applications are. You can access your web-based documents from any computer, wherever you might be. So it's a lot easier to edit that work document at home or access your home budget while on the road.

Some other advantages of cloud apps are that they can run on any computer at any location, and they don't take up any hard disk space. This is especially important if you have a device without traditional hard disk storage, such as a tablet, ultrabook, or smartphone. Just point your web browser to the cloud app and start running—no installation required.

It isn't all positive, however. The primary downside of running cloud apps is that you need a stable Internet connection to do so. If you can't connect to the Internet, you can't access the cloud, and you can't run any apps. So if you're planning on getting work done on your next plane trip, cloud apps might not be the way to go.

For most other uses, however, cloud apps represent a viable alternative to traditional hard disk–based computer programs. Most cloud apps are low cost or free to use, and they offer much the same functionality as their more traditional software cousins.

What types of cloud apps are available? You name it, it's there. Later chapters talk about cloud-based office productivity apps, cloud-based calendars, and more. Just make sure you're connected to the Internet, then launch Internet Explorer and get ready to go.

THE ABSOLUTE MINIMUM

Here are the key points to remember from this chapter:

- You can purchase, download, and install Windows 8 apps from Microsoft's Windows Store.

- Traditional software apps come on either CD or DVD and install automatically when you insert the installation disk into your computer's CD/DVD drive.

- You can download many software apps from the Internet just by clicking a button (and providing your credit card number).

- Web-based or cloud apps don't install on your PC; instead they run over the Internet within your web browser.

23

DOING OFFICE WORK

When it comes to doing office work—writing letters and reports, crunching budgets, and creating presentations—you need a particular type of app called an *office suite*. In reality, an office suite is a combination of different programs, each designed to perform a specific task.

The most common office suite components are a *word processor* (for writing letters and memos), a *spreadsheet* (for crunching numbers), and a *presentation program* (for creating and giving presentations to small and large groups). With these office apps installed on your computer, you're ready to do just about anything you might be asked to do in the workplace.

What kind of office suite should you use? It all depends on how often and for what purposes you'll be using it.

Working with Microsoft Office

The most popular office suite today is Microsoft Office, which comes to you from the same folks who produce Microsoft Windows. Office has three main components—Word (word processing), Excel (spreadsheet), and PowerPoint (presentations), which means it should be able to handle just about anything you can throw at it.

Microsoft Office actually comes in two flavors. You can purchase Office as traditional desktop software (expensive but fully featured) or in a web-based version (free but somewhat limited, feature-wise). Both versions have their advantages and disadvantages.

Using Office on the Desktop

For most experienced computer users, there's only one office suite that matters, and it's the software version of Microsoft Office. This is the office suite you find used in 90% or more of the world's offices; it doesn't matter whether it's a large office or a small one, Microsoft Office reigns supreme.

The version of Office that reigns supreme is the traditional desktop software version. This is a software program—actually, a group of programs—that you install on your computer, typically from an installation CD or DVD.

There are several different editions of the Microsoft Office suite, each containing its own unique bundle of programs. Which Office programs you get depends on the edition of Office you have. Table 23.1 details the different editions for the current version, Microsoft Office 2010.

TABLE 23.1 Microsoft Office 2010 Editions

Edition	Applications Included	Price
Office Home and Student	Word (word processing) Excel (spreadsheet) PowerPoint (presentations) OneNote (notes)	$119.99
Office Home and Business	Word (word processing) Excel (spreadsheet) PowerPoint (presentations) OneNote (notes) Outlook (email and calendar)	$199.99

TABLE 23.1 (continued)

Edition	Applications Included	Price
Office Professional	Word (word processing)	$349.99
	Excel (spreadsheet)	
	PowerPoint (presentations)	
	OneNote (notes)	
	Outlook (email and calendar)	
	Access (database)	
	Publisher (desktop publishing)	

For most home users, the Home and Student Edition is the right fit—it includes the three major apps and is somewhat affordable. If you need an email client, too, then go for the slightly more expensive Home and Business Edition. And if you also need database and desktop publishing functionality, go all the way to the much more expensive Professional Edition.

 NOTE Many new PCs come with a trial version of Office (typically the Home and Student Edition) preinstalled. You can use this version for 90 days at no charge; at that point, you have the option of purchasing the software or having the trial version deactivated.

Using Office on the Web

If you don't want to go to all the trouble of purchasing and installing an expensive piece of software, you can still use Microsoft Office on the Web. Microsoft offers a web-based version of Office, dubbed Microsoft Office Web Apps, via its SkyDrive cloud-based storage system.

This web-based version of Office is free, which is always appealing. The individual apps, however, don't come with all the sophisticated functionality of the software versions, so there's a trade-off. Bottom line, if you're not a power user, you might be able to get by with the free Office Web Apps instead of purchasing and installing the full Office version on CD/DVD.

You access Office Web Apps from within Internet Explorer. Launch the web browser and go to skydrive.live.com. You now see all the files you've previously uploaded to SkyDrive, organized in the folders you created, as shown in Figure 23.1. Note that Word, Excel, and PowerPoint files are displayed with icons that include the app graphics, so you can quickly see what kind of file you're looking at.

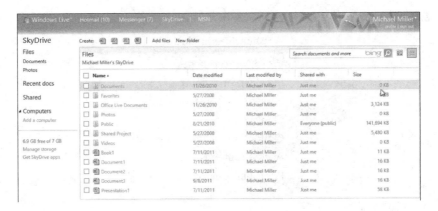

FIGURE 23.1

Working with Office documents in Microsoft SkyDrive.

NOTE You can also open and edit existing documents using the SkyDrive app in Windows 8. However, at this writing, you can't use the SkyDrive app to create new documents; you have to do this from within Internet Explorer.

To open an existing document, double-click it with your mouse. To open a new document of a given type (Word, Excel, PowerPoint, or OneNote), click the appropriate icon in the Create bar at the top of the screen.

The designated app opens in Internet Explorer. You can begin to enter text and numbers to create the content of the new document. We'll look at each of the three major Office Web Apps next.

NOTE The next few sections of this chapter focus on the Web-based versions of Microsoft Word, Microsoft Excel, and Microsoft PowerPoint. You can learn more about Office Web Apps at office.microsoft.com/en-us/web-apps/.

Which Version of Office Should You Use?

Given the choice of a free web-based version of Microsoft Office or a somewhat expensive desktop version, many users choose the web-based Office. There's a good argument for that—free is always more attractive than paid.

In the case of Office Web Apps, what you get is kind of a basic version of the full-featured Office you can buy in a store. For most users, Office Web Apps offers all the features you need; it's great for doing letters and memos, home budgets and planning, and even basic presentations. There's the added plus that you can run Office Web Apps on any Windows-based PC or tablet with having to install anything. Getting up and running is as quick and easy as clicking a few buttons.

If your needs are more sophisticated, however, the paid desktop version of Office is the way to go. There are so many advanced functions in the Office software that it's unlikely you'll ever use them all. But if your work involves creating brochures or newsletters, fancy comparison spreadsheets, or sophisticated presentations with animations and such, you have to go the Office software route; you just can't do some of this stuff in the web-based version.

Word Processing with Microsoft Word

When you want to write a letter, fire off a quick memo, create a report, or create a newsletter, you use a word processing app. For most computer users, that means Microsoft Word—in either its web-based or traditional desktop versions.

Exploring the Word Workspace

Before we get started, let's take a quick tour of the Word workspace—so you know what's what and what's where.

If you're using the web-based version of Word, dubbed Word Web App, you see the screen shown in Figure 23.2. At the top of the screen is the Ribbon, which provides all the buttons and controls you need to create and edit a document. Different tabs on the Ribbon display different collections of functions; click a tab, such as File, Home, Insert, or View, to access commands associated with that particular operation.

Beneath the Ribbon is the document itself. Begin typing at the cursor.

The software version of Word has a similar interface. As you can see in Figure 23.3, the Word software uses a similar Ribbon, but with a few more tabs— Page Layout, References, Mailings, and Review. This is because of the added functionality of the desktop version of Word; you can do more sophisticated desktop publishing–like stuff with the traditional Word program than you can with the Word Web App.

Whichever version of Word you're using, click a tab on the Ribbon to access all the related commands. For example, the File tab contains basic file opening and saving operations; the Home tab contains most of the editing and formatting functions you use on a daily basis; the Insert tab contains commands to add images and tables to a document; and the View tab contains commands that enable you to change how a document is viewed or displayed.

Ribbon tabs

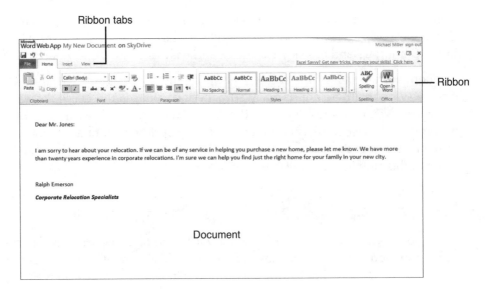

FIGURE 23.2

The Word Web App workspace—all functions are on the Ribbon.

Ribbon tabs

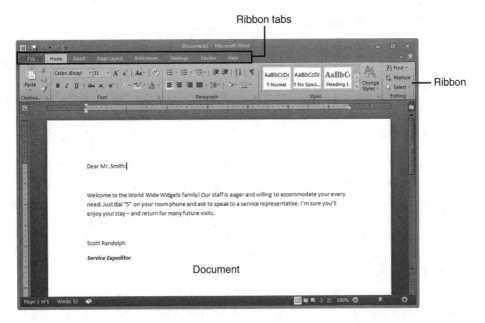

FIGURE 23.3

The traditional Word desktop workspace—similar but not identical to the web-based version.

TIP If you're not sure just what button on a Ribbon or toolbar does what, you're not alone—those little graphics are sometimes difficult to decipher. To display the name of any specific button, just hover your cursor over the button until the descriptive *ScreenTip* appears.

Working with Documents

Anything you create with Word is called a *document*. A document is nothing more than a computer file that can be copied, moved, and deleted—or edited—from within Word.

To create a new document in the Word Web App, follow these steps:

1. From the main SkyDrive page (skydrive.live.com), click the Word icon in the Create bar.

2. When the New Microsoft Word Document dialog box appears, enter a name for this new document and click the Create button.

To create a new document in the desktop version of Word, follow these steps:

1. Click the File tab on the Ribbon.

2. When the File screen appears, click New.

3. Word now displays a selection of available *templates*. If you want to base your document on one of these templates, double-click it now. Otherwise, double-click Blank Document.

Opening an existing document is easy in the Word Web App; just go to the main SkyDrive page, navigate to the document, and click it. In the desktop version of Word, select the File tab and click Open; when the Open dialog box appears, navigate to and select the file you want to open, then click the Open button.

Of course, you must save to a file every document you make that you want to keep. To do this, select the File tab and click Save.

NOTE The first time you save a file in the desktop version of Word, you're prompted to specify a filename and location.

Entering Text

You enter text in a Word document at the *insertion point*, which appears onscreen as a blinking cursor. When you start typing on your keyboard, the new text is added at the insertion point.

You move the insertion point with your mouse by clicking a new position in your text. You move the insertion point with your keyboard by using your keyboard's arrow keys.

Editing Text

After you've entered your text, it's time to edit. With Word you can delete, cut, copy, and paste text—or graphics—to and from anywhere in your document, or between documents.

Before you can edit text, though, you have to *select* the text to edit. The easiest way to select text is with your mouse; just hold down your mouse button and drag the cursor over the text you want to select. You also can select text using your keyboard; use the Shift key—in combination with other keys—to highlight blocks of text. For example, Shift+left arrow selects one character to the left; Shift+End selects all text to the end of the current line.

Any text you select appears as white text against a black highlight. After you've selected a block of text, you can then edit it in a number of ways, as detailed in Table 23.2.

TABLE 23.2   Word Editing Operations

Operation	Keystroke
Delete	Del
Copy	Ctrl+Ins or Ctrl+C
Cut	Shift+Del or Ctrl+X
Paste	Shift+Ins or Ctrl+V

Formatting Text

After your text is entered and edited, you can use Word's numerous formatting options to add some pizzazz to your document. Fortunately, formatting text is easy.

When you want to format your text, select the Home Ribbon. This Ribbon includes buttons for bold, italic, and underline, as well as font, font size, and font color. To format a block of text, highlight the text and then click the desired format button.

Checking Spelling and Grammar

If you're not a great speller, you'll appreciate Word's automatic spell checking. You can see it right onscreen; just deliberately misspell a word, and you see a squiggly red line under the misspelling. That's Word telling you you've made a spelling error.

When you see that squiggly red line, position your cursor on top of the misspelled word and then right-click your mouse. Word displays a pop-up menu with its suggestions for spelling corrections. You can choose a replacement word from the list or return to your document and manually change the misspelling.

Sometimes Word meets a word it doesn't recognize, even though the word is spelled correctly. In these instances, you can add the new word to Word's spelling dictionary by right-clicking the word and selecting Add from the pop-up menu.

 NOTE   The desktop version of Word also includes a built-in grammar checker. When Word identifies bad grammar in your document, it underlines the offending passage with a green squiggly line. Right-click anywhere in the passage to view Word's grammatical suggestions.

Printing Your Document

When you've finished editing your document, you can instruct Word to send a copy to your printer. To print a document, select the File tab and click Print. The document is sent to your printer, and a hardcopy should be in your hands shortly.

Working with Pictures

Although memos and letters might look fine if they contain nothing but text, you might want to jazz up other types of documents—newsletters, reports, and so on.

The easiest way to add a graphic to your document is to use Word's built-in Clip Art Gallery. The Clip Art Gallery is a collection of ready-to-use illustrations and photos, organized by topic, that you can paste directly into your Word documents.

To insert a piece of clip art, select the Insert Ribbon and click the Clip Art button; the Insert Clip Art dialog box (or, in the desktop version, the Clip Art pane) displays.

Enter one or more keywords into the search box and then press the Enter key. Pictures matching your criteria display, as shown in Figure 23.4. Double-click a graphic to insert it into your document.

FIGURE 23.4

Searching for clip art.

You're not limited to using graphics from the Clip Art Gallery. Word enables you to insert any type of graphics file into your document—including GIF, JPG, BMP, TIF, and other popular graphics formats.

To insert a graphics file into your document, select the Insert Ribbon and click the Picture button. When the Files page appears, navigate to and select the picture you want to insert. Click the Open button.

 TIP To move your picture to another position in your document, use your mouse to drag it to its new position. You also can resize the graphic by clicking the picture and then dragging a selection handle to resize that side or corner of the graphic.

Number Crunching with Microsoft Excel

When you're on your computer and want to crunch some numbers, you use a program called a *spreadsheet*. Microsoft Excel is the spreadsheet program in the Microsoft Office suite, and it's available in both web-based and traditional desktop versions.

Exploring the Excel Workspace

A spreadsheet is nothing more than a giant list. Your list can contain just about any type of data you can think of—text, numbers, and even dates. You can take any of the numbers on your list and use them to calculate new numbers. You can sort the items on your list, pretty them up, and print the important points in a report. You can even graph your numbers in a pie, line, or bar chart!

In a spreadsheet, everything is stored in little boxes called *cells*. Your spreadsheet is divided into lots of these cells, each located in a specific location on a giant grid made of *rows* and *columns*. Each cell represents the intersection of a particular row and column.

As you can see in Figure 23.5, each column has an alphabetic label (A, B, C, and so on). Each row, on the other hand, has a numeric label (1, 2, 3, and so on). The location of each cell is the combination of its column and row locations. For example, the cell in the upper-left corner of the spreadsheet is in column A and row 1; therefore, its location is signified as A1. The cell to the right of it is B1, and the cell below A1 is A2.

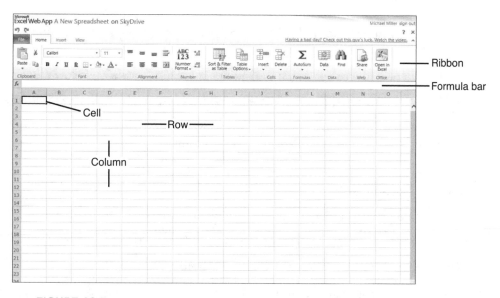

FIGURE 23.5

An Excel spreadsheet—divided into many rows and columns.

Entering Data

Entering text or numbers into a spreadsheet is easy. Just remember that data is entered into each cell individually—then you can fill up a spreadsheet with hundreds or thousands of cells filled with their own data.

To enter data into a specific cell, follow these steps:

1. Select the cell you want to enter data into.

2. Type your text or numbers into the cell; what you type is echoed in the Formula bar at the top of the screen.

3. When you're done typing data into the cell, press Enter.

 TIP You can enter numbers and text directly into the selected cell, or into the Formula bar at the top of the spreadsheet. The Formula bar echoes the contents of the active cell.

Inserting and Deleting Rows and Columns

Sometimes you need to go back to an existing spreadsheet and insert some new information.

To insert a new row or column in the middle of your spreadsheet, follow these steps:

1. Click the row or column header after where you want to make the insertion.

2. Select the Home Ribbon and click the down arrow below the Insert button; then select either Insert Rows or Insert Columns.

Excel now inserts a new row or column either above or to the left of the row or column you selected.

To delete an existing row or column, follow these steps:

1. Click the header for the row or column you want to delete.

2. Select the Home Ribbon and click the Delete button.

The row or column you selected is deleted, and all other rows or columns move up or over to fill the space.

Adjusting Column Width

If the data you enter into a cell is too long, you only see the first part of that data—there'll be a bit to the right that looks cut off. It's not cut off, of course; it just can't be seen because it's longer than the current column is wide.

You can fix this problem by adjusting the column width. Wider columns allow more data to be shown; with narrow columns you can display more columns per page.

To change the column width, move your cursor to the column header, and position it on the dividing line on the right side of the column you want to adjust. When the cursor changes shape, click the left button on your mouse and drag the column divider to the right (to make a wider column) or to the left (to make a smaller column). Release the mouse button when the column is the desired width.

 TIP To make a column the exact width for the longest amount of data entered, position your cursor over the dividing line to the right of the column header and double-click your mouse. This makes the column width automatically "fit" your current data.

Using Formulas and Functions

Excel lets you enter just about any type of algebraic formula into any cell. You can use these formulas to add, subtract, multiply, divide, and perform any nested combination of those operations.

Excel knows that you're entering a formula when you type an equal sign (=) into any cell. You start your formula with the equal sign and enter your operations *after* the equal sign.

For example, if you want to add 1 plus 2, enter this formula into a cell: **=1+2**. When you press Enter, the formula disappears from the cell—and the result, or *value*, is displayed.

Table 23.3 shows the algebraic operators you can use in Excel formulas.

TABLE 23.3 Excel Operators

Operation	Operator
Add	+
Subtract	–
Multiply	*
Divide	/

So if you want to multiply 10 by 5, enter **=10*5**. If you want to divide 10 by 5, enter **=10/5**.

Including Other Cells in a Formula

If all you're doing is adding and subtracting numbers, you might as well use a calculator. Where a spreadsheet becomes truly useful is when you use it to perform operations based on the contents of specific cells.

To perform calculations using values from cells in your spreadsheet, you enter the cell location into the formula. For example, if you want to add cells A1 and A2, enter this formula: **=A1+A2**. And if the numbers in either cell A1 or A2 change, the total automatically changes, as well.

An even easier way to perform operations involving spreadsheet cells is to select them with your mouse while you're entering the formula. To do this, follow these steps:

1. Select the cell that will contain the formula.

2. Type =.

3. Click the first cell you want to include in your formula; that cell location is automatically entered in your formula.

4. Type an algebraic operator, such as +, −, *, or /.

5. Click the second cell you want to include in your formula.

6. Repeat steps 4 and 5 to include other cells in your formula.

7. Press Enter when your formula is complete.

Quick Addition with AutoSum

The most common operation in any spreadsheet is the addition of a group of numbers. Excel makes summing up a row or column of numbers easy via the AutoSum function.

All you have to do is follow these steps:

1. Select the cell at the end of a row or column of numbers, where you want the total to appear.

2. Select the Home Ribbon and click the AutoSum button.

Excel automatically sums all the preceding numbers and places the total in the selected cell.

Excel's AutoSum also includes a few other automatic calculations. When you click the down arrow on the bottom of the AutoSum button, you can perform the following operations:

- **Average**, which calculates the average of the selected cells

- **Count Numbers**, which counts the number of selected cells

- **Max**, which returns the largest value in the selected cells

- **Min**, which returns the smallest value in the selected cells

 TIP   When you're referencing consecutive cells in a formula, you can just enter the first and last number or the series separated by a colon. For example, cells A1 through A4 can be entered as A1:A4.

Using Functions

In addition to the basic algebraic operators previously discussed, Excel includes a variety of *functions* that replace the complex steps present in many formulas. For example, if you want to total all the cells in column A, you could enter the formula **=A1+A2+A3+A4**. Or, you could use the SUM function, which lets you sum a column or row of numbers without having to type every cell into the formula. (And when you use AutoSum, it's simply applying the SUM function.)

In short, a function is a type of prebuilt formula.

You enter a function in the following format: **=function(argument)**, where **function** is the name of the function and **argument** is the range of cells or other data you want to calculate. Using the last example, to sum cells A1 through A4, you'd use the following function-based formula: **=sum(A1,A2,A3,A4)**.

Excel includes hundreds of functions. You can access and insert any of Excel's functions by following these steps:

1. Select the cell where you want to insert the function.

2. Select the Home Ribbon and click the down arrow beneath the AutoSum button and select More Functions.

3. When the Insert Function dialog box appears, as shown in Figure 24.6, pull down the Select a Category list to display the functions of a particular type.

4. Click the function you want to insert.

5. If the function has related arguments, a Function Arguments dialog box displays; enter the arguments and click OK.

6. The function you selected is inserted into the current cell. You can manually enter the cells or numbers into the function's argument.

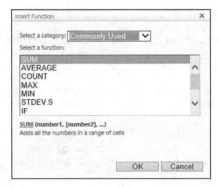

FIGURE 23.6

Choose from hundreds of functions in Excel.

 TIP In the desktop version of Excel, you can access more functions directly from the Formula Ribbon.

Formatting Your Spreadsheet

You don't have to settle for boring-looking spreadsheets. You can format how the data appears in your spreadsheet—including the format of any numbers you enter.

When you enter a number into a cell, Excel applies what it calls a "general" format to the number—it just displays the number, right-aligned, with no commas or dollar signs. You can, however, select a specific number format to apply to any cells in your spreadsheet that contain numbers.

All of Excel's number formatting options are in the Number section of the Home Ribbon. Click the dollar sign button to choose an accounting format, the percent button to choose a percentage format, the comma button to choose a comma format, or the General button to choose from all available formats. You can also click the Increase Decimal and Decrease Decimal buttons to move the decimal point left or right.

You can also apply a variety of other formatting options to the contents of your cells. You can make your text bold or italic, change the font type or size, or even add shading or borders to selected cells.

These formatting options are found in the Font and Alignment sections of the Home Ribbon. Just select the cell(s) you want to format; then click the appropriate formatting button.

Creating a Chart

Numbers are fine, but sometimes the story behind the numbers can be better told with a picture. The way you take a picture of numbers is with a *chart*, such as the one shown in Figure 23.7.

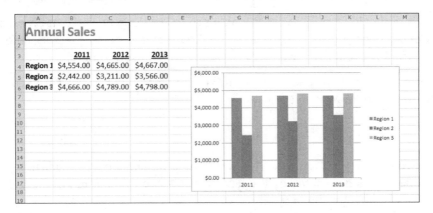

FIGURE 23.7

Some numbers are better represented via a chart.

You create a chart based on numbers you've previously entered into your Excel spreadsheet. It works like this:

1. Select the range of cells you want to include in your chart. (If the range has a header row or column, include that row or column when selecting the cells.)

2. Select the Insert Ribbon, shown in Figure 23.8.

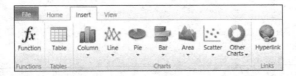

FIGURE 23.8

Select the type of chart you want to insert.

3. In the Charts section of the Ribbon, click the button for the type of chart you want to create.

4. Excel displays a variety of charts within that general category. Select the type of chart you want.

5. When the chart appears in your worksheet, select the Design Ribbon to edit the chart's type, layout, and style.

Giving Presentations with Microsoft PowerPoint

When you need to present information to a group of people, the hip way to do it is with a PowerPoint presentation. Microsoft PowerPoint is a presentation program—that is, an app you can use to both create and give presentations.

If you work in an office, you probably see at least one PowerPoint presentation a week—if not one a day. Teachers use PowerPoint to present lesson materials in class. Kids even use PowerPoint to prepare what used to be oral reports.

So get with the program—and learn how to create your own great-looking presentations with PowerPoint!

Exploring the PowerPoint Workspace

As you can see in Figure 23.9, PowerPoint looks like the other Office apps. The workspace is dominated by the Ribbon at the top of the screen, with the current slide displayed in the middle.

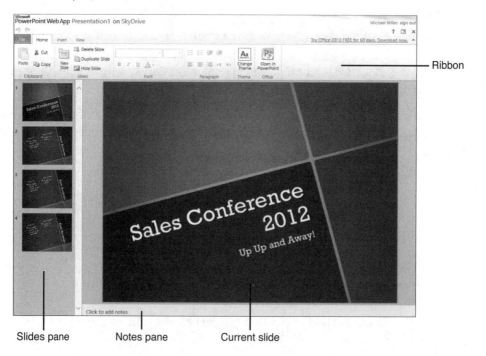

FIGURE 23.9

The PowerPoint workspace.

On the left side of the workspace is something unique to PowerPoint—the Slides pane, which displays all the slides in your presentation, one after another. Below the current slide is a Notes pane, which lets you enter presentation notes.

Applying a Theme

You don't have to reinvent the wheel when it comes to designing the look of your presentation. PowerPoint includes a number of slide *themes* that you can apply to any presentation, blank or otherwise. A theme specifies the color scheme, fonts, layout, and background for each slide you create in your presentation.

 NOTE In the desktop version of PowerPoint, themes are located on the Design Ribbon.

To apply a new theme to your current presentation, select the Home Ribbon and click the Change Theme button. This displays the Select Theme dialog box, shown in Figure 23.10; select the theme you want and then click the Apply button.

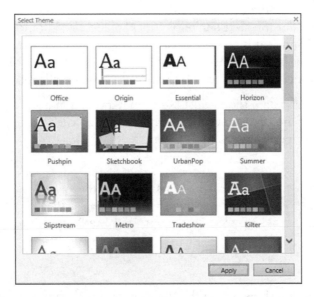

FIGURE 23.10

Selecting a new theme in the PowerPoint Web App.

It's that simple. All the colors, fonts, and everything else from the theme are automatically applied to all the slides in your presentation—and every new slide you add also carries the selected design.

NOTE Don't confuse the slide *layout*, which defines which elements appear on the slide, with the slide *template*, which defines the colors and fonts used.

Inserting New Slides

When you create a new presentation, PowerPoint starts with a single slide—the *title slide*. Naturally, you need to insert additional slides to create a complete presentation. PowerPoint lets you insert different types of slides, with different types of layouts for different types of information.

To insert a new slide, all you have to do is select the Home Ribbon and click the New Slide button. This displays the New Slide dialog box; select the slide layout you want, then click the Add Slide button.

Adding and Formatting Text

You can enter text for a slide directly into that slide. When PowerPoint creates a new slide, the areas for text entry are designated with boilerplate text—"Click to add title" (for the slide's title) or "Click to add text" (for regular text or bullet points). Adding text is as easy as clicking the boilerplate text and then entering your own words and numbers. Press Enter to move to a new line or bullet. To enter a sub-bullet, press the Tab key first; to back up a level, press Shift+Tab.

Formatting text on a slide is just like formatting text in a word processing document. Select the text you want to format and then click the appropriate button in the Font section of the Home Ribbon.

TIP The desktop version of PowerPoint enables you to add animated transitions between slides. The PowerPoint Web App does not have this feature. If you want to use slide transitions you'll have to switch to the desktop PowerPoint software.

Start the Show!

To run your slideshow, select the View tab and click the Slide Show button. (In the desktop version, click the Slide Show button at the very bottom of the workspace.) To move from one slide to the next, all you have to do is click your mouse.

Exploring Other Office Suites

Microsoft Office is just one of several office suites on the market today. You might also want to check out the following competing suites:

- **Google Drive** (drive.google.com, free)—This is the primary web-based competitor to Office Web Apps. It's free to use and based totally in the cloud. Includes Google Docs (word processor), Google Spreadsheets, and Google Presentations.

- **WordPerfect Office Home and Student Edition** (www.corel.com, $99.99)— This is a set of traditional desktop programs, including WordPerfect (word processor), Quattro Pro (spreadsheet), Presentations, and Corel WordPerfect Lightning (notes). Also available in Standard, Professional, and Legal editions.

- **Zoho Office** (www.zoho.com, free)—Another popular web-based office suite. Includes word processor, spreadsheet, presentations, and other apps.

 CAUTION Note that if you use Microsoft Office on another computer (at the office, for example), you might not be able to edit your Office documents with one of these other office suites. If you need full compatibility for Office documents, stick with the Microsoft Office suite.

THE ABSOLUTE MINIMUM

Here are the key points to remember from this chapter:

- To perform common work-related tasks, you need the individual apps that make up an office suite.

- The most popular office suite today is Microsoft Office, which is available in either web-based or traditional desktop software versions.

- Microsoft Word is the word processor in Microsoft Office, used to write letters and reports.

- Microsoft Excel is Office's spreadsheet program, used for budgets and other number crunching.

- Microsoft PowerPoint is used to create and give presentations.

- Other popular office suites include the WordPerfect Office software and the web-based Google Drive and Zoho Office.

STAYING ORGANIZED

In today's hectic world, you need to stay organized. Fortunately, you can use your new computer to help you plan your schedule—to track appointments, manage your to-do list, and such. It's all a matter of entering the proper information into the appropriate app, and letting your computer do its thing.

There are a number of different ways to use your computer to organize your day. Windows 8 includes a pretty good Calendar app that a lot of people like; there are also various web-based calendars and task management apps you might find worthwhile.

Using Windows 8's Calendar App

Let's start with the Calendar app included with Windows 8. Like most Windows 8-specific apps, it's integrated well into the Windows system.

This integration starts on the Start screen. As you can see in Figure 24.1, the Calendar tile is "live"—that is, it displays a scrolling list of upcoming appointments. This way you can see what's coming up, without even having to launch the app.

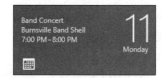

FIGURE 24.1

The "live" tile for the Calendar app.

Displaying Different Views

When you click or tap the Calendar tile, you see a monthly calendar, like the one in Figure 24.2. All your scheduled appointments are listed here. To scroll back or forward through the months, use your keyboard's left and right arrow keys or swipe the screen (on a touchscreen device). To re-center the calendar on the current day, display the Options bar then click or tap Today.

FIGURE 24.2

The Calendar app in monthly view.

You can also display your calendar in weekly or daily views. Right-click anywhere on the screen to display the Options bar, shown in Figure 24.3. Click or tap the desired view—Day, Week, or Month. (Figure 24.4 shows the daily view; Figure 24.5 shows the weekly view.)

FIGURE 24.3

The Calendar app's Options bar.

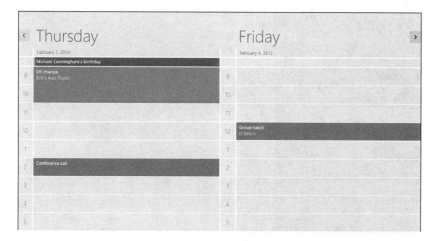

FIGURE 24.4

The Calendar app in daily view. (Actually displays two days side by side.)

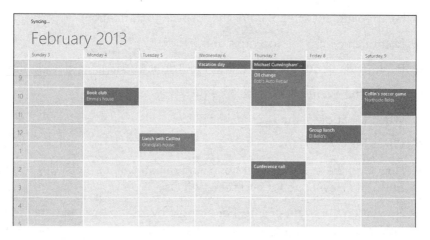

FIGURE 24.5

The Calendar app in weekly view.

To view more details about an appointment, click or tap the item. The appointment screen opens; you can then edit anything about the appointment. Click or tap the save button to save your changes.

Creating a New Appointment

To create a new appointment, click or tap the day of the appointment. (If you're in daily or weekly views, click or tap the day and time you want the appointment to start.) The appointment screen displays (see Figure 24.6).

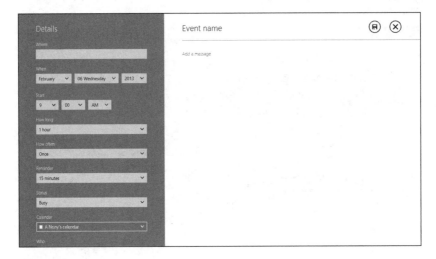

FIGURE 24.6

Creating a new appointment.

On the appointment screen, enter the following information:

- Event name, into the top right of the form.

- Information about the event, into the Add a Message section on the right.

- Where the event takes place.

- When (what date) the event takes place.

- When the event starts.

- How long the event lasts, in hours and minutes. If it's an all-day event, pull down the How Long list and select All Day.

- How often the event occurs. For a single event, accept the default Once option. For recurring events, pull down the How Often list and select a frequency.

- Use the Reminder list to set a reminder for a specific amount of time before the event starts.

- Set your status for this event; the default setting is Busy.

- Pull down the Calendar list and select which calendar you want to use for this event.

- If you want to invite others to this event, enter their email addresses into the Who box.

- If you'd prefer to keep this event private, check the Private box.

When you're done entering information about this event, click or tap the Save button on the top right.

 NOTE The Windows 8 Calendar app automatically connects to other calendars associated with your Microsoft Account, including your Hotmail Calendar and Google Calendar, and displays events from those calendars. Connected calendars are shown in the Calendar list on the appointment page.

Using Web-Based Calendars

The Windows 8 Calendar app is nice, and it's free, but it's not the most versatile calendar out there. When you have a lot of public or community events you share with other people, it makes sense to go to a web-based calendar. It's one thing to keep a private schedule on a single PC, but most of us have schedules that include a lot of public or shared events. In addition, if you keep a personal calendar on your home PC, you can't reference it from work or when you're traveling. That limits the calendar program's usefulness.

This is why, instead of using a calendar that's wedded to a single computer, many users prefer web-based calendars. A web-based calendar stores your appointments on the Internet, where you can access them from any computer or device that has an Internet connection. This enables you to check your schedule when you're on the road, even if your assistant in the office or your spouse at home has added new appointments since you left. Web-based calendars are also extremely easy to share with other users in any location, which make them great for collaborative projects.

Most web-based calendars are free and offer similar online sharing and collaboration features. The most popular of these calendars include

- 30Boxes (www.30boxes.com)

- Famundo (www.famundo.com)

- Google Calendar (calendar.google.com), shown in Figure 24.7.

- Hotmail Calendar (mail.live.com/mail/calendar.aspx)

- Hunt Calendars (www.huntcal.com)

- Yahoo! Calendar (calendar.yahoo.com)

- Zoho Calendar (calendar.zoho.com)

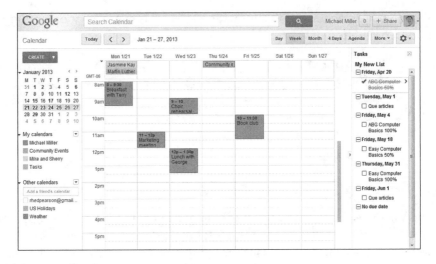

FIGURE 24.7

Google Calendar—one of the most popular web-based calendars.

Using Web-Based To-Do Lists

Just as you can track your appointments with a web-based calendar, you can track your to-do lists with web-based to-do lists. These apps enable you to manage everything from simple to-do lists to complex group tasks, and you can do it over the Internet so you can collaborate with other users.

The most popular of these web-based task management applications include the following:

- Bla-Bla List (www.blablalist.com)

- HiTask (www.hitask.com)

- Hiveminder (www.hiveminder.com)

- iPrioritize (www.iprioritize.com)

- Remember the Milk (www.rememberthemilk.com)

- Trackslife (www.trackslife.com)

- Vitalist (www.vitalist.com)

- Voo2Do (www.voo2do.com)

- Zoho Planner (planner.zoho.com)

 TIP Some web-based calendars, such as Google Calendar, also offer task management and to-do list functions.

THE ABSOLUTE MINIMUM

Here are the key points to remember from this chapter:

- The Windows 8 Calendar app is a good, basic way to manage your schedule and appointments.

- Web-based calendars enable you to access your schedule from any computer, and you can collaborate with others on public calendars.

- Web-based task management services help you manage your to-do lists.

25

VIEWING AND SHARING DIGITAL PHOTOS

In the old days, if you wanted to share your photos with friends and family, you had to have extra prints made and then hand them out or mail them off, as appropriate. This approach is not only time-consuming, it's costly; you have to pay money for each extra print you make.

In today's age of digital photography, it's a whole lot easier to view and share your photos on your computer, over the Internet. In fact, you can even edit your digital photos to eliminate red eye and such before you share them. It's a whole new digital world out there—all you need is a digital camera and your new computer.

Transferring Pictures from Your Digital Camera

If you want to edit or print your digital photos, you need to connect that digital camera to your PC—which is relatively easy to do. You can transfer digital photos directly from your camera's memory card, download pictures from your camera via a USB connection, or even scan existing photo prints.

Connecting via USB

Connecting a digital camera to your PC is easy. All you have to do is connect a USB cable from your camera to a USB port on your computer. With this type of setup, Windows recognizes your camera or scanner as soon as you plug it in and installs the appropriate drivers automatically.

When you connect a USB cable between your camera and your PC, Windows should recognize when your camera is connected and automatically download the pictures in your camera, while displaying a dialog box that notifies you of what's going on. That's unless you have another photo management program installed.

Some digital cameras come with their own proprietary picture management programs. If you've installed such a program on your PC, this is the program that probably launches when you connect your camera to your computer. If this program launches and asks to download the pictures from your camera, follow the onscreen instructions to proceed.

You might also have installed a third-party photo editing program, such as Adobe Photoshop Elements. If so, this might be the program that launches when you connect your camera to your PC. Follow the onscreen instructions to proceed.

 CAUTION   Depending on the apps you have installed on your system, you might get multiple prompts to download photos when you connect your camera. If this happens, pick the program you'd prefer to work with and close the other dialog boxes.

Transferring Pictures from a Memory Card

Copying digital pictures via USB cable is nice—if your camera supports this method. For many users, an easier approach is to use a memory card reader. Many PCs have memory card readers built in; if yours doesn't, you can always add a low-cost external memory reader via USB. You then insert the memory card from your digital camera into the memory card reader, and your PC recognizes the card as if it were another hard disk.

In many cases Windows recognizes a memory card full of photos and asks if you want to download them. If not, you can use File Explorer to copy files from the memory card to your computer. Just open File Explorer and click the drive icon for the memory card. This displays the card's contents, typically in a subfolder labeled DCIM. You can then move, copy, and delete the photos stored on the card, as you would with any other type of file in Windows.

Scanning a Picture

If your photos are of the old-fashioned print variety, you can still turn them into digital files using a flatbed scanner. The scanning starts automatically when you press the Scan button on your scanner. Your print photo is saved as a digital file for future use.

Note that some third-party software programs, such as Adobe Photoshop Elements, also let you scan photos from the program. In most instances, scanning via one of these programs offers more options than scanning via Windows; you can change the resolution (in dots per inch) of the scanned image, crop the image, even adjust brightness and contrast if you want. If you're scanning a lot of old, washed-out prints, this approach might produce better results.

 NOTE By default, Windows stores all your pictures in the Pictures library, which you can access from File Explorer. This folder includes a number of features specific to the management of picture files, as well as all the normal file-related tasks, such as copying, moving, or even deleting your photos.

Viewing Your Photos in Windows

Viewing photos in Windows 8 is a snap. All you have to do is click or tap the Photos tile on the Start page; the Photos app, which you use for viewing photos, launches.

As you can see in Figure 25.1, the Photos app consolidates photos stored in a number of places. In particular, you see photos stored

- On your computer, in the Pictures library

- Online on Facebook, if you're a member

- Online on Flickr, if you have an account on that site

- Online in your SkyDrive account, if you've uploaded any photos there.

- On any external device connected to your computer, such as a USB drive or memory card.

FIGURE 25.1

Viewing photo locations with the Photos app.

NOTE Flickr (www.flickr.com) is a popular photo sharing site for digital photography enthusiasts. Learn more later in this chapter.

The number of photos for each location is noted as a small number beneath the main tile. Click or tap any of these tiles to see specific folders stored at that location. Continue clicking and tapping to view the contents of a given folder or subfolder.

Figure 25.2 shows the individual pictures within a folder. Scroll left or right to view additional photos. Click or tap a photo to view it full-screen; you can then use your mouse, keyboard, or finger to scroll left or right to additional pictures. Press Esc to exit full-screen mode.

You can, if you like, view all the pictures on your computer (including those contained in additional subfolders) by date. Display the Options bar, shown in Figure 25.3, then click or tap Browse by Date. You now see tiles organized by month (most recent first), as shown in Figure 25.4; click or tap a tile to view all photos taken that month.

TIP Here's another fun way to view your photos. Click or tap Slide Show in the Options bar and Windows displays your photos one at a time, full-screen, in random order. Playing a slide show like this can be quite relaxing when the rest of your work is done.

FIGURE 25.2

Scrolling through your pictures with the Photos app.

FIGURE 25.3

The Options bar in the Photos app.

FIGURE 25.4

Viewing photos by date.

If you find a picture you'd like to delete, it's easy enough to get rid of it. Just right-click the picture to select it; this also displays the Options bar with three new items on the left, as shown in Figure 25.5. Click or tap Delete to delete the selected item(s).

 NOTE If you have a pure touchscreen device, you can't delete photos this easily. Instead, you have to display the photo first, and then swipe up from the bottom of the screen to display the Options bar. From there you can tap Delete to get rid of the picture.

FIGURE 25.5

Deleting a picture in the Photos app.

Editing Your Digital Photos

The Windows Photos app is for viewing photos only. If you need to edit your photos, you need a full-featured photo editing program. This type of program lets you edit your photos to remove red eye, crop out unwanted elements, adjust color and brightness, and so forth. Many of these programs also enable you to organize your photos and make photo prints on your PC's printer.

When it comes to picking a photo editing program, you have a lot of choices. You can choose a low-priced, consumer-oriented program or a high-priced program targeted at professional photographers. For most users, the low-priced programs do everything you need. The most popular of these include the following:

- Adobe Photoshop Elements (www.adobe.com), $99.99

- Paint Shop Pro (www.corel.com), $79.99

- Photo Explosion Deluxe (www.novadevelopment.com), $49.95

- Picasa (www.picasa.com), free

 NOTE Don't confuse the affordable Adobe Photoshop Elements with the much higher-priced (and more sophisticated) Adobe Photoshop CS, which is used by most professional photographers.

You can also find photo editing programs in the Windows Store. Look in the Photo section of the store.

For example, Picasa, shown in Figure 25.6, runs on the traditional Windows desktop and enables you to both organize and edit your digital photos. After you select a photo in the photo organizer, you can perform all sorts of fixes. As you can see in Figure 25.7, Picasa enables you to crop or straighten a photo, remove red eye, adjust contrast and color, and more. You can even apply a variety of special effects. It's pretty much a matter of clicking or tapping the button for the fix or effect you want to apply.

FIGURE 25.6

Organizing your digital photos with Picasa.

 NOTE Picasa is a free photo editing program from the folks at Google. It accompanies Google's free online photo-sharing site, Picasa Web Albums (picasaweb.photo.com).

Note that all of these programs perform most of the same functions. It's really a matter of finding one that feels comfortable to you—and fits within your budget. (That's why Picasa is nice—it's free!)

FIGURE 25.7

Using Picasa to edit a photo.

Printing Your Photos

After you've touched up (or otherwise manipulated) your photos, it's time to print them.

Choosing the Right Printer and Paper

If you have a color printer, you can make good-quality prints of your image files. Even a low-priced color inkjet can make surprisingly good prints, although the better your printer, the better the results.

Some manufacturers sell printers specifically designed for photographic prints. These printers use special photo print paper and output prints that are almost indistinguishable from those you get from a professional photo processor. If you take a lot of digital photos, one of these printers might be a good investment.

The quality of your prints is also affected by the type of paper you use. Printing on standard laser or inkjet paper is okay for making proofs, but you'll want to use a thicker, waxier paper for those prints you want to keep. Check with your printer's manufacturer to see what type of paper it recommends for the best quality photo prints.

Making the Print

You can't print directly from the Windows 8 Photos app. You can, however, open File Explorer and print from there. Just follow these steps:

1. From within File Explorer, navigate to the Pictures library and select the picture you want to print.

2. Select the Share tab and click Print to display the Print Pictures window, shown in Figure 25.8.

FIGURE 25.8

Printing a photo from File Explorer.

3. Select your printer from the Printer list.

4. Select a layout from the right-hand column—that is, how many and what size images to print on the page.

5. Click the Print button.

NOTE The layout options available depend on the size of your original photo and the size paper you're using. In most instances, you can choose from a full-page photo, two 4" × 6" photos, two 5" × 7" photos, one 8" × 10" photo, four 3.5" × 5" photos, nine wallet-sized photos, or 35 photos on a contact sheet. (This last option is useful if you selected more than one photo to print.)

Printing Photos Professionally

If you don't have your own photo-quality printer, you can use a professional photo-processing service to print your photos. You can create prints from your digital photos in two primary ways:

- Copy your image files to CD or memory card and deliver the CD or card by hand to your local photo finisher.

- Go to the website of an online photo-finishing service, and transfer your image files over the Internet.

The first option is convenient for many people, especially because numerous drug-stores, supermarkets, and discount stores (including Target and Walmart) offer onsite photo printing services. Often the printing service is via a self-serve kiosk; just insert your CD or memory card, follow the onscreen instructions, and come back a half-hour later for your finished prints.

The second option is also convenient, if you don't mind waiting a few days for your prints to arrive. You never have to leave your house; you upload your photo files from your computer over the Internet and then receive your prints in your postal mailbox.

 TIP Some photo services, particularly those associated with retail chains, offer the option of picking up your prints at a local store—often with same-day service!

There are a number of photo printing services online, including the following:

- dotPhoto (www.dotphoto.com)

- Nations Photo Lab (www.nationsphotolab.com)

- Shutterfly (www.shutterfly.com)

- Snapfish (www.snapfish.com)

To print a photo online, you start by using Internet Explorer to go to the site and sign up for a free account. After you create your account, choose which photos on your PC you want to print. After the photos are selected, the site automatically uploads them from your PC to the website. You can then select how many and what size prints you want. Enter your shipping information and credit card number, and you're good to go.

For example, Shutterfly, shown in Figure 25.9, makes it easy to order prints at a variety of sizes—4" × 6", 5" × 7", 8" × 10", 11" × 14", 16" × 20", 20" ×30", and wallet-sized—in either matte or glossy finish. Choose the size and quantity you want for each print and then enter your payment and shipping information.

FIGURE 25.9

Ordering photo prints from Shutterfly.

Most sites ship within a day or two of receiving your order; add shipping time, and you should receive your prints in less than a week. Shipping is typically via the U.S. Postal Service or some similar shipping service.

Sharing Photos at an Online Photo Site

You don't have to print your photos to share them with friends. There are a number of photo sharing websites that let you upload your photos and then share them with the people you love.

These photo sharing sites let you store your photos in online photo albums, which can then be viewed by any number of visitors via their web browsers—for free. Some of these sites also offer photo printing services, and some sell photo-related items, such as picture tee shirts, calendars, mugs, and so on. Most of these sites are free to use; they make their money by selling prints and other merchandise.

To use a photo sharing site, you start by signing up for a free account. After your account is created, choose which photos on your PC you want to share. After the photos are selected, the site automatically uploads them from your PC to the website. You then organize the photos into photo albums, each of which has its own unique URL. You can then email the URL to your friends and family; when they access the photo site, they view your photos on their computer screens.

The most popular of these photo sharing sites include

- DropShots (www.dropshots.com)
- Flickr (www.flickr.com)

- Fotki (www.fotki.com)

- FotoTime (www.fototime.com)

- Photobucket (www.photobucket.com)

- Picturetrail (www.picturetrail.com)

- Webshots (www.webshots.com)

Of all these sites, Flickr is arguably the most popular, especially among professional photographers and serious hobbyists. As you can see in Figure 25.10, Flickr
lets you organize your photos into topic-oriented galleries, and then you can share
complete galleries or individual photos with others. Friends and family can download or print the photos they like.

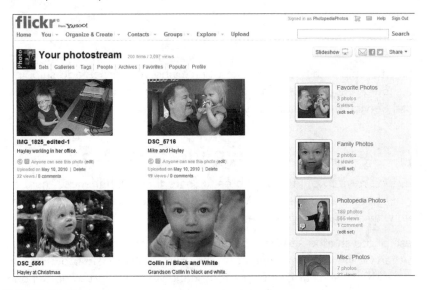

FIGURE 25.10

Sharing photos at Flickr.

Emailing Digital Photos

There's another way to share your digital photos that doesn't involve any uploading or websites. I'm talking about sharing via email; all you have to do is attach
your photos to an email message you create in your regular email program and
then send that message to as many recipients as you want.

You learned how to attach files to email messages in Chapter 16, "Sending and Receiving Email." Because a digital photo is just another type of computer file, the process is the same when you want to send a photo. Create a new message in your email program or web mail service, click the attachments button, and then select those photos you want to attach. Click the Send button, and your message is sent on its way, complete with the photos you selected.

As easy as this process is, you need to be aware of one issue before you start emailing your photos far and wide—the size of the photo files you email.

If you're emailing photos pretty much as they were shot with your camera, you're probably emailing some large files. This can be a problem if you or your recipients are using a slow dial-up Internet connection; the larger the attached files, the longer it takes to send or receive an email message. In addition, some ISPs have trouble handling messages that are too large; you want to avoid messages more than 1 or 2MB in size.

 NOTE You can use most photo editing programs to resize your pictures.

For this reason, you probably want to resize your photos before you email them. If your recipients will be viewing your photos only on their computer screens, you should make your photos no larger than the typical screen—no more than 1024 pixels wide or 768 pixels tall. Anything larger won't fit on a typical computer screen.

On the other hand, if your recipients will be printing the photos, you probably don't want to resize them—or at least not that much. A photo resized to 1024×768 pixels doesn't have enough picture resolution to create a detailed print. You should keep your photos at or near their original size if someone is going to print them; any significant resizing results in fuzzy prints.

THE ABSOLUTE MINIMUM

Here are the key points to remember from this chapter:

- You can transfer photos from your digital camera to your PC via a USB connection or by using your camera's memory card.

- The Windows 8 Photos app enables you to view digital photos stored on your computer or uploaded to Facebook and other sites.

- You need to install a separate photo editing program, such as Picasa or Adobe Photoshop Elements, if you want to crop or otherwise edit your photos.

- To print your photos on your home printer, use File Explorer.

- You can order photo prints from a variety of online printing services, or from your local drugstore, supermarket, or department store.

- You can share your photos with multiple people by uploading them to an online photo sharing website.

- You can also send photos as email attachments—as long as the files aren't too big.

IN THIS CHAPTER

- Using the Music App
- Playing Music from Your Library
- Purchasing Music Online
- Playing, Ripping, and Burning Music CDs

26

PLAYING MUSIC IN WINDOWS

Your personal computer is a full-featured digital music machine. You can use your PC to play music from CDs, create your own digital music library, and download music from the Internet. You can even make your own audio "mix" CDs from the music stored on your computer, which you can then play in your home or car.

There are actually several different ways to do all this, depending on which apps you choose to use. This chapter tells you how to listen to music using Windows 8's Music app—which is probably the easiest way to enjoy the music you love.

Using the Music App

Windows 8 features a central hub for all your music-related activities. That hub is the Music app, which you can click or tap from the Windows Start screen.

The Music app has four separate components:

- My Music, shown in Figure 26.1, houses your digital music collection—those albums and tracks you've downloaded from the Web or ripped from your own CDs. Your newest music is featured on the main screen; click or tap an album cover to play that album. To view your entire music collection, click or tap the My Music header.

- Spotlight, shown in Figure 26.2, displays the currently-playing track and whatever else Microsoft wants to highlight. (There's typically an advertisement shoehorned into this section, as well.)

- New Releases, shown in Figure 26.3, highlights new releases from major artists.

- Popular, shown in Figure 26.4, features tracks and albums for purchase and download. Click or tap a tile to view information about that item; click or tap the section header to see more available music.

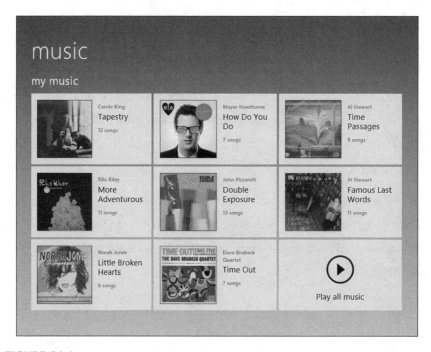

FIGURE 26.1

The My Music section of the main Music app screen.

FIGURE 26.2

The Spotlight section of the main Music app screen.

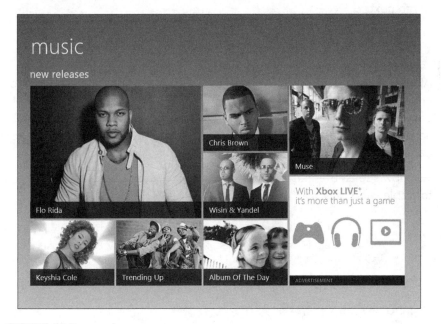

FIGURE 26.3

The New Releases section of the main Music app screen.

FIGURE 26.4

The Popular section of the main Music app screen.

You scroll left and right to view each of these sections—which we'll look at in depth next.

Playing Music from Your Library

All the music you've purchased and downloaded online, as well as music you've ripped from your own CDs, is stored in your Music library on your computer's hard drive. You can view and play music from your library using the Music app. All you have to do is launch the Music app, scroll to the My Music section of the main page, and click or tap the My Music heading.

You now see all the music stored on your computer. There are a number of ways to display and play your music.

 TIP You can play all the music in your library directly from the main Music screen. Just click or tap the Play All Music tile to begin playback.

Viewing Your Music Library

The default view, shown in Figure 26.5, displays all your music by the date you added it—that is, the newest albums and tracks are listed first. Scroll left or right to view your entire collection. To play an album, click or tap the album cover; a new tile displays as shown in Figure 26.6. Click or tap Play to play the album; alternatively, click or tap Add to Now Playing to add the album to any music currently playing. Tap or click Artist Details to learn more about the artist. (Figure 26.7 shows a typical artist page; scroll right to the Discography section to view all the artist's albums available for purchase.)

FIGURE 26.5

The default view of your music library—viewing all your albums in order added.

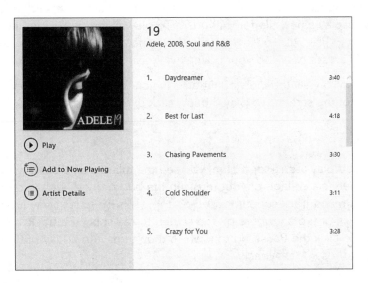

FIGURE 26.6

Getting ready to play an album.

FIGURE 26.7

Viewing a typical artist page.

To display your music in a different order, tap or click Date Added. You can then opt to display your music in alphabetical (A to Z) order, or by artist, release year, or genre.

By default, the Music app displays albums. If you'd rather view the artists you have in your collection, click Artists at the top left corner of the screen. The app displays an alphabetical list of artists, as shown in Figure 26.8; click or tap an artist's tile to display a new tile for that artist. To play all the tracks by that artist, in order, click or tap Play All. To view details about the artist, click or tap Artist Details. To add this artist's music to your now playing list, click or tap Add to Now Playing.

You can also view the individual tracks in your collection. Just click or tap Songs at the top of the screen. To play a track, click or tap it and then click Play.

Playing Music

When you play a track or album, you see the full-screen display shown in Figure 26.9. There's a collage of your music in the background, with information about the album and track superimposed on top. (This bit fades away after a few seconds; click or tap anywhere on the screen to redisplay the track info.) To pause playback, click the Pause button, which then turns into a Play button; click the Play button to resume playback.

FIGURE 26.8

Viewing the artists in your music library.

FIGURE 26.9

Playing an album.

You can also "scrub" through a track to get to a different point in playback. Just click or tap the green scrub control and drag it forward or backward to the point you wish.

To skip to the next track, click or tap the big right arrow to the right of the Pause control. To return to the previous track, click or tap the big left arrow on the left.

You can access more playback-related controls in the Options bar, shown in Figure 26.10, which you display by right-clicking the screen. From here you can pause or resume playback, go to the next or previous track, or even choose to "shuffle" the tracks in random order. Just click or tap the appropriate control in the Options bar.

FIGURE 26.10

Controlling playback from the Options bar.

To return to your music library, click or tap the Return arrow at the top of the screen, you return to your music library.

 TIP You can switch to any other app in Windows, or to the Start screen, while your music is playing. To pause or change the playback, however, you have to switch back to the Music app.

Purchasing Music Online

The Windows 8 Music app also enables you (actually, encourages you) to purchase more music online. You can purchase individual tracks or complete albums from Microsoft's Zune Music store.

Both the New Releases and Popular sections of the main Music screen link to purchasing opportunities. Click or tap an individual tile to purchase that item. Click or tap either the New Releases or Popular headers to view more items for purchase.

What you see next is a collection of featured albums, like the one in Figure 26.11. You can browse these featured albums by genre, by clicking or tapping the appropriate genre along the side of the screen. You can also display individual songs and songs by artists by clicking or tapping Show Albums and selecting instead Show Songs or Show Artists.

When you find an item you want to buy, click or tap it. The tile shown in Figure 26.12 displays; you can then opt to view artist details, play a preview of selected tracks, or buy the album.

FIGURE 26.11

Viewing featured albums.

FIGURE 26.12

Viewing album details.

If you decide to make a purchase, you see the Confirm Purchase screen shown in Figure 26.13. At this point you're faced with the conundrum that is the Zune Music store, primarily that you don't pay with actual dollars. Instead, you have to purchase Microsoft Points which are kind of like a credit in the store. Assuming you don't have any points built up, you need to click or tap the Buy Points button, buy an appropriate number of points, and then proceed from there.

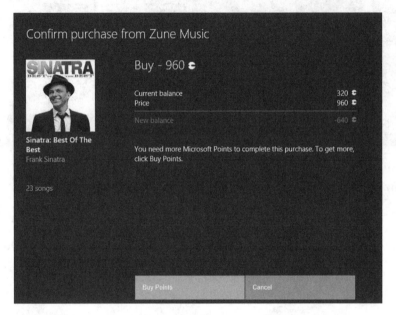

FIGURE 26.13

Purchasing an album.

 NOTE   It costs $4.99 to purchase 400 Microsoft Points, or $9.99 to purchase 800 Points. A typical album costs 800 Microsoft Points, which equates to a $9.99 purchase.

After you make the purchase, the album is downloaded to your computer and added to your music library. This takes a few minutes; when the download is complete, you can play your new album.

Playing, Ripping, and Burning Music CDs

How do you get music into your Music library? One way is to purchase tracks online, as just discussed. Another way is to "rip" music from those compact discs you already own. Or, if you like, you can just play those CDs directly from Windows.

Playing a CD

Unfortunately, the Windows 8 Music app doesn't play physical CDs, only digital music stored on your computer. To play a CD, you have to use Windows Media Player (WMP), an app that runs on the traditional desktop.

Fortunately, music playback via WMP is somewhat automatic when you insert a CD into your computer's disc drive. When you insert a CD you see a notification box that asks you want you want to do. Select the play music option, and WMP launches on the Windows desktop.

As you can see in Figure 26.14, WMP defaults to what is called the Now Playing window. This is a simple and compact playback window that takes up a lot less desktop space than the normal WMP window. To switch to the larger WMP window, click the Switch to Library button in the upper-right corner. As you can see in Figure 26.15, the larger WMP window displays more information about the currently playing album, including a full track list.

To pause playback (in either window), click the Pause button; click Play again to resume playback. To skip to the next track, click the Next button. To replay the last track, click the Previous button. You stop playback completely by clicking the Stop button.

FIGURE 26.14

Playing a CD in WMP's Now Playing window.

FIGURE 26.15

The same CD displayed in the main WMP window.

 TIP   To play the songs on a CD in a random order, click the Shuffle button on the far left of the transport panel of the larger WMP window. WMP also offers a repeat function, which repeats the selected song(s) over and over. You activate this function by clicking the Repeat button, which is next to the Shuffle button in the transport panel.

Ripping a CD to Your Music Library

You also use WMP to "rip" physical CDs to the digital music library on your computer. When you rip a CD, you make a digital copy of the CD's music on your PC's hard drive. It's actually a fairly easy process—and a great way to preserve your physical music collection in today's digital world.

Before you begin ripping, however, you have to tell WMP what format you want to use for your ripped files. You also have to choose the quality level (the *bitrate*) for the recording.

Let's start with the file format. Windows Media Player enables you to rip audio files in a number of different formats: MP3, WMA, or WAV. For most users, Window's proprietary WMA format is good, although if you want to ensure almost-universal compatibility with your iPod or iPhone or other music player, the MP3 format is better.

To select a file format, open Windows Media Player (the large version), click Rip Settings and then click Format. You can select either the Windows Media Audio or MP3 format. Next, click Rip Settings, Audio Quality and then select the desired bitrate; the available options vary by the type of file you select, but, in general, the higher the bitrate, the better sounding the music.

TIP   When using the normal WMA format, a quality level of 128Kbps or 160Kbps is typically a good choice.

After you've set the format and bit rate, it's time to start ripping. All you have to do is insert the CD you want to copy into your PC's CD drive and, when the Now Playing window appears, click Rip CD (at the top of the window).

TIP   You can also rip a CD from the main WMP window. Just check all the tracks you want to copy and then click the Rip CD button on the toolbar.

Windows Media Player now extracts the selected tracks from the CD and converts them from their original CD Audio format to the file format you selected, sampled at the bitrate you selected. The converted files are written to your PC's hard disk and added to your computer's Music library—from there you can play the ripped tracks from the Windows 8 Music app.

TIP   Make sure you're connected to the Internet before you start ripping so that WMP can download album and track details. (If you don't connect, you can't encode track names or CD cover art.)

Burning Your Own CDs

If you can copy tracks from a CD to your hard disk, what's to stop you from going in the other direction—copying files from your hard disk to a recordable/rewritable CD?

This process of recording your own custom CDs is called *burning* a CD. Unlike CD ripping, CD burning doesn't require you to set a lot of format options. That's because whatever format the original file is in (WMA, MP3, or WAV) when it gets copied to CD is encoded into the CDDA (CD Digital Audio) format. All music CDs use the CDDA format, so if you're burning an MP3 or WMA file, Windows Media Player translates it to CDDA before the copy is made.

There are no quality levels to set, either. All CDDA-format files are encoded at the same bit rate. So you really don't have configuration to do—other than deciding which songs you want to copy.

Here's all you have to do to burn a CD:

1. Insert a blank CD-R disc into your PC's CD drive.

2. Open Windows Media Player. (You can do this from Windows' All Apps screen.)

3. Click the Burn tab, shown in Figure 26.16.

4. Drag the desired tracks, albums, or playlists from the Content pane to the Burn List in the List pane.

5. Click and drag items within the Burn List to place them in the desired playback order.

6. When you're ready to burn the CD, click the Start Burn button.

FIGURE 26.16

Creating a Burn List in Windows Media Player.

WMP now inspects the files you want to copy, converts them to CDDA format, and copies them to your CD. When the entire burning process is done, WMP displays a message to that effect and ejects the newly burned CD from the disc drive.

THE ABSOLUTE MINIMUM

Here are the key points to remember from this chapter:

- You can play all the music stored on your PC with Windows 8's Music app.

- The Music app enables you to view your music collection in a number of different ways, including by album, artist, song, or genre.

- You can also use the Music app to purchase and download new music from Microsoft's Zune Music store.

- The Music app doesn't play music CDs, however; for that, you have to use the Windows Media Player program, which runs on the traditional desktop.

- You can also use the Windows Media Player to copy songs from a CD to your hard disk—a process called *ripping*.

- The process of copying digital audio files from your hard disk to a blank CD is called *burning*—which you also do via Windows Media Player.

27

PLAYING MUSIC WITH iTUNES

The Windows 8 Music app isn't the only way to play music on your PC. If you're the proud owner of an Apple iPod or iPhone, you're probably already familiar with the iTunes program, which functions kind of like Windows Media Player, but specifically for Apple's portable devices. It lets you play, download, rip, and burn digital music on your PC—and synchronize that music to your iPod or iPhone.

Navigating iTunes

You run iTunes on the Windows desktop. As you can see in Figure 27.1, the iTunes window is divided into two or three panes. (The third pane is optional.)

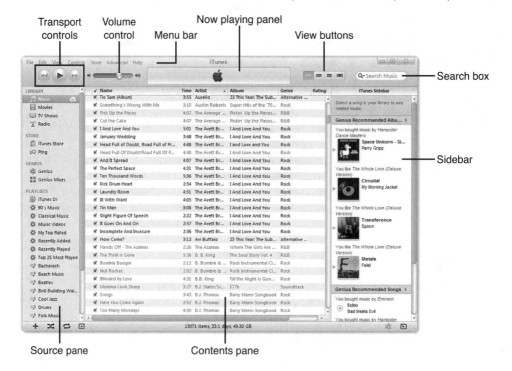

FIGURE 27.1

The iTunes player, with contents in song list view.

 NOTE The iTunes software is not included with Windows 8; you have to download it separately using Internet Explorer. Fortunately, the iTunes software is free. Go to www.apple.com/itunes/download/ for more information and to download the program.

The left pane (dubbed the Source pane) is for navigation, and includes the following sections:

- **Library**—Displays either your Music, Movies, TV Shows, Radio, or Apps libraries—that is, all those items stored on your computer.

- **Store**—Connects to and displays the iTunes Store or, optionally, iTunes Ping.

NOTE Ping is the social networking arm of iTunes; it displays recent activity from your favorite artists.

- **Genius**—Genius is iTune's recommendation engine; it recommends artists and tracks related to other music you're listening to. Click Genius to create and play Genius playlists (automatic playlists based on a selection), or click Genius Mixes to play pre-selected mixes based on your library's contents.

- **Playlist**—This section displays all the playlists you've created or that iTunes has created for you automatically. Click a playlist to view, edit, and play it.

 NOTE When you connect your iPod, iPhone, or iPad, there's an additional section for your connected device, as we discuss later in this chapter.

The center pane displays the contents of whatever you've selected in the Source pane. For example, if you select Music in the Library section, the center pane displays all the music in your library. If you select iTunes Store from the Store section, it connects to and display's Apple's iTunes Store.

You can, if you like, change how the contents in the center pane are displayed. Just click one of the four buttons at the top right of the window. You can choose any one of the following four views:

- **Song list**—Displays all tracks in a long list. You can sort the song list by track name, track time, artist, album title, genre, rating, and number of plays.

- **Album list**—Displays all tracks sorted by album. That is, the list is sorted by album, with the tracks for each album listed within each album's section.

- **Grid**—Displays album, artist, genre, or composer thumbnails, as shown in Figure 27.2. Click each thumbnail to see the tracks within.

- **Cover flow**—Somewhat unique to iTunes, a "flow" of album covers, as shown in Figure 27.3. Flip left and right through the covers using your mouse or the left and right arrow buttons on your computer keyboard. Contents for the selected album are displayed in a list beneath the covers.

At the very top of the iTunes window is a menu bar, with pull-down menus for common functions. Beneath that are iTunes's transport controls (Rewind, Play/Pause, Fast Forward), the volume control slider, the now playing pane, buttons for changing the display of the contents pane, and a search box. At the very bottom of the window are buttons for Create a Playlist, Shuffle, Repeat, and Show/Hide Artwork; stats for your library; and more buttons to Show Genius and Show/Hide Sidebar. (That's the right sidebar.)

FIGURE 27.2

iTunes in grid view, displaying artist thumbnails.

FIGURE 27.3

iTunes in cover flow view.

That right sidebar is imaginatively named the iTunes Sidebar. It displays information related to the current selection, Genius results (if you have that feature enabled), and Ping results about your favorite artists.

Playing Music from Your Library

Playing songs with iTunes is relatively easy. Make sure you have Music selected in the Library section of the Source pane, and then iTunes displays all the music you have stored on your computer. Depending on the view you've selected, you might see individual tracks, albums, or artists.

If you're displaying an album or artist, click the thumbnail for that album or artist to view all related songs. To play a track, either double-click it or select it and then click the Play button in the transport controls.

Downloading Music from the iTunes Store

When you want to add new music to your library, you can either rip music from a CD (discussed later in this chapter) or purchase new digital music online—which you can do from Apple's iTunes Store. The iTunes Store is the largest online music store today, with more than 20 million tracks available for downloading at prices ranging from 69 cents to $1.29 each. (It also offers complete albums for download, too.) It's a much bigger store than any local music store you've ever frequented.

 TIP The iTunes Store offers more than just music for download. iTunes also sells movies, TV shows, music videos, podcasts, audiobooks, and ebooks. You even get access to iTunes U, which offers all manner of textbooks, courses, and educational materials, and Apple's App Store for the iPhone and iPad.

Navigating the iTunes Store

You access the iTunes Store from the iTunes software. All you have to do is click iTunes Store in the navigation sidebar.

As you can see in Figure 27.4, the main page of the iTunes Store offers access to just about everything offered. Main sections of the home page include the following:

- **Navigation bar** with links to Home, Music, Movies, TV Shows, App Store, Books, Podcasts, iTunes U, and Ping (iTune's social network for sharing music).

- **New Releases** by category—Music, Movies, TV Shows, and selected categories. Click the See All link to view all new releases, or scroll to the bottom of the page to see tracks that are Free on iTunes this week.

- **Quick Links** to key operations—Redeem (gift cards), Buy iTunes Gifts, Power Search, Browse, Account, Support, Free Book, iTunes LP (big album art for selected items), Inside iTunes (blog), iTunes Match, Purchased, My Wish List, Recent Activity, My Alerts, Recommendations for You, and Complete My Album (purchase additional tracks from an album from which you've purchased single tracks).

- **Top Charts** for Singles, Movies, and TV Shows.

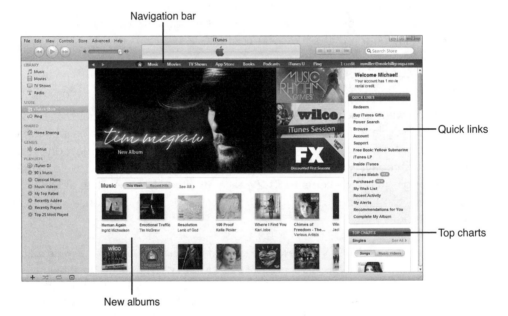

FIGURE 27.4

The home page of the iTunes Store

There are three navigational buttons at the left side of the iTunes Store navigation bar. Click the Back button to return to the previous store page, click the Forward button to go to the next store page (after you've clicked the Back button), and click the Home button to return to the store's home page.

In addition, your username (email address) appears at the right side of the navigation bar. Click the down arrow next to your name, which appears when you hover the mouse over your email address, to access your account information (Account), redeem gift cards (Redeem), access your wish list (Wish List), or log out of your account (Sign Out).

Finally, at the top-right corner of the iTunes window itself is a search box. Use this to search the iTunes Store for specific tracks, artists, albums, and such.

 NOTE Before you can purchase items from the iTunes Store, you have to create an Apple account. You might be prompted to do this the first time you click to purchase, or you can create your account manually, at any time, by clicking the Sign In button at the top right of the iTunes window and, when prompted, clicking the Create New Account button.

Purchasing Items from the iTunes Store

To find items for download, you can either browse or search the store. To search for specific items or artists, use the search box in the top-right corner of the iTunes window. To browse the store, you can either click or tap the down arrow next to Music on the navigation bar and then select a genre, or you can click or tap Browse in the Quick Links box on the home page and work through the different genres from there.

Whether you search or browse for music, you eventually end up with either a track list or an artist page, like the one shown in Figure 27.5. The artist page is particularly useful, as this page enables you to purchase complete albums. To view information about an album, click or tap the album title or cover thumbnail; to purchase the album, click or tap the Buy Album button. When you select an album, iTunes displays all the tracks for that album in a track list.

FIGURE 27.5

An artist page in the iTunes Store.

Alternatively, you can display all tracks for an artist by clicking or tapping the See All link in the Songs section of the artist page. You can then purchase individual tracks; just click or tap the Buy button next to the desired track.

After you choose to purchase a track or album, you're prompted as to whether you really want to make the purchase. (This ensures you don't click or tap the Buy button by mistake.) When you confirm your intention, iTunes automatically charges your credit card and begins downloading the purchased music. Your purchased tracks or albums are automatically added to your iTunes music library.

Using iTunes to Play, Rip, and Burn CDs

You can also use iTunes with compact discs—that is, to play, rip, or burn music on CD.

Playing a CD

When you insert a CD into your PC's CD drive, that CD automatically appears in the iTunes window. To start playback, all you have to do is click the Play button. You can then use the transport controls to pause the CD or go backward and forward through the tracks. Naturally, the volume control adjusts the playback level.

 TIP   To play the songs on a CD in a random order, click the Shuffle button at the bottom left of the iTunes window. iTunes also offers a repeat function, which repeats the selected song(s) over and over. You activate this function by clicking the Repeat button, which is next to the Shuffle button.

Ripping Songs from CD to Your PC

iTunes makes copying songs from CD to your PC's hard drive relatively easy. Before you rip a CD, however, you first have to configure iTunes to use the desired file format and bitrate for the songs it rips.

To do this, select Edit, Preferences to open the General Preferences dialog box and then select the General tab. Go to the When You Insert a CD section and click the Import Settings button.

When the Import Settings dialog box appears, as shown in Figure 27.6, pull down the Import Using list and select the desired file type. The best choices are either AAC Encoder (for Apple's standard file format) or MP3 Encoder (works with virtually all music player devices and programs).

FIGURE 27.6

Configuring iTunes for ripping.

Next, pull down the Setting list and select the desired rip quality, which differs depending on the file type you selected. For example, if you selected the AAC Encoder, you have the option of High Quality (128Kbps), iTunes Plus (256Kbps), Spoken Podcast (64Kbps), or Custom (anything from 64Kbps to 320Kbps). Click OK when done.

When everything is properly configured, all you have to do to rip a CD is insert that CD into your computer's CD/DVD drive. As you can see in Figure 27.7, all the tracks from the CD are now listed in the iTunes window. Check those tracks you want to copy and click the Import CD button at the bottom of the iTunes window.

FIGURE 27.7

Getting ready to rip a CD with iTunes.

iTunes now extracts the selected tracks from the CD and converts them from their original CD Audio format to the file format you selected, sampled at the bitrate you selected. The converted files are written to your PC's hard disk and automatically added to the iTunes library.

 TIP Make sure you're connected to the Internet before you start ripping so that your program can download album and track details. If you don't connect, you won't encode track names or CD cover art, which means you'll have to do it manually, later.

Burning Your Own CDs

Burning music from your PC to a blank CD is also easy with iTunes. Here's how to do it:

1. In iTunes, create a new playlist containing all the songs you want to burn to CD. Make sure that your playlist is less than 80 minutes long.

2. Insert a blank CD-R disc into your PC's CD drive.

3. Select the playlist that contains the songs you want to burn, as shown in Figure 27.8, and make sure that all the songs in the playlist are checked.

4. Select File, Burn Playlist to Disc.

iTunes now converts the selected files to CDDA format and copies them to your blank CD. When the entire burning process is done, iTunes displays a message to that effect and ejects the newly burned CD from the disc drive.

FIGURE 27.8

Burning a playlist of songs to CD.

Syncing Music from Your PC to Your iPod or iPhone

The main reason to use the iTunes software is because you own an iPhone or iPod music player. You use the iTunes software to manage the music stored on your portable device.

Getting Connected

You start by connecting your iPod or iPhone to your computer via the supplied cable which connects between your portable device and a USB port on your computer. When your iPod is connected to your PC, the portable device automatically enters a special sync/charge mode. Your PC should automatically recognize your device and launch the iTunes software.

Within iTunes, a new Devices section appears in the Source pane, with your iPod or iPhone listed. In addition, the main window changes to display information about your iPod in a series of tabs, as shown in Figure 27.9.

 CAUTION   Do not disconnect your iPod from your computer until synchronization is complete, otherwise you might corrupt the files on your iPod.

FIGURE 27.9

Viewing information about a connected iPhone in iTunes.

The Summary tab displays the name, capacity, version information, serial number, and such for your iPod or iPhone. In addition, the Version section lets you update your device's firmware or restore the device to its factory condition (useful if you have corrupted data or some sort of operational problem).

At the bottom of the Summary tab is a visual representation of what's currently stored on your iPod or iPhone. You'll see how much total space is available, how much space is devoted to each type of media (audio, video, photos, apps, books, and other), and how much free space is left to use.

 NOTE Connecting your iPod or iPhone to your PC also recharges the device's battery. Even if you don't need to sync your device, you still need to connect it to your PC to recharge it—or use the power adapter to recharge it directly from a wall outlet.

Configuring Sync Options

Scroll down to the Options section of the Summary tab to determine how your iPod or iPhone syncs to your computer. The following options are available:

- **Open iTunes when this iPod/iPhone is connected**, the default operational mode.

- **Sync with this iPod/iPhone over Wi-Fi,** available for devices with Wi-Fi connectivity; enables you to perform the sync operation over your wireless network, no cables needed.

- **Sync only checked songs and videos**, which is useful when you're syncing a device that has less storage capacity than you have songs stored on your PC. When this option is selected, only those tracks you've checked in your iTunes library are copied to your portable device. When this option is not selected, all the songs in your library are automatically transferred to your iPod or iPhone— which works well if you have a larger-capacity device (or a smaller music library).

- **Prefer standard definition videos**, which keeps you from filling up your portable device with large HD video files.

- **Convert higher bit rate songs to XXX AAC**, which is an easy way to load lower bitrate versions of files stored on your computer at a higher bitrate—and save storage space on your i-device.

- **Manually manage music and videos**, which you can use to sync only selected tracks to your portable device.

If you have a large-capacity iPod classic and you want to transfer all the songs on your PC to the iPod, uncheck all but the first option. If you have a smaller-capacity iPod nano or iPod shuffle, or want to transfer only selected songs to your iPod, check the first and second options. If you want to manage the music already stored on your iPod, check the first and third options.

Syncing Your Music

To configure what music files are synced, you need to access the Music tab, shown in Figure 27.10. From here, you can choose to sync everything in your music library or just selected playlists, artists, albums, or genres—that is, those items checked in your iTunes library. You can also choose to include music videos in your sync, if you wish.

FIGURE 27.10

Selecting music sync options in iTunes.

 TIP   After you make a change on the Music, Movies, or similar tabs, click or tap the Apply button to register the change and make the new sync.

When everything is synced, you can disconnect your iPod or iPhone from your PC, plug in your earbuds, and start listening. You don't need to resync until you add new music to your iTunes library!

THE ABSOLUTE MINIMUM

Here are the key points to remember from this chapter:

- iTunes is a music player/management program designed specifically to work with Apple's iPod and iPhone devices.

- You can use iTunes to manage and play music from the music library stored on your PC.

- You also use iTunes to purchase and download digital music from Apple's iTunes Store.

- The iTunes program can also be used to play, rip, and burn music CDs.

- If you have an iPod or iPhone, you use the iTunes software to manage and synchronize the music on your portable device.

28

PLAYING MUSIC ONLINE

You don't have to own a song or album to play it on your PC. There's another way to listen to music on your computer—online, via streaming music services.

A streaming music service is the online equivalent of listening to AM or FM radio. In some instances you choose the music you want to listen to; in other cases, you just sit back and listen to whatever's served up—just like old school radio.

What makes streaming music different from downloading or ripping music is that you don't store any files on your computer; it all comes at you in real time, over the Internet. It's a great way to hear a lot of music at relatively low cost.

Listening to Streaming Music Online

There are two primary types of delivery services for streaming audio over the Internet. You can listen to music from a streaming music service, or from an Internet radio station. (And, yes, there is some overlap between the two.)

Understanding Streaming Music Services

A streaming music service is typically a paid service that enables you to listen to an unlimited amount of music, which is streamed over the Internet, for a flat monthly subscription fee. (Some call these "all you can eat" plans.) Most services let you browse or search for specific tracks or albums, or music by a given artist or in a given genre. Some services let you create playlists of your favorite tracks; some even create custom "radio stations" based on your listening habits. A few services are social in nature, in that they let you share your favorite music with friends on Facebook and other social networks.

You access most streaming music services from Internet Explorer or any other web browser. In most instances, listening is as easy as going to the music service's website, searching for the music you want, and clicking or tapping the play button.

 NOTE Some online music services, such as Spotify, require you to install an app on your computer to access their music.

Exploring Streaming Music Services

There are a lot of similarities between the major streaming music services. Although a few are free, most cost anywhere from $5 to $10 per month, depending on services offered. Most offer between 10 and 15 million individual tracks for listening. And most let you create online "radio stations" on the fly, based on the tracks or artists you select.

Table 28.1 compares the most popular streaming music services today.

 NOTE While Pandora is a free service, it does have a paid option, dubbed Pandora One, that offers ad-free radio stations, higher quality audio, and more personalization. Pandora One runs $3.99 per month, or $36 for a one-year subscription.

TABLE 28.1 Streaming Music Services

Service	URL	Price	Selection (number of tracks available)
Grooveshark	www.grooveshark.com	$6.00–$9.00/month, plus free plan	15 million
Last.fm	www.last.fm	Free	12 million
MOG	www.mog.com	$4.99–$9.99/month, plus free plan	14 million
Pandora Radio	www.pandora.com	Free	900,000
Raditaz	www.raditaz.com	Free	14 million
Rara.com	www.rara.com	$4.99–$9.99/month	10 million
Rdio	www.rdio.com	$4.99–$9.99/month, plus free plan	12 million
Rhapsody	www.rhapsody.com	$9.99–$14.99/month	14 million
Slacker Radio	www.slacker.com	$3.99–$9.99/month, plus free plan	8 million
Spotify	www.spotify.com	$4.99–$9.99/month, plus free plan	15 million
Turntable.fm	www.turntable.fm	Free	11 million
Zune Music Pass	www.zune.net	$9.99/month	11 million

Getting to Know Spotify

Of these services, Spotify is arguably the most popular. As you can see in Figure 28.1, you access Spotify with its own app, which runs on the traditional Windows desktop. Spotify offers three different plans: Free (limited to 10 hours of listening each month), Unlimited ($4.99/month, unlimited listening), and Premium ($9.99, adds smartphone access). You can listen to music that Spotify suggests, search for specific music, or listen to music shared from other users. (Figure 28.2 shows the result of a music search—Spotify returns playlists, artists, albums, and individual tracks that match your query.)

When you find a track you like, you can then launch a Spotify radio station based on that track or artist. As you can see in Figure 28.3, a radio station includes tracks by the same artist, as well as similar tracks by other artists. It's a great way to hear new music, as well as the music you love.

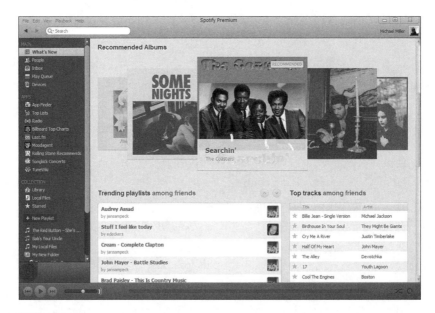

FIGURE 28.1

Listening to streaming music with Spotify.

FIGURE 28.2

Searching for music on Spotify.

FIGURE 28.3

Listening to a Spotify radio station.

Other online music services function similarly, of course. Most offer some sort of free plan or trial period you can use to check out what's available before you sign up for a paid plan. If you like what's there, you get access to a ton of music for a low monthly price.

Listening to Internet Radio

The other form of streaming music is so-called Internet radio. This is the online equivalent of terrestrial AM/FM radio, full of all sorts of radio stations that operate over the Web using streaming audio technology.

Some Internet radio stations exist solely online. Others simulcast existing AM/FM stations. And some let you create your own personal stations, just for you, in real time. It's an interesting way to hear old favorites and new music alike, town to town and up and down the dial—over the Internet, on your own PC, through Internet Explorer or a similar web browser.

Exploring Web-Only Radio Stations

There are a large number of Internet radio stations that create their own original radio programming and beam it over the Internet. This programming is typically genre-specific music; many of these sites offer dozens (or hundreds) of channels, each devoted to a specific type of music. So whether you're interested in '70s pop hits or classic polka tunes, one of these sites probably has a channel just for you!

Here's a short list of some of the most popular Internet-only radio sites:

- **AccuRadio** (www.accuradio.com)—Listen to programmed stations (typically by genre) or create your own custom stations.

- **AOL Radio** (music.aol.com/radioguide/)—A large number of genre-specific radio stations, created specifically for online listening.

- **Goom Radio** (www.goomradio.us)—A variety of genre-specific Internet radio stations, as well as user-created stations.

- **iHeartRadio** (www.iheart.com)—Presents more than 850 terrestrial and web-only stations, plus user-created custom stations.

- **Jango** (www.jango.com)—A mix of genre-based stations and user-personalized programming.

- **Live365** (www.live365.com)—As shown in Figure 28.4, one of the largest Internet radio sites, with more than 5,000 stations in more than 260 different genres.

FIGURE 28.4

The many online stations available on Live365.

- **RadioMOI** (www.radiomoi.com)—Features a mix of programmed channels (browsable by genre) and on-demand content.

- **SHOUTcast** (www.shoutcast.com)—Part of the AOL empire and one of the oldest and most reliable Internet radio sites. Amalgamates more than 50,000 free Internet radio stations in a single site. You can browse by genre or search by station, artist, or genre.

Listening to AM/FM and Satellite Radio Online

Most traditional AM and FM radio stations simulcast their programming over the Internet. This is a great way to get local news and views or listen to your local DJs while you're on your computer. Of course, you're not limited to listening to just *your* local stations; via the magic of the Internet, you can listen to local stations from anywhere in the world, in real time.

Here's a list of resources for AM/FM stations online:

- **Live Radio on the Internet** (www.live-radio.net)—A great guide to AM/FM simulcasts from all around the globe.

- **Online Radio Stations** (www.webradios.com)—Listings of local radio stations online, by location or genre.

- **radio-locator** (www.radio-locator.com)—A search engine with links to more than 10,000 AM and FM stations, searchable by city or ZIP Code, country, or call letters.

- **Sirius/XM Radio** (www.siriusxm.com/player/)—Satellite radio online, with more than 130 channels of music, news, and talk—including several web-only channels that aren't available via normal satellite radio. (Available only if you have a Sirius/XM subscription.)

- **TuneIn Radio** (www.tunein.com)—This site lets you browse local stations in any city or state, as well as listen to local police and fire bands. As you can see in Figure 28.5, many stations show what's currently playing, which is great when you're browsing for something interesting to listen to.

All you have to do is point Internet Explorer to your website of choice and search for stations in a specific locale. Listening in is a matter of clicking the station you want.

FIGURE 28.5

Browsing through local radio stations with TuneIn Radio.

THE ABSOLUTE MINIMUM

Here are the key points to remember from this chapter:

- Streaming music services let you listen to music in real time over the Internet.

- Most streaming music services let you listen to an unlimited number of songs for a low monthly fee.

- Internet radio stations offer a variety of programming accessible from your web browser.

- You can listen to most local AM and FM radio stations over the Internet.

29

WATCHING VIDEOS IN WINDOWS

As you've learned, your new PC is great for listening to your favorite music. It's also great for watching videos—either those downloaded to your PC or, as you learn in the next chapter, those streamed over the Internet.

The easiest way to watch videos on your computer is to use Windows 8's Video app. This app enables you to play videos you've downloaded to your PC, as well as enabling you to purchase new videos to watch.

Using the Windows 8 Video App

You launch the Video app from the Windows 8 Start screen, by clicking or tapping the Video tile. When the app launches, you can scroll through the multiple parts of the Video screen:

- **My Videos**, shown in Figure 29.1, enables you to view videos you've previously added to your computer's Video library—both your own videos and videos you've purchased online. Click or tap one of the featured videos to view. Alternatively, click or tap the My Videos header to see all the videos in your library.

FIGURE 29.1

The My Videos section of the Video app.

- **Spotlight**, shown in Figure 29.2, displays featured films and TV shows available for purchase and download.

- **Movies Marketplace**, shown in Figure 29.3, enables you to purchase movies to watch on your computer. Click or tap to purchase any featured movie. Alternatively, click or tap Show More to see more movies for purchase.

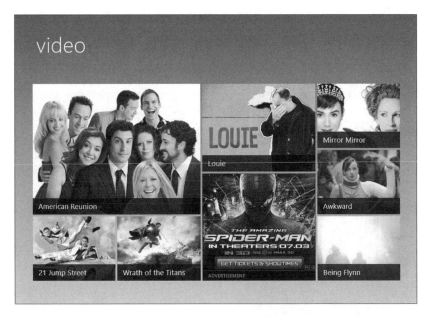

FIGURE 29.2

The Showcase section of the Video app.

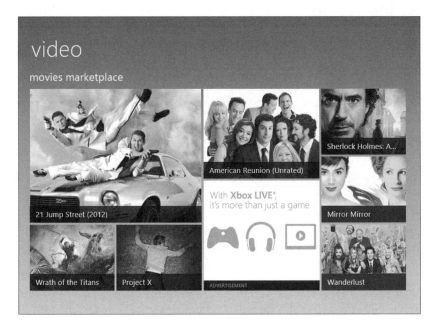

FIGURE 29.3

The Movies Marketplace section of the Video app.

- **TV Marketplace**, shown in Figure 29.4, enables you to purchase individual episodes and complete seasons of popular TV shows to watch on your computer. Click or tap to purchase any featured show. Alternatively, click or tap Show More to see more TV programming available for purchase.

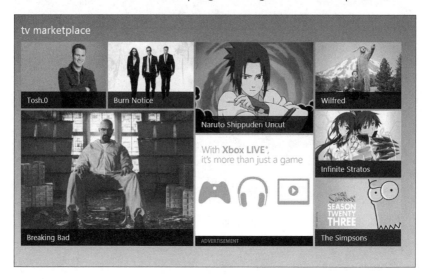

FIGURE 29.4

The TV Marketplace section of the Video app.

Viewing Movies in Your Collection

All movies you've purchased and downloaded to your PC are stored in your Video library, and you access them via the My Videos section of the Video app. This is also where you play any home movies you've saved to your computer.

To view all the videos in your collection, open the Video app, scroll to the My Videos section, and click or tap My Videos. You now see your video collection, as shown in Figure 29.5, organized by Movies, TV, and Other; click or tap a selection at the top of the screen to view that particular type of video. By default, your videos are sorted in alphabetical order; to sort by date added instead, click or tap the down arrow next to A to Z and select Date Added.

To play a video, click or tap its tile. Figure 29.6 shows a video during playback, which fills up the entire computer screen. Click or tap the screen to display the playback controls. You can pause or resume playback, or tap the left or right arrows to jump back 15 seconds or forward 30 seconds in the video. (This is great for skipping recorded commercials.) There's also a scrub control you can drag left or right to skip to a specific point in the video.

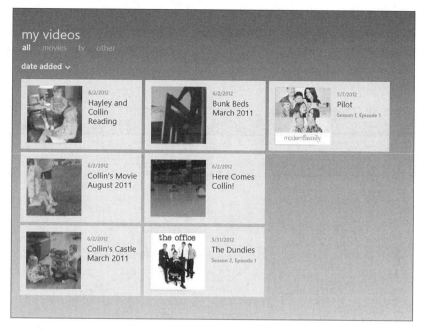

FIGURE 29.5

Browsing videos in your collection.

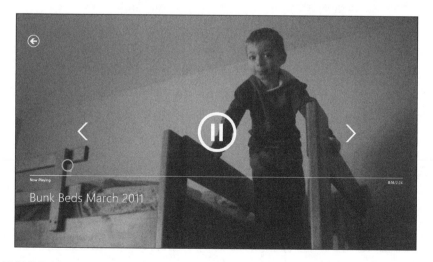

FIGURE 29.6

Playing a video, with playback controls onscreen.

While a video is playing or selected, you can also right-click the screen to display the Options bar, shown in Figure 29.7. (On a touchscreen device, drag your finger up from the bottom of the screen to display the Options bar.) This provides additional controls to Repeat the video, view the Previous and Next videos, and to Pause or Play the video.

FIGURE 29.7

More playback controls in the Options bar.

Purchasing Movies and TV Programming

The Video app also provides a front end to Microsoft's Zune Movies store, where you can purchase movies and TV shows for download to your computer. Just scroll to the Movie Marketplace or TV Marketplace section of the Video app and click or tap Show More.

What you see next is a list of featured movies or TV shows in the store, as shown in Figure 29.8. You can also display Top movies or shows, programming by Genres, or programming by Studios (in the movie marketplace) or Networks (in the TV marketplace), by tapping the tabs at the top of the screen.

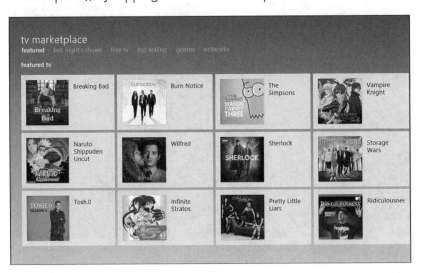

FIGURE 29.8

Items for purchase in the TV marketplace.

When you click or tap the tile for an item, you see the larger info tile shown in Figure 29.9. Click or tap Series Details or Movie Details to view more information about the item. In the case of a movie, you typically have the option of playing the movie's trailer before you decide to purchase. In the case of a TV show, you can usually view and purchase either individual episodes or entire seasons.

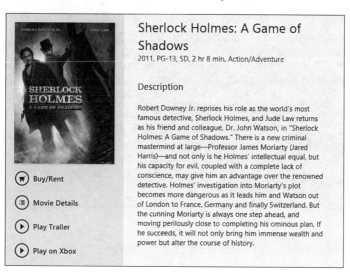

FIGURE 29.9

Display the purchase information tile for a movie.

Figure 29.10 shows a typical purchase screen for an individual TV episode. Just as it is with purchasing music, you don't pay for the movie or TV show directly. Instead, you have to purchase the proper amount of Microsoft Points required for the item. You get 400 points for $4.99; a typical TV episode costs 240 points (approximately $3), while a typical movie costs 360 points (approximately $4). Movies are typically "rented" for a limited time (14 days), rather than downloaded for you to own permanently.

After you've purchased an item, you typically have the option of either playing the item now, via streaming video, or downloading it to your PC. Downloading makes sense if you have a lot of free hard disk space on your PC; streaming makes sense if you have little or no hard disk space, as with an ultrabook or tablet.

Whether you decide to download or stream, movies and TV shows you've purchased appear in the Collection section of the Video app. Select either Movies or TV at the top of the screen to see the items you've purchased.

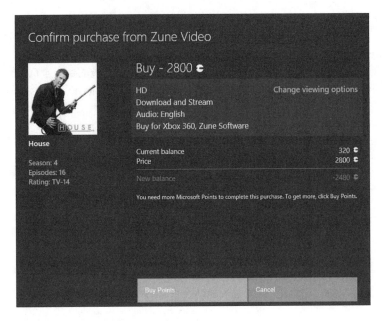

FIGURE 29.10

Getting ready to purchase an episode of a TV series.

 NOTE There are lots of other sites online that let you purchase or "rent" movies and TV shows for viewing on your PC. For example, if you have an iPhone or iPod, you can purchase video programming from the iTunes Store.

Making Your Own Home Movies

If you have a video camcorder, it's easy to download movies from your camcorder to your PC and then edit them into professional-looking videos. Assuming that you have a digital camcorder (most sold in the past few years are digital), when you make a recording, you're actually saving what you record to a video file stored on the camcorder.

Connecting Your Camcorder to Your PC

Most camcorders today record either to a built-in hard disk or memory card. You can connect the camcorder directly to your PC using the supplied USB connection. Or, if the camcorder records to memory card, insert the camcorder's memory card into your computer's memory card reader.

In the case of a direct connection, use the software that came with the camcorder to transfer the digital movie files from the camcorder to your computer's hard drive. If you're using a memory card, you can copy files from the card to your computer using Windows Explorer.

Choosing a Video-Editing Program

Although you can view "raw" video transferred to your PC, you might want to edit your videos into more professional-looking productions. You might, for example, want to cut out some boring footage, combine two or more clips, insert transitions between clips, and even add titles and credits to your movie.

You can do all of these things—and more—with a PC-based video-editing program. These programs perform many of the same functions as the professional editing consoles you might find at your local television station. Today's video-editing programs are surprisingly easy to use—and the results are amazing!

The most popular Windows-compatible video-editing programs are quite affordable—typically $100 or less. The most popular of these include the following:

- Adobe Premiere Elements (www.adobe.com, $99.99)

- Pinnacle Studio HD (www.pinnaclesys.com, $59.95)

- Sony Vegas Movie Studio HD (www.sonycreativesoftware.com, $44.95)

- VideoStudio Express (www.corel.com, $39.99)

- Windows Live Movie Maker (download.live.com, free)

Most of these video-editing programs work in much the same fashion. You select the video files you want to include in your movie and then drag and drop the clips onto a timeline of some sort. You can then rearrange and trim the clips and add transitions from clip to clip. You can create titles and insert them at the front of the video; likewise, you can insert credits at the end. Depending on the program, additional special effects and editing functions might be available. (Figure 29.11 shows the editing window for Adobe Premiere Elements.)

It's all easier to do than you'd think, and the results can approach professional quality. Naturally, all the home movies you create in this fashion can be viewed with Windows' Video app; just go to the Collection section.

FIGURE 29.11

Editing movies with Adobe Premiere Elements.

Playing DVD Movies on Your PC

What about watching old-fashioned DVD movies on your PC? Well, previous versions of Windows included the necessary technology to play DVDs, but Windows 8 does not. This means that you can't use Windows 8 itself to play DVDs on your computer—although DVD playback is still possible.

If you want to watch DVDs on a Windows 8 computer, you need to use a third-party program. You might already have such a program installed; many PC manufacturers include DVD or media player programs as part of the package with new computers. Look on the Start screen for a tile labeled "movies" or "movie player" or "media player" or something like that.

If your computer did not come with a movie player app, you can easily install such a program to play DVD movies. There are a number of popular programs out there, including the following:

- BlazeDVD (www.blazevideo.com, $49.95)

- PowerDVD (www.cyberlink.com, $49.95)

- Roxio CinePlayer (www.roxio.com, $29.99)

- WinDVD (www.corel.com, $49.99)

- Zoom Player (www.inmatrix.com, free)

All of these players work in pretty much the same fashion. Insert your DVD and the player should launch automatically. Playback controls are typically at the bottom of the playback window; you can choose to watch a movie in a window on the desktop or full screen.

THE ABSOLUTE MINIMUM

Here are the key points to remember from this chapter:

- The Windows 8 Video app lets you view movies, TV shows, and other videos stored on your computer.

- You can also use the Video app to purchase movies and TV shows online.

- If you want to edit home movies for viewing on your computer, install and use a video-editing app, such as Adobe Premiere Elements.

- Windows 8 does not include the capability to watch movies on DVD. If you want to watch DVD movies, you need to install a third-party DVD player app.

30

WATCHING TV AND MOVIES ONLINE

Want to rewatch last night's episode of *The Daily Show*? Or the entire first season of your favorite television series? How about a classic music video from your favorite band? Or that latest "viral video" you've been hearing about?

Here's the latest hot thing on the Web—watching your favorite television programs, films, and videos via your web browser. Assuming you have a fast enough Internet connection, you can find tens of thousands of free and paid videos to watch at dozens of different websites.

Looking for Videos on the Web

The first trick to viewing videos online is to find some videos you want to watch. This isn't difficult; many sites specialize in online videos, and many regular websites offer videos as part of their regular content.

 NOTE   Many sites freely offer their web-based videos. Others charge a fee to view or download their videos. Browse around before you enter your credit card number.

Videos on Regular Websites

For example, the CBS News site (www.cbsnews.com) features all sorts of videos on its home page. As you can see in Figure 30.1, you can watch the most recent broadcasts of *60 Minutes*, *CBS This Morning*, and the *CBS Evening News*, along with individual segments from each program and special web-only newscasts. All you have to do is select the video you want to watch and then click or tap the Play button on the embedded video player; there's no separate software to launch.

Similarly, you can go to the NBC website (www.nbc.com) to view full episodes of its top prime-time shows. Missed this week's episode of *The Office* or *Saturday Night Live*? They're available online, for free—as you can see in Figure 30.2.

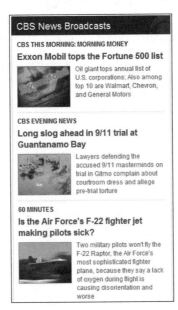

FIGURE 30.1

Watch news broadcasts for free at the CBS News website.

FIGURE 30.2

Prime-time shows online at NBC's website.

Most network TV sites have similar free video offerings. Check out ABC.com (abc.go.com), CBS.com (www.cbs.com), Fox on Demand (www.fox.com), and Comedy Central (www.comedycentral.com). For your favorite music videos, both current and classic, you can't beat MTV.com (www.mtv.com) and VH1.com (www.vh1.com). And to get your daily sports fix, check out the videos on the ESPN website (espn.go.com).

Video-Only Websites

Then there are the websites that specialize in web-based videos. These sites offer videos, videos, and nothing but videos—often for free.

The most popular of these online video sites include

- AOL Video (video.aol.com)

- Hulu (www.hulu.com)

- Metacafe (www.metacafe.com)

- Veoh (www.veoh.com)

- Vevo (www.vevo.com)

- Vimeo (www.vimeo.com)

- Yahoo! Screen (screen.yahoo.com)

- YouTube (www.youtube.com)

Some of these sites offer commercial videos—TV shows and movies. Others offer a larger mix of homemade videos.

For example, Hulu (shown in Figure 30.3) offers episodes from major-network TV shows, as well as new and classic feature films. YouTube, on the other hand, offers millions of free videos uploaded by its users.

FIGURE 30.3

TV shows and movies for online viewing at Hulu.

Whichever service you use, you typically watch the videos in your web browser, using a technique called *streaming video*. This means that there's no downloading necessary (except, perhaps, for an initial plug-in to enable video streaming); the video streams from the website to your computer in real time. Just click the Play button and settle back to watch the show.

 NOTE Sites that offer videos for sale, such as the iTunes Store, let you download the videos to your PC. After they're downloaded, you can watch any video at your leisure and (in some instances) copy the video to your iPod for portable viewing. Learn more in the "Downloading Videos from the iTunes Store" section, later in this chapter.

Viewing Videos on YouTube

Unquestionably, the biggest video site on the Web is YouTube (www.youtube.com), shown in Figure 30.4. What's cool about YouTube is that the majority of the videos are uploaded by other users, so you get a real mix of professional-quality and amateur clips.

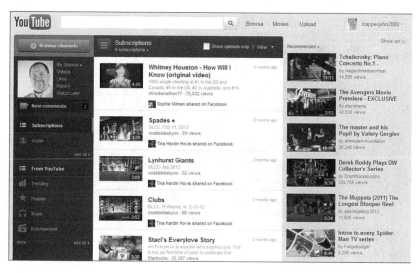

FIGURE 30.4

View user-uploaded videos at YouTube.

Searching for Videos

Looking for an early performance clip of the Beatles? Or a classic toy commercial from the 1970s? Or maybe a homemade mashup of news clips with a hip hop soundtrack? Or something to do with dancing monkeys? What you're looking for is probably somewhere on YouTube; all you have to do is search for it, using the top-of-page search box.

The results of your search are shown on a separate page. Each matching video is listed with a representative thumbnail image, the length of the video, a short description (and descriptive tags), the name of the user who uploaded the video, and a viewer rating (from zero to five stars).

 CAUTION Although YouTube has strict content policies and a self-policing community, there are no parental controls on the site—so it's viewer beware!

Viewing Videos

When you find a video you like, click or tap the image or title, and a new page appears. As you can see in Figure 30.5, this page includes an embedded video player, which starts playing the video automatically. Use the Pause and Play controls as necessary.

FIGURE 30.5

Watching a video on YouTube.

TIP Most YouTube videos can also be watched full-screen; just click the full-screen button beneath the video. If a video is available in high-definition, click the Change Quality button to view it in all its high-resolution, widescreen glory.

Sharing Videos

Videos become viral when they're shared between hundreds and thousands of users—and the easiest way to share a YouTube video is via email. YouTube enables you to send an email containing a link to the video you like to your friends. When a friend receives this email, he or she can click the link in the message to go to YouTube and play the video.

When you want to share a video, go to that video's page, and click or tap the Share button underneath the YouTube video player. When the Share tab expands, click or tap the Email button and then enter the email addresses of the intended recipients into the To box. (Separate multiple addresses with commas.) Enter a personal message if you want and then click or tap the Send button. In a few minutes your recipients will receive the message, complete with a link to the selected video.

You can also share a given video via Facebook, Twitter, and Google+. Click or tap the Share button and then the button for your social network of choice.

Uploading Your Own Videos to YouTube

Anyone can upload a movie or video to the YouTube site. After the video is uploaded, users can view the video—and if you're lucky, the video will go viral!

You can shoot YouTube videos with any computer webcam or consumer camcorder. YouTube accepts videos in just about any format, as long as each video is no more than 10 minutes long.

Uploading is easy. Just follow these steps:

1. Click the Upload link at the top of any YouTube page.

2. When the next page appears, click Select Files from Your Computer.

3. When the Upload page appears, navigate to and select the file to upload and then click the Open button.

4. While the video uploads, you're prompted to enter information about the video, including title, description, tags, category, and privacy level. Do so, and then click or tap the Save Changes button.

That's it. After the video uploads, YouTube converts it to the proper viewing format and creates a viewing page for the video. To view your video, click or tap the My Videos link on any YouTube page, and then click or tap the thumbnail for your new video.

THE ABSOLUTE MINIMUM

Here are the key points to remember from this chapter:

- Numerous websites offer videos for online viewing.

- Most major TV networks offer episodes of their top series online, either on their own sites or at sites such as Hulu.

- The most popular video download site today is YouTube—which also lets you upload your own videos for others to view.

31

PROTECTING AGAINST COMPUTER ATTACKS, MALWARE, AND SPAM

As you've seen, a lot of what you'll do on your computer revolves around the Internet. Unfortunately, when you connect your computer to the Internet, you open a whole new can of worms—literally. Computer worms, viruses, spyware, spam, and the like can attack your computer and cause it to run slowly or not at all. In addition to these malicious software programs (called *malware*) that can infect your computer, you're likely to come across all manner of inappropriate content that you'd probably rather avoid. It can be a nasty world online, if you let it.

Fortunately, it's easy to protect your computer and your family from these dangers. All you need are a few software utilities—and a lot of common sense!

Safeguarding Your System from Computer Viruses

A *computer virus* is a malicious software program designed to do damage to your computer system by deleting files or even taking over your PC to launch attacks on other systems. A virus attacks your computer when you launch an infected software program, launching a "payload" that oftentimes is catastrophic.

Signs of Infection

How do you know whether your computer system has been infected with a virus?

In general, whenever your computer starts acting different from normal, it's possible that you have a virus. You might see strange messages or graphics displayed on your computer screen or find that normally well-behaved programs are acting erratically. You might discover that certain files have gone missing from your hard disk or that your system is acting sluggish—or failing to start at all. You might even find that your friends are receiving emails from you (that you never sent) that have suspicious files attached.

If your computer exhibits one or more of these symptoms—especially if you've just downloaded a file from the Internet or received a suspicious email message—the prognosis is not good. Your computer is probably infected.

 NOTE Many computer attacks today are executed using personal computers compromised by a computer virus. These so-called *zombie computers* are operated via remote control in an ad hoc attack network called a *botnet*. A firewall program protects against incoming attacks and botnet controllers.

How to Catch a Virus

Whenever you share data with another computer or computer user (which you do all the time when you're connected to the Internet), you risk exposing your computer to potential viruses. There are many ways you can share data and many ways a virus can be transmitted:

- Opening an infected file attached to an email message or instant message
- Launching an infected program file downloaded from the Internet
- Sharing a USB memory drive or data CD that contains an infected file
- Sharing over a network a computer file that contains an infection

Of all these methods, the most common means of virus infection is via email—with instant messaging close behind. Whenever you open a file attached to an email message or instant message, you stand a good chance of infecting your computer system with a virus—even if the file was sent by someone you know and trust. That's because many viruses "spoof" the sender's name, thus making you think the file is from a friend or colleague. The bottom line is that no email or instant message attachment is safe unless you were expressly expecting it.

Practicing Safe Computing

Because you're not going to completely quit doing any of these activities, you'll never be 100% safe from the threat of computer viruses. There are, however, some steps you can take to reduce your risk:

- Don't open email attachments from people you don't know—or even from people you *do* know, if you aren't expecting them. That's because some viruses can hijack the address book on an infected PC, thus sending out infected email that the owner isn't even aware of. Just looking at an email message won't harm anything; the damage comes when you open a file attached to the email.

- Don't accept files sent to you via instant messaging; like email attachments, files sent via IM can be easily infected with viruses and spyware.

- Download files only from reliable file archive websites, such as Download.com (www.download.com) and Tucows (www.tucows.com/downloads/).

- Don't access or download files from music and video file-sharing networks, which are notoriously virus- and spyware-ridden. Instead, download music and movies from legitimate sites, such as the iTunes Store and Amazon MP3 Store.

- Don't execute programs you find in Usenet newsgroups or posted to web message boards or blogs.

- Don't click links sent to you from strangers via instant messaging or in a chat room.

- Share USB drives, CDs, and files only with users you know and trust.

- Use antivirus software—and keep it up-to-date with the most recent virus definitions.

These precautions—especially the first one about not opening email attachments—should provide good insurance against the threat of computer viruses.

CAUTION If you remember nothing else from this chapter, remember this: Never open an unexpected file attachment. Period!

Disinfecting Your System with Antivirus Software

Antivirus software programs are capable of detecting known viruses and protecting your system against new, unknown viruses. These programs check your system for viruses each time your system is booted and can be configured to check any programs you download from the Internet. They're also used to disinfect your system if it becomes infected with a virus.

Fortunately, Windows 8 comes with its own built-in antivirus utility. It's called Windows Defender, and you can see it in action by going to the All Apps page, scrolling to the Apps section, and clicking or tapping Windows Defender.

 NOTE Windows Defender may or may not be activated on your new PC. Some computer manufacturers prefer to include third-party antivirus software, and thus disable Windows Defender by default.

As you can see in Figure 31.1, Windows Defender runs in the background, monitoring your computer against all sorts of malware, including both viruses and spyware. Although Defender automatically scans your system on its own schedule, you can also opt to perform a manual scan at any time by clicking the Scan Now button.

Of course, you're not locked into using Microsoft's anti-malware solution. There are a lot of third-party antivirus programs available, including the following:

- AVG Anti-Virus (www.avg.com)
- Avira Antivirus (www.avira.com)
- Kaspersky Anti-Virus (www.kaspersky.com)
- McAfee AntiVirus Plus (www.mcafee.com)
- Norton AntiVirus (www.symantec.com)
- Trend Micro Titanium (www.trendmicro.com)

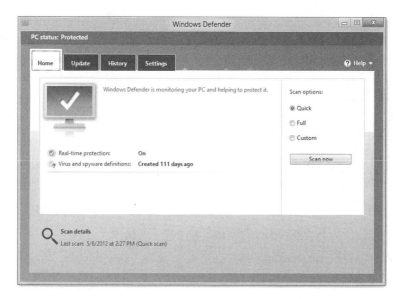

FIGURE 31.1

Windows Defender—Windows 8's built-in anti-malware utility.

CAUTION Your antivirus software is next to useless if you don't update it at least weekly. An outdated antivirus program won't be capable of recognizing—and protecting against—the very latest computer viruses.

Whichever antivirus program you choose, you need to configure it to go online periodically to update the virus definition database the program uses to look for known virus files. Because new viruses are created every week, this file of known viruses must be updated accordingly.

Hunting Down Spyware

Even more pernicious than computer viruses is the proliferation of *spyware*. A spyware program installs itself on your computer and then surreptitiously sends information about the way you use your PC to some interested third party. Spyware typically gets installed in the background when you're installing another program. Peer-to-peer music-trading networks (*not* legitimate online music stores, such as the iTunes Store) are one of the biggest sources of spyware; when you install the file-trading software, the spyware is also installed.

Having spyware on your system is nasty—almost as bad as being infected with a computer virus. Some spyware programs even hijack your computer and launch pop-up windows and advertisements when you visit certain web pages. If there's spyware on your computer, you definitely want to get rid of it.

Unfortunately, many antivirus programs won't catch spyware because spyware isn't a virus. To track down and uninstall these programs, then, you might need to run a separate anti-spyware utility.

 NOTE Windows Defender, included free in Windows 8, guards against both viruses and spyware.

Here are some of the best of these spyware fighters:

- Ad-Aware (www.lavasoftusa.com)

- Spybot Search & Destroy (www.safer-networking.org)

- Webroot Spy Sweeper (www.webroot.com)

In addition, some of the major Internet security suites, such as Norton Internet Security and McAfee Total Protection, include anti-spyware modules. Check the program's feature list before you buy.

Defending Against Computer Attacks

Connecting to the Internet is a two-way street—not only can your PC access other computers online, but other computers can also access *your* PC. Which means that, unless you take proper precautions, malicious hackers can read your private data, damage your system hardware and software, and even use your system (via remote control) to cause damage to other computers.

You protect your system against outside attack by blocking the path of attack with a *firewall*. A firewall is a software program that forms a virtual barrier between your computer and the Internet. The firewall selectively filters the data that is passed between both ends of the connection and protects your system against outside attack.

Using the Windows Firewall

Fortunately for all of us, Microsoft builds a firewall utility into Windows. The Windows Firewall is activated by default, although you can always check to make sure that it's up and working properly. You do this by opening the Control Panel and selecting System and Security, Windows Firewall.

Using Third-Party Firewall Software

For most users, the Windows Firewall is more than enough protection against computer attacks. That said, a number of third-party firewall programs also are available, most of which are more robust and offer more protection than Windows' built-in firewall. The best of these programs include

- McAfee Total Protection (www.mcafee.com)

- Norton Internet Security (www.symantec.com)

- ZoneAlarm Free Firewall (www.zonelabs.com)

 NOTE   If you're running a third-party firewall program, you might need to turn off the Windows Firewall.

Fighting Email Spam

If you're like most users, well over half the messages delivered to your email inbox are unsolicited, unauthorized, and unwanted—in other words, *spam*. These spam messages are the online equivalent of the junk mail you receive in your postal mailbox, and it's a huge problem.

Although it's probably impossible to do away with 100% of the spam you receive (you can't completely stop junk mail, either), there are steps you can take to reduce the amount of spam you have to deal with. The heavier your spam load, the more steps you can take.

Protecting Your Email Address

Spammers accumulate email addresses via a variety of methods. Some use high-tech methods to harvest email addresses listed on public web pages and message board postings. Others use the tried-and-true approach of buying names from list brokers. Still others automatically generate addresses using a "dictionary" of common names and email domains.

One way to reduce the amount of spam you receive is to limit the public use of your email address. It's a simple fact: The more you expose your email address, the more likely it is that a spammer will find it—and use it.

To this end, you should avoid putting your email address on your web page or your company's web page. You should also avoid including your email address in postings you make to web-based message boards or Usenet newsgroups. In addition, you should most definitely not include your email address in any of the conversations you have in chat rooms or via instant messaging.

Another strategy is to actually use *two* email addresses. Take your main email address (the one you get from your ISP) and hand it out only to a close circle of friends and family; do *not* use this address to post public messages or to register at websites. Then obtain a second email address (you can get a free one at Hotmail or Gmail) and use that one for all your public activity. When you post on a message board or newsgroup, use the second address. When you order something from an online merchant, use the second address. When you register for website access, use the second address. Over time, the second address will attract the spam; your first email address will remain private and relatively spam-free.

TIP If you do have to leave your email address in a public forum, you can insert a spamblock into your address—an unexpected word or phrase that, although easily removed, will confuse the software spammers use to harvest addresses. For example, if your email address is johnjones@myisp.com, you might change the address to read johnSPAMBLOCKjones@myisp.com. Other users will know to remove the SPAMBLOCK from the address before emailing you, but the spam harvesting software will be foiled.

Blocking Spammers in Your Email Programs

Most email software and web-based email services include some sort of spam filtering. You should always enable the anti-spam features in your email program or service, which should block most of the unwanted messages you might otherwise receive.

TIP It's a good idea to review messages in your spam folder periodically, to make sure no legitimate messages have been accidentally sent there.

Resisting Phishing Scams

Phishing is a technique used by online scam artists to steal your identity by tricking you into disclosing valuable personal information, such as passwords, credit card numbers, and other financial data. If you're not careful, you can mistake a phishing email for a real one—and open yourself up to identity theft.

A phishing scam typically starts with a phony email message that appears to be from a legitimate source, such as your bank, eBay, PayPal, or other official institution. When you click the link in the phishing email, you're taken to a fake website masquerading as the real site, complete with logos and official-looking text. You're encouraged to enter your personal information into the forms on the web page; when you do so, your information is sent to the scammer, and you're now a victim of identity theft. When your data falls into the hands of criminals, it can be used to hack into your online accounts, make unauthorized charges on your credit card, and maybe even drain your bank account.

Until recently, the only guard against phishing scams was common sense. That is, you should never click through a link in an email message that asks for any type of personal information—whether that be your bank account number or eBay password. Even if the email *looks* official, it probably isn't; legitimate institutions and websites never include this kind of link in their official messages. Instead, you should access your personal information only by using your web browser to go directly to the website in question. Don't link there!

Fortunately, Windows offers some protection against phishing scams, in the form of a SmartScreen Filter that alerts you to potential phishing sites. When you attempt to visit a known or suspected phishing site, the browser displays a warning message. Do not enter information into these suspected phishing sites—return to your home page, instead!

But even with these protections, you also need to use your head. Don't click through suspicious email links, and don't give out your personal information and passwords unless you're sure you're dealing with an official (and not just an official-looking) site!

Shielding Your Children from Inappropriate Content

The Internet contains an almost limitless supply of information on its tens of billions of web pages. Although most of these pages contain useful information, it's a sad fact that the content of some pages can be quite offensive to some people—and that there are some Internet users who prey on unsuspecting youths.

As a responsible parent, you want to protect your children from any of the bad stuff (and bad people) online, while still allowing access to all the good stuff. How do you do this?

Using Content-Filtering Software

If you can't trust your children to always click away from inappropriate web content, you can choose to install software on your computer that performs filtering functions for all your online sessions. These safe-surfing programs guard against either a preselected list of inappropriate sites or a preselected list of topics—and then block access to sites that meet the selected criteria. After you have the software installed, your kids won't be able to access the really bad sites on the Web.

The most popular filtering programs include the following:

- CyberPatrol (www.cyberpatrol.com)

- CYBERsitter (www.cybersitter.com)

- Net Nanny (www.netnanny.com)

In addition, many of the big Internet security suites (such as those from McAfee and Norton/Symantec) offer built-in content-filtering modules.

Kids-Safe Searching

If you don't want to go to all the trouble of using content-filtering software, you can at least steer your children to some of the safer sites on the Web. The best of these sites offer kid-safe searching so that all inappropriate sites are filtered out of the search results.

The best of these kids-safe search and directory sites include

- Ask Kids (www.askkids.com)

- Fact Monster (www.factmonster.com)

- Google SafeSearch (www.google.com; go to the Preferences page and then choose a SafeSearch Filtering option)

- Yahoo! Kids (kids.yahoo.com)

 TIP A kids-safe search site is often good to use as the start page for your children's browser because it is a launching pad to guaranteed safe content.

Encouraging Safe Computing

Although using content-filtering software and kids-safe websites are good steps, the most important thing you can do, as a parent, is to create an environment that encourages appropriate use of the Internet. Nothing replaces traditional parental supervision, and at the end of the day, you have to take responsibility for your children's online activities. Provide the guidance they need to make the Internet a fun and educational place to visit—and your entire family will be better for it.

Here are some guidelines you can follow to ensure a safer surfing experience for your family:

- Make sure that your children know never to give out identifying information (home address, school name, telephone number, and so on) or to send their photos to other users online. This includes not putting overly personal information (and photos!) on their MySpace and Facebook pages.

- Provide each of your children with an online pseudonym so they don't have to use their real names online.

- Don't let your children arrange face-to-face meetings with other computer users without parental permission and supervision. If a meeting is arranged, make the first one in a public place, and be sure to accompany your child.

- Teach your children that people online might not always be who they seem; just because someone says that she's a 10-year-old girl doesn't necessarily mean that she really is 10 years old, or a girl.

- Consider making Internet surfing an activity you do together with your younger children—or turn it into a family activity by putting your kids' PC in a public room (such as a living room or den) rather than in a private bedroom.

- Set reasonable rules and guidelines for your kids' computer use. Consider limiting the number of minutes/hours they can spend online each day.

- Monitor your children's Internet activities. Ask them to keep a log of all websites they visit or check their browser history; oversee any chat sessions they participate in; check out any files they download; even consider sharing an email account (especially with younger children) so that you can oversee their messages.

- Don't let your children respond to messages that are suggestive, obscene, belligerent, or threatening—or that make them feel uncomfortable in any way. Encourage your children to tell you if they receive any such messages, and then report the senders to your ISP.

- Install content-filtering software on your PC, and set up one of the kid-safe search sites (discussed earlier in this section) as your browser's start page.

Teach your children that Internet access is not a right; it should be a privilege earned by your children and kept only when their use of it matches your expectations.

THE ABSOLUTE MINIMUM

Here are the key points to remember from this chapter:

- Avoid computer viruses by not opening unsolicited email attachments and by using an antivirus software program.

- Use anti-spyware tools to track down and remove spyware programs from your computer.

- Windows 8 has its own Windows Defender anti-malware utility.

- Protect your computer from an Internet-based attack by turning on the Windows Firewall or using a third-party firewall program.

- Fight email spam by keeping your email address as private as possible and utilizing your email program's spam filter.

- Avoid falling for phishing scams characterized by fake—but official-looking—email messages.

- To protect against inappropriate content on the Internet, install content-filtering software—and make sure that your children use kid-safe websites.

32

PERFORMING ROUTINE MAINTENANCE AND DEALING WITH COMMON PROBLEMS

"An ounce of prevention is worth a pound of cure."

That old adage might seem trite and clichéd, but it's also true—especially when it comes to your computer system. Spending a few minutes a week on preventive maintenance can save you from costly computer problems in the future.

To make this chore a little easier, Windows includes several utilities to help you keep your system running smoothly. You should use these tools as part of your regular maintenance routine—or if you experience specific problems with your computer system.

And if you experience more serious problems—well, try not to panic. There are ways to fix most issues you encounter, without necessarily calling in the tech support guys.

Maintaining Your Computer

Most computers these days, especially those running Windows 8, don't require a lot of handholding to keep them up and running. That said, there's a little bit of routine maintenance you might want to undertake—just to make sure your system remains in its optimal operating condition.

Cleaning Up Unused Files

Most desktop and notebook computers have pretty big hard disks; ultrabooks and tablets do not. But even if your computer has a tremendous amount of storage, it's still easy to end up with too many useless files and programs taking up too much disk space.

Fortunately, Windows includes a utility that identifies and deletes unused files. The Disk Cleanup tool is what you want to use when you need to free up extra hard disk space for more frequently used files.

To use Disk Cleanup, follow these steps:

1. From the Control Panel, click System and Security.

2. On the next screen, scroll to the Administrative Tools section and click Free Up Disk Space.

3. When prompted, select the drive you want to clean up and then click OK.

4. Disk Cleanup automatically analyzes the contents of your hard disk drive. When it's finished analyzing, it presents its results in the Disk Cleanup dialog box, shown in Figure 32.1.

    NOTE You can safely choose to delete all the files found by Disk Cleanup except the setup log files, which are sometimes needed by the Windows operating system.

5. You have the option of permanently deleting various types of files: downloaded program files, temporary Internet files, offline web pages, deleted files in the Recycle Bin, and so forth. Select which files you want to delete.

6. Click OK to begin deleting.

FIGURE 32.1

Use Disk Cleanup to delete unused files from your hard disk.

Removing Unused Programs

Another way to free up valuable hard disk space is to delete those programs you never use. This is accomplished using the Uninstall or Change a Program utilities in Windows. Use the following steps.

 TIP Most brand-new PCs come with unwanted programs and trial versions installed at the factory. Many users choose to delete these "bloatware" programs when they first run their PCs.

1. From the Windows Control Panel, click Uninstall a Program (in the Programs section).

2. When the next screen appears, as shown in Figure 32.2, click the program you want to delete.

3. Click Uninstall.

FIGURE 32.2

Uninstall any program you're no longer using.

Making Your Hard Disk Run Better by Defragmenting

If you think that your computer is taking longer than usual to open files or notice that your hard drive light stays on longer than usual, you might need to *defragment* your hard drive.

File fragmentation is sort of like taking the pieces of a jigsaw puzzle and storing them in different boxes along with pieces from other puzzles. The more dispersed the pieces are, the longer it takes to put the puzzle together. Spreading the bits and pieces of a file around your hard disk occurs whenever you install, delete, or run an application or when you edit, move, copy, or delete a file.

If you notice that your system takes longer and longer to open and close files or run applications, it's because these file fragments are spread all over the place. You fix the problem when you put all the pieces of the puzzle back in the right boxes—which you do by defragmenting your hard disk.

To defragment your hard disk, use the Disk Defragmenter utility. In Windows 8, Disk Defragmenter runs periodically in the background, automatically defragging your hard disk whenever your computer is turned on. You can also choose to run the utility manually, to affect more immediate results.

To run Disk Defragmenter manually, follow these steps:

1. From the Control Panel, click System and Security.

2. On the next screen, scroll to the Administrative Tools section and click Defragment Your Hard Drive.

3. When the Optimize Drives window appears, as shown in Figure 32.3, select the drive you want to defragment.

4. Click the Optimize button.

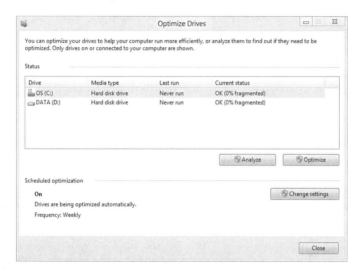

FIGURE 32.3

Defragmenting a hard drive.

Defragmenting your drive can take a while, especially if you have a large hard drive or your drive is really fragmented. So, you might want to start the utility and let it run overnight while you're sleeping.

Performing a Hard Disk Checkup with ScanDisk

Any time you run an application, move or delete a file, or accidentally turn the power off while the system is running, you run the risk of introducing errors to your hard disk. These errors can make it harder to open files, slow down your hard disk, or cause your system to freeze when you open or save a file or an application.

Fortunately, you can find and fix most of these errors directly from within Windows. All you have to do is run the built-in ScanDisk utility.

To find and fix errors on your hard drive, follow these steps:

1. Launch Windows Explorer and click Computer in the navigation sidebar.

2. Right-click the icon for the drive you want to scan and then select Properties from the pop-up menu.

3. When the Properties dialog box appears, select the Tools tab.

4. Click the Check button in the Error-Checking section.

5. When the Check Disk dialog box appears, check both the options (Automatically Fix File System Errors and Scan for and Attempt Recovery of Bad Sectors).

6. Click Start.

Windows now scans your hard disk and attempts to fix any errors it encounters. Note that you might be prompted to reboot your PC if you're checking your computer's C: drive.

Using the Windows Action Center

In Windows 8, the best way to manage your PC's maintenance and security is via the Action Center utility. As you can see in Figure 32.4, the Action Center centralizes a lot of maintenance operations, error reporting, and troubleshooting operations.

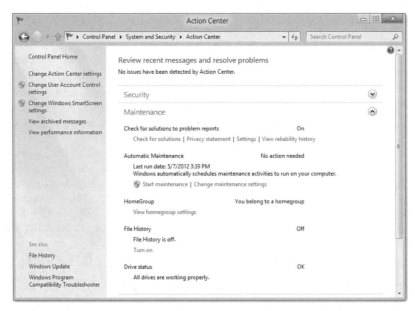

FIGURE 32.4

Monitoring your system's maintenance with the Windows Action Center.

To access the Action Center, open the Windows Control Panel and select System & Security, Action Center. The Action Center alerts you to any action you need to take to protect and maintain your system.

Keeping Your Hardware in Tip-Top Condition

There's also a fair amount of preventive maintenance you can physically perform on your computer hardware. It's simple stuff, but it can really extend the life of your PC.

System Unit

The system unit on a desktop PC—or the entire unit of a notebook or tablet computer—has a lot of sensitive electronics inside, from memory chips to disk drives to power supplies. Check out these maintenance tips to keep your system unit from flaking out on you:

- Position your computer in a clean, dust-free environment. Keep it away from direct sunlight and strong magnetic fields. In addition, make sure that your system unit and your monitor have plenty of air flow around them to keep them from overheating.

- Hook up your system unit to a surge suppressor to avoid damaging power spikes.

- Avoid turning on and off your system unit too often; it's better to leave it on all the time than incur frequent "power on" stress to all those delicate components. However…

- Turn off your system unit if you're going to be away for an extended period—anything longer than a few days.

- Check all your cable connections periodically. Make sure that all the connectors are firmly connected and all the screws properly screwed—and make sure that your cables aren't stretched too tight or bent in ways that could damage the wires inside.

Keyboard

Even something as simple as your computer keyboard requires a little preventive maintenance from time to time. Check out these tips:

- Keep your keyboard away from young children and pets—they can get dirt and hair and Play-Doh all over the place, and they have a tendency to put way too much pressure on the keys.

- Keep your keyboard away from dust, dirt, smoke, direct sunlight, and other harmful environmental stuff. You might even consider putting a dust cover on your keyboard when it's not in use.

- Use a small vacuum cleaner to periodically sweep the dirt from your keyboard. (Alternatively, you can use compressed air to *blow* the dirt away.) Use a cotton swab or soft cloth to clean between the keys. If necessary, remove the keycaps to clean the switches underneath.

- If you spill something on your keyboard, disconnect it immediately and wipe up the spill. Use a soft cloth to get between the keys; if necessary, use a screwdriver to pop off the keycaps and wipe up any seepage underneath. Let the keyboard dry thoroughly before trying to use it again.

Display

If you think of your computer display as a little television set, you're on the right track. Just treat your screen as you do your TV, and you'll be okay. That said, look at these preventive maintenance tips:

- As with all other important system components, keep your monitor away from direct sunlight, dust, and smoke. Make sure that it has plenty of ventilation, especially around the back; don't cover the rear cooling vents with paper or any other object, and don't set anything bigger than a small plush toy on top of the cabinet.

- Don't place strong magnets in close proximity to your monitor. (This includes external speakers.)

- With your monitor turned off, periodically clean the monitor screen. For an LCD flat-panel monitor, use water to dampen a lint-free cloth, and then wipe the screen; do not spray liquid directly on the screen. Do not use any cleaner that contains alcohol or ammonia; these chemicals may damage an LCD screen. (You can, however, use commercial cleaning wipes specially formulated for LCD screens.)

- Don't forget to adjust the brightness and contrast controls on your monitor every now and then. Any controls can get out of whack—plus, your monitor's performance will change as it ages, and simple adjustments can often keep it looking as good as new.

Printer

Your printer is a complex device with a lot of moving parts. Follow these tips to keep your printouts in good shape:

- Use a soft cloth, mini-vacuum cleaner, or compressed air to clean the inside and outside of your printer on a periodic basis. In particular, make sure that you clean the paper path of all paper shavings and dust.

- If you have an ink-jet printer, periodically clean the ink jets. Run your printer's cartridge cleaning utility, or use a small pin to make sure that they don't get clogged.

- If you have a laser printer, replace the toner cartridge as needed. When you replace the cartridge, remember to clean the printer cleaning bar and other related parts, per the manufacturer's instructions.

- Don't use alcohol or other solvents to clean rubber or plastic parts—you'll do more harm than good!

Maintaining a Notebook PC

All the previous tips hold for both desktop and notebook PCs. If you have a notebook PC, however, there are additional steps you need to take to keep everything working in prime condition.

Using the Windows Mobility Center

Let's start with all the various settings that are unique to a notebook PC—power plan, display brightness, presentation settings, and so forth. Windows puts all these settings into a single control panel called the Windows Mobility Center. As you can see in Figure 32.5, you can use the Mobility Center to configure and manage just about everything that makes your notebook run better.

To access the Windows Mobility Center, go to the All Apps screen, scroll to the Windows Accessories section, and click or tap Mobility Center. Click or tap the button or adjust the slider for whichever option you need to change.

 NOTE   Some notebook manufacturers add their own mobile configuration settings to the Windows Mobility Center.

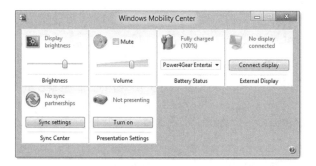

FIGURE 32.5

Manage key notebook PC settings with the Windows Mobility Center.

Conserving Battery Life

One of the key issues with a notebook PC is battery life. It's especially important if you use your notebook a lot on the road.

Any notebook, even a desktop replacement model, gives you at least an hour of operation before the battery powers down. If you need more battery life than that, here are some things you can try:

- **Change your power scheme**—Windows includes several built-in power schemes that manage key functions to provide either longer battery life or better performance. (It's always a trade-off between the two.) You can switch power schemes from the Windows Mobility Center (in the Battery Status section) or by clicking the Power icon in the notification area of the Windows taskbar on the traditional desktop.

- **Dim your screen**—The brighter your screen, the more power your PC uses. Conserve on power usage by dialing down the brightness level of your notebook's screen.

- **Turn it off when you're not using it**—A PC sitting idle is still using power. If you're going to be away from the keyboard for more than a few minutes, turn off the notebook to conserve power—or put the PC into sleep mode, which also cuts power use.

- **Don't do anything taxing**—Anytime you write or read a file from your notebook's hard disk, you use power. The same goes with using the CD or DVD drive; every spin of the drive drains the battery. If you use your notebook to watch DVD movies, don't expect the batteries to last as long as if you were just checking email or surfing the Web.

- **Buy a bigger battery**—Many notebook manufacturers sell batteries that have various capacities. You might be able to buy a longer-lasting battery than the one that came in the box.

- **Buy a second battery**—When the first battery is drained, remove it and plug in a fresh one.

- **Buy a smaller notebook**—Ultrabook models use less power and have longer battery life than do traditional notebooks, which in turn are less power-hungry than desktop replacement models. The smaller the screen and the less power-ful the CPU, the longer the notebook's battery life.

If worse comes to worst, keep an eye out for an available power outlet. Most coffee shops and airport lounges have at least one seat next to a power outlet; just carry your notebook's AC adapter with you and be ready to plug in when you can.

Securing Your Notebook

One of the great things about a notebook PC is that it's small and easily portable. One of the bad things about a notebook PC is that it's small and easily portable—which makes it attractive to thieves. Take care to protect your notebook when you're using it in public, which may mean investing in a notebook lock or some similar sort of antitheft device. Of course, just being vigilant helps; never leave your notebook unattended in a coffee shop or airport terminal.

In addition, be careful about transmitting private data over a public Wi-Fi network. Avoid the temptation to do your online shopping (and transmit your credit card number) from your local coffee shop; wait until you're safely connected to your home network before you send your private data over the Wi-Fi airwaves.

How to Troubleshoot Computer Problems

Computers aren't perfect. It's possible—although unlikely—that at some point in time, something will go wrong with your PC. It might refuse to start, it might freeze up, it might crash and go dead. Yikes!

When something goes wrong with your computer, there's no need to panic (even though that's what you'll probably feel like doing). Most PC problems have easy-to-find causes and simple solutions. The key thing is to keep your wits about you and attack the situation calmly and logically—following the advice you'll find in this chapter.

No matter what kind of computer-related problem you're experiencing, there are six basic steps you should take to track down the cause of the problem. Work through these steps calmly and deliberately, and you're likely to find what's causing the current problem—and then be in a good position to fix it yourself:

1. **Don't panic!**—Just because there's something wrong with your PC is no reason to fly off the handle. Chances are there's nothing seriously wrong. Besides, getting all panicky won't solve anything. Keep your wits about you and proceed logically, and you can probably find what's causing your problem and get it fixed.

2. **Check for operator errors**—In other words, something *you* did wrong. Maybe you clicked the wrong button, pressed the wrong key, or plugged something into the wrong jack or port. Retrace your steps and try to duplicate your problem. Chances are the problem won't recur if you don't make the same mistake twice.

3. **Check that everything is plugged into the proper place and that the system unit itself is getting power**—Take special care to ensure that all your cables are *securely* connected—loose connections can cause all sorts of strange results.

4. **Make sure you have the latest versions of all the software installed on your system**—While you're at it, make sure you have the latest versions of device drivers installed for all the peripherals on your system.

5. **Try to isolate the problem by when and how it occurs**—Walk through each step of the process to see if you can identify a particular program or driver that might be causing the problem.

6. **When all else fails, call in professional help**—If you think it's a Windows-related problem, contact Microsoft's technical support department. If you think it's a problem with a particular program, contact the tech support department of the program's manufacturer. If you think it's a hardware-related problem, contact the manufacturer of your PC or the dealer you bought it from. The pros are there for a reason—when you need technical support, go and get it.

 CAUTION   Not all tech support is free. Unless you have a brand new PC or brand new software, expect to pay a fee for technical support.

Troubleshooting in Safe Mode

If you're having trouble getting Windows to start, it's probably because some setting is wrong or some driver is malfunctioning. The problem is, how do you get into Windows to fix what's wrong, when you can't even start Windows?

The solution is to hijack your computer before Windows gets hold of it and force it to start *without* whatever is causing the problem. You do this by watching the screen as your computer boots up and pressing the F8 key just before Windows starts to load. This displays the Windows startup menu, where you select Safe mode.

Safe mode is a special mode of operation that loads Windows in a very simple configuration. When in Safe mode you can look for device conflicts, restore incorrect or corrupted device drivers, or restore your system to a prior working configuration (using the System Restore utility, discussed later in this chapter).

 NOTE Depending on the severity of your system problem, Windows might start in Safe mode automatically.

What to Do When Windows Freezes or Crashes

Probably the most common computer trouble is the freeze-up. That's what happens when your PC just stops dead in its tracks. The screen looks normal, but nothing works—you can't type onscreen, you can't click any buttons, nothing's happening. Even worse is when Windows crashes on you—just shuts down with no warning.

If your system freezes or crashes, the good news is that there's probably nothing wrong with your computer hardware. The bad news is that there's probably something funky happening with your operating system.

This doesn't mean your system is broken. It's just a glitch. And you can recover from glitches. Just remember not to panic and to approach the situation calmly and rationally.

What Causes Windows to Freeze?

If Windows up and freezes, what's the likely cause? There can be many different causes of a Windows freeze, including the following:

- You might be running an older software program or game that isn't compatible with your version of Windows. If so, upgrade the program.

- A memory conflict might exist between applications, or between an application and Windows. Try running fewer programs at once, or running problematic programs one at a time to avoid potential memory conflicts.

- You might not have enough memory installed on your system. Upgrade the amount of memory in your PC.

- You might not have enough free hard disk space on your computer. Delete any unnecessary files from your hard drive.

- Your hard disk might be developing errors or bad sectors. Check your hard disk for errors, as described in the "Perform a Hard Disk Checkup with ScanDisk" section earlier in this chapter.

Dealing with Frozen Windows

When Windows freezes, you need to get it unfrozen and up and running again. The way to do this is to shut down your computer.

In older versions of Windows, you could force a shutdown by holding down the Ctrl+Alt+Del keys. That doesn't work in Windows 8; instead, you need to press the Windows key and your PC's power button simultaneously. If that doesn't work, just press and hold the power button until the PC shuts down.

If your system crashes or freezes frequently, however, you should call in a pro. These kinds of problems can be tough to track down by yourself when you're dealing with Windows.

Dealing with a Frozen Program

Sometimes Windows works fine but an individual software program freezes. Fortunately, recent versions of Windows present an exceptionally safe environment; when an individual application crashes or freezes, it seldom messes up your entire system. You can use a utility called the Windows Task Manager to close the problem application without affecting other Windows programs.

When a Windows application freezes or crashes, press Ctrl+Alt+Del, and when the next screen appears, click or tap Task Manager; this opens the Windows Task Manager, shown in Figure 32.6. Select the task that's frozen and then click or tap the End Task button. That should do the trick.

If you have multiple applications that crash on a regular basis, the situation can often be attributed to insufficient memory. See your computer dealer about adding more RAM to your system.

FIGURE 32.6

Use the Windows Task Manager to end nonresponding programs.

Dealing with a Major Crash

Perhaps the worst thing that can happen to your computer system is that it crashes—completely shuts down—without warning. If this happens to you, start by not panicking. Stay calm, take a few deep breaths, and then get ready to get going again.

You should always wait about 60 seconds after a computer crashes before you try to turn on your system again. This gives all the components time to settle down and—in some cases—reset themselves. Just sit back and count to 60 (slowly); then press your system unit's "on" button.

Nine times out of ten, your system will boot up normally, as if nothing unusual has happened. If this is what happens for you, great! If, on the other hand, your system doesn't come back up normally, you'll need to start troubleshooting the underlying problem, as discussed previously.

Even if your system comes back up as usual, the sudden crash might have done some damage. A system crash can sometimes damage any software program that was running at the time, as well as any documents that were open when the crash occurred. You might have to reinstall a damaged program or recover a damaged document from a backup file.

Restoring, Resetting, or Refreshing Your System

If you experience severe or recurring system crashes, it's time to take serious action. In Windows 8 there are three options for dealing with serious problems—in terms of severity, you can opt to restore, reset, or completely refresh your system.

Restoring Your System to a Previous State

The least intrusive course of action when your system crashes is to use Microsoft's System Restore utility. This utility can automatically restore your system to the state it was in before the crash occurred—and save you the trouble of reinstalling any damaged software programs. It's a great safety net for when things go wrong.

System Restore works by monitoring your system and noting any changes that are made when you install new applications. Each time it notes a change, it automatically creates what it calls a *restore point*. A restore point is basically a "snapshot" of key system files (including the Windows Registry) just before the new application is installed.

If something in your system goes bad, you can run System Restore to set things right. Pick a restore point before the problem occurred (such as right before a new installation), and System Restore will undo any changes made to monitored files since the restore point was created. This restores your system to its preinstallation—that is, *working*—condition.

To restore your system from a restore point, follow these steps:

1. From the Windows Control Panel, click System and Security, then System.

2. From the left-hand pane, click Advanced System Settings. This opens the System Properties window, with the System Protection tab selected.

3. Click the System Restore button to display the System Restore window, shown in Figure 32.7.

4. You can now choose to restore to the Windows recommended restore point or to a different restore point. (Check the Choose a Different Restore Point option.) Make your choice and click Next.

5. When the confirmation screen appears, click the Finish button.

 CAUTION System Restore helps you recover any damaged programs and system files, but it doesn't help you recover damaged documents or data files.

FIGURE 32.7

Use the System Restore utility to restore damaged programs or system files.

Windows now starts to restore your system. You should make sure that all open programs are closed because Windows needs to be restarted during this process.

When the process is complete, your system should be back in decent working shape. Note, however, that it might take a half-hour or more to complete a system restore—so you'll have time to order a pizza and eat dinner before the operation is done!

Refreshing System Files

New to Windows 8 is the ability to "refresh" your system with the current versions of important system files. Windows 8's Refresh PC utility works by checking whether key system files are working properly or not. If it finds any issues, it attempts to repair those files—and only those files.

 NOTE The Refresh PC utility doesn't remove any of your personal files or documents. It only refreshes Windows system files.

To refresh your system, follow these steps:

1. Display the Charms Bar and select Settings.

2. When the next panel appears, click or tap More PC Settings to display the PC Settings page.

3. Select the General tab.

4. Scroll down to the Refresh Your PC Without Affecting Your Files section, shown in Figure 32.8, and click or tap Get Started.

5. Windows tells you what it's going to do. Click or tap Next to proceed.

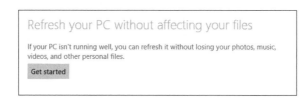

Refresh your PC without affecting your files

If your PC isn't running well, you can refresh it without losing your photos, music, videos, and other personal files.

Get started

FIGURE 32.8

Getting ready to refresh your system.

Windows prepares your system for the refresh; this might take a few minutes. Your computer eventually restarts. When you see the Start screen, your system is refreshed.

Resetting Your System to Its Original Condition

Resetting your system is more drastic than simply refreshing it. The Reset PC utility wipes your hard disk clean and reinstalls Windows from scratch. That leaves you with a completely reset system—but without any of the apps you've installed or the files you created.

 CAUTION The Reset PC utility completely deletes any files, documents, and programs you have on your system. Back up your files before taking this extreme step, and then restore your files from the backup and reinstall all the apps you use.

To reset your system, follow these steps:

1. Display the Charms Bar and select Settings.

2. When the next panel appears, click or tap More PC Settings to display the PC Settings page.

3. Select the General tab.

4. Scroll down to the Reset Your PC and Start Over section, shown in Figure 32.9, and click or tap Get Started.

5. Windows tells you what it's going to do. Click or tap Next to proceed.

6. If your PC has more than one drive, you're prompted to remove files from all drives or only the drive where Windows is installed. Make your choice.

7. Windows asks how you want to remove your personal files—thoroughly or quickly. For most situations quickly is fine.

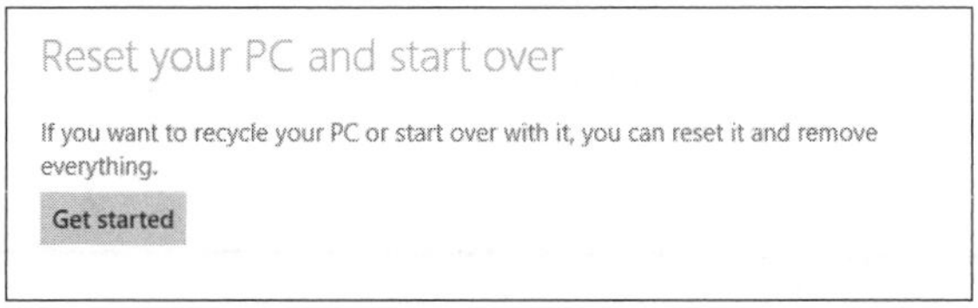

Reset your PC and start over

If you want to recycle your PC or start over with it, you can reset it and remove everything.

Get started

FIGURE 32.9

Getting ready to reset your system to factory-fresh condition.

Windows begins resetting your system by deleting everything on your hard drive and reinstalling the Windows operating system. This might take some time. When the process is complete, you need to re-enter your Windows product key and other personal information—but you'll have a like-new system, ready to start using again.

THE ABSOLUTE MINIMUM

Here are the key points to remember from this chapter:

- Dedicating a few minutes a week to PC maintenance can prevent serious problems from occurring in the future.

- Windows includes a number of utilities you can use to keep your hard drive in tip-top shape.

- Make sure that you keep all your computer hardware away from direct sunlight, dust, and smoke, and make sure that your system unit has plenty of ventilation.

- If you have a notebook PC, take appropriate steps to conserve battery life—and keep your PC safe from thieves!

- You can shut down frozen programs from the Windows Task Manager, which you display by pressing Ctrl+Alt+Del.

- Some problems can be fixed from Windows Safe mode; to enter Safe mode, restart your computer and press F8 before the Windows start screen appears.

- If your system has serious problems, you can opt to restore, refresh, or completely reset Windows to its original factory condition.

Index

X

Y

Z

Computer
Basics

Updated for Windows 8

ABSOLUTE BEGINNER'S GUIDE

No experience necessary!

Sixth Edition

Michael Miller

que

FREE
Online Edition

Your purchase of **Computer Basics Absolute Beginner's Guide, Windows 8 Edition** includes access to a free online edition for 45 days through the **Safari Books Online** subscription service. Nearly every Que book is available online through **Safari Books Online**, along with thousands of books and videos from publishers such as Addison-Wesley Professional, Cisco Press, Exam Cram, IBM Press, O'Reilly Media, Prentice Hall, Sams, and VMware Press.

Safari Books Online is a digital library providing searchable, on-demand access to thousands of technology, digital media, and professional development books and videos from leading publishers. With one monthly or yearly subscription price, you get unlimited access to learning tools and information on topics including mobile app and software development, tips and tricks on using your favorite gadgets, networking, project management, graphic design, and much more.

Activate your FREE Online Edition at
informit.com/safarifree

STEP 1:   Enter the coupon code: MNJQXAA.

STEP 2:   New Safari users, complete the brief registration form.
Safari subscribers, just log in.

If you have difficulty registering on Safari or accessing the online edition,
please e-mail customer-service@safaribooksonline.com